CONTRACEPTION VS. TRADITION

1969

CONTRACEPTION VS. TRADITION

A Catholic Critique

G. EGNER

HERDER AND HERDER

1967
HERDER AND HERDER NEW YORK
232 Madison Avenue, New York 10016

Library of Congress Catalog Card Number: 67-14144

Manufactured in the United States of America

A man like that will be quite unaware of how the people next door behave—he will scarcely know whether they are human beings or creatures of some other species. But when it comes to "the nature of man" or "specifically human activity and experience", he will spend himself in laborious investigations.

Plato, *Theaetetus*

Contents

Preface

In the summer of 1963 I wrote a critique of arguments used to support the standard Catholic position about the morality of contraception. Subsequent exchange of views with friends convinced me that a lengthier analysis of the question was needed, and the result is this book, of which the manuscript was finished by Easter 1964. An appendix was added shortly afterwards to take account of the increase which that year saw in discussion of birth-regulation. The debate has since been extended to an unprecedented degree, and it is no part of my theme to give a history of it. But I have followed the first appendix with two others, in which I discuss two recent works, one a philosophical defence of the prohibition of contraception, the other a history of this prohibition in Catholic theology. I have also modified the text in many places so as to give consideration, not only to a situation that is continually developing, but to criticisms made by readers of the first draft. The vehement dissent of some of these from my opinions obliges me to confine responsibility for what follows to myself: but it does not prevent me from thanking them all for their generosity. I should like to extend these thanks to others who helped to prepare the text for publication, or undertook the tedious but unavoidable task of linguistic revision.

G. EGNER

Abbreviations

See also Appendix to Chapter 1 (pp. 19–24 below)

CAR	F. Hürth, SJ, "Inquisitio critica in moralitatem 'Amplexus Reservati' ", *Periodica*, 41 (1952)
CD	F. Hürth, SJ, "Dubia Matrimonialia", *Periodica*, 38 (1949)
CG	St Thomas Aquinas, *Summa Contra Gentiles*
CM	F. Hürth, SJ, "Adnotationes ad Allocutiones . . . ad Obstetrices . . .", *Periodica* 40 (1951)
CR	*The Clergy Review*
D	Denzinger and Schönmetzer, *Enchiridion Symbolorum* (1963)
DM	St Thomas Aquinas, *Quaestio Disputata de Malo*
"Doctors"	Address of Pius XII to Catholic Doctors (1949)
EOM	F. Hürth, SJ, "De Finibus Matrimonii", *Periodica*, 33 (1944)
"Fertility"	Address of Pius XII to the Congress on Fertility and Sterility (1956)
"Haematologists"	Address of Pius XII to the Society of Haematology (1958)
L	S. de Lestapis, SJ, *Family Planning and Modern Problems*, tr. R. F. Trevett, London (1961)
"Marriage"	Pius XI, Encyclical *Casti Connubii* (1930)
"Midwives"	Address of Pius XII to Catholic midwives (1951)
R	J. Rock, *The Time Has Come*, London (1963)
Sent	St Thomas Aquinas, *Commentarium in Libros Sententiarum*
ST	St Thomas Aquinas, *Summa Theologiae*
"Urologists"	Address of Pius XII to Urologists (1951)

1

Introduction

1. The state of the question

> "That birth-control stuff [he said] . . . They claimed it was against nature, but I claim, if that's so, an operation's against nature. I told my old man that when he was having his kidney stones out. You ought to have heard him yell!" [Mary McCarthy, *On the Contrary*, p. 71.]

The speaker was a lapsed Catholic, and his argument was crude enough—but its very crudeness seems to make it typical of the dissatisfaction felt by so many Catholics, lapsed or not, at what they are taught about contraception. What the Church teaches, they are bound to respect; but they find it hard to do so when the teaching is presented in the context of reasons and proofs which seem open to such obvious ripostes. Is not shaving unnatural? And chewing-gum an abuse of the masticatory organs? Are not the calculations and apparatus required for the safe period just as artificial as contraceptive appliances? And is not the safe period itself a thwarting of the generative act? Or is it lawful just because it is not safe? We are all familiar with such remarks, and whatever may be their strength or weakness, they are symptoms of a widespread uneasiness which the standard answers and explanations seem incapable of quieting. Recently, this disquiet has been voiced with a new frankness. Catholic newspapers and magazines have devoted pages to debates on the matter, and public argument has disclosed the presence of far-reaching dissent, even where no infraction of the Church's discipline is made or contemplated.

For all this, the topic still suffers from a lack of analysis and discussion. Disciplinary regulations have in the past led to a silence which excluded that critical appraisal and modification to which statements are subjected in serious argument, and by which they are sharpened and corrected. The recent freedom of debate has, unfortunately, done little to mend matters. Correspondence-columns and articles in newspapers cannot provide that sustained and close examination which so difficult and complex a question demands; they can only point to obscurities, they cannot illuminate them. This lack of rigorous and protracted debate has produced a shoddiness and debasement in standards of argument here. Words like "nature", "chastity", "generosity", "frustrate", and "self-indulgence", are used to end debates instead of to advance them; presuppositions about human beings and human life slip by unscrutinized; faults in logic are committed which would not escape detection where a tradition of scrupulous and open discussion existed. Yet without such scrutiny, no satisfactory ventilation of the matter can be expected, and what debate there is will lack, not only rigour, but any attempt to seize the general principles involved in it. Accounts of the hardship caused by the present state of affairs; testimonies to the damage done by contraception; objections to patristic opinions about sex; debates about the natural law; hopeful casuistry about licit uses for sterilizing drugs—these and other topics which have appeared so often in recent discussions are not likely to lead to any conclusion if they are submitted in isolation. The whole question needs examining, and examining as a whole; nor can the examination, if it is to be just, avoid being lengthy.

This book is a contribution to such an examination, and I should like at this point to show how its theme is developed. Let me begin with some terminological matters. I shall in future refer to the common Roman Catholic teaching on birth regulation as "the Roman Position", which I shall abbreviate to "the RP". What exactly the RP is will become clearer as the essay proceeds. It is, of course, permissible to define it as "the prohibition of unnatural means of controlling conception", but of little profit here, where the meaning of "unnatural" has yet to be examined. We have a rough idea of it to start with—a condemnation of actions which are considered to disturb the pattern of the sexual act, of which interrupted intercourse and condoms are held to be clear instances. The word "contraception" I shall use simply as a function of the expression "the RP". That is to say, by "contraception" I mean "those methods of preventing conception which the RP condemns". Nothing more is claimed by this definition; for instance, the distinction between condoms and sterilizing drugs will be duly investigated when the time comes. By "controlling conception", "preventing conception", "regulating conception" and "birth control" I mean any method, lawful or unlawful, of governing human procreation which does not involve an attack on the fertilised ovum.

For the rest of this chapter, I state the philosophical background to the concept of nature so often used in arguments about the RP, and I then give some examples of how the appeal made to it by moral theologians affects debates between them. As an appendix to the chapter I give an account of works I have consulted and an estimate of their standing; this I regard as important, for discussions of the RP are often vitiated by an undiscriminating appeal to sources which differ greatly in authority and reliability. (For convenient reference, an alphabetical list of all works consulted is given in an index on p. 275 of this book.)

In the next four chapters I state and analyse the rational arguments used in support of the RP: the values claimed to be bound up with it; the accordance of it with nature; the distinction it preserves between artificial and natural sterility; and the protection alleged to be afforded by it to the virtue of chastity. Of these chapters, the longest (chap. 3) is devoted to that "appeal to nature" which is the chief rational defence of the RP. That on sterility (chap. 4) tries to corroborate some conclusions of the preceding chapter, and touches on topics (like sterilising drugs and the safe period) which are examined again later on. The account of the place held by the virtue of chastity in argument for the RP (chap. 5) links the analyses of its rational apologetic with the study of its chief dogmatic defence—the appeal to tradition. To this topic I devote the sixth chapter: I try to show what form the appeal takes, and what are its presuppositions; to state more precisely what the tradition is; to show why it forms the strongest defence of the RP, and in what way, if any, it might be open to revaluation. Having examined both the rational and dogmatic arguments for the RP, I turn in the last two chapters to a survey of present possibilities. Chapter 7 contains an account of some recent pronouncements on the RP (including the controversy over sterilizing drugs), and of ways in which opinions seem likely to develop—an appendix to this chapter says something of points raised in the most recent debates of all. And in Chapter 8 I try to state what I think are the scope and limits of arguments about the RP, and what is required if such arguments are to be profitable.

Let me briefly state the thesis of this book. The rational apologetic for the RP I cannot accept, and I suggest that the appeal to tradition, while uniquely powerful, might not be as irremovable an obstacle in the way of change as is usually supposed. Recent speculation about the RP has usually taken the form of suggestions for the employment of sterilizants, or proposals for a rethinking of attitudes to these; for better or worse, what I have to say faces the question at a deeper level. That is why I should not like the novelty and perhaps unacceptability of my conclusions to stand in the way of an impartial appraisal of a number of themes to be found in the essay. My treatment of them is, I think, independent of my general position, and I submit that they could be of interest even to those who reject that position. I mention some of them here: in Chapter 3, the claim that neo-scholastic philosophy shares with traditional empiricism a defective criterion of significance and purpose; in Chapter 6, the analysis of the form taken by appeals to tradition, the suggestion that Aquinas did not teach the "argument from nature", and the account of Augustine's views on the use of marriage; and in Chapter 7, the diagnosis of why steroid drugs have aroused so much interest, and the critique of some uses of intentional concepts in debates over the RP. These topics I should like to be evaluated for their own sake, not just as elements in a larger argument.

The essay itself will show that I regard the appeal to tradition, not only as the one acceptable defence of the RP, but as a defence whose force can be adequately appraised only by the authoritative teaching of the Church, not by any individual enquirer. To reject the rational apologetic for the RP is, I am going to suggest, a matter for philosophical decision, and a question soluble in philosophical terms. But the appeal to tradition is different in kind. It is the witness of what has been taught and believed in the Church, and only the teaching Church can, in the last analysis, decide what status is to be accorded it. Nor is such a decision an academic piece of history or theology; it is itself part of the tradition that it evaluates. Consequently, when

I say that, in questioning the force of this appeal as commonly made, I submit my views to those of the Church, I am asserting an integral part of my thesis, not just adding a postscript dictated by prudence or good manners. Of its very nature, the appeal to tradition cannot be definitively appraised by human means; all that can be done—all that I have tried to do—is to suggest that the appeal as it stands is indecisive, so that an authoritative intervention of the Church is needed to resolve its ambiguities.

The borderland between philosophy and theology yields difficult questions, yet it is just here that the understandable demands of pastoral practice call for easy and brief solutions. The demands must be resisted if discussion is to be worth while. Claims made in such discussion must be subjected to the same impartial examination as that given to any assertion of history or logic. It is only in this way that the many and diverse elements in arguments about the RP can be disentangled and separately evaluated; it is only in this way that an end can be made to confusion between a doctrine and arguments adduced in its favour. I have called the last section of the final chapter "A Plea for Discussion", and I could have used this as a title for the whole work. Where I cannot convince, let me at least help to provoke informed and serious debate.

In the next section of this chapter, something of the philosophical background to the "argument from nature"—the doctrine of the natural law—is examined; while in the section after that I try to show what kind of moral criterion Nature turns out to be in the debates of moral theologians.

2. *The philosophical background*

When defenders of the RP use concepts like "natural", "frustration", or "artificial" they are appealing implicitly or explicitly to the tradition of ethical teaching known as the natural law. It would be hard to think of a word with a greater motley of uses than "nature", and it would be just as hard to give a full account of the origin and content of the moral theory concerning the law of nature. Fortunately, there is no need to embark here on so formidable a task. It will be enough to give an outline of the theory as presented by Aquinas, since it is his speculations more than anyone else's which have shaped Catholic use of the concept, and it is his application of it to chastity which has been adopted—and adapted—to defend the RP. First, then, for what Aquinas says about the natural law; then for his application of it to sexual behaviour.

God is the creator of the world, and it is God's providence which dictates the order of things in it; the divine reason may be compared to the skill of a craftsman with which he produces an artefact, and it is this divine direction of things which may be called the eternal law. Not that the world is eternal; but God, who is eternal, has made the world in the way he has chosen. (*ST* 1/2.93.)[1] Now, this direction or government by God has two very different senses. For objects on earth other than men, it simply means that they behave as God made them: but man is distinguished from the rest by possessing reason, and by his ability to be in a sense his own providence—to plan and to make decisions for himself. He needs something more of the eternal law than a way of behaving, he needs a conscious share in the ordering reason of God. The share of the eternal law which man enjoys is called by Aquinas the natural law. (*ST* 1/2.91.2.) It is not a full knowledge of the eternal law which he has—that would entail in some sense a vision of God—but a natural inclination towards the fulfilment of himself, which is the practical reason man has concerning good and evil. The basic precept of the practical reason—undemonstrable because it would have to be assumed in any demonstration—is that good is to be done and evil avoided. This apparently vacuous precept is given content by the natural inclinations of man, which determine commands of the natural law. Thus, the instinct for self-preservation he shares with all things; sexual activity and family life he has in common with other animals; and he alone is inclined towards rational society and the worship of God. (*ST* 1/2.94.2.)

Aquinas does not, of course, suggest that every inclination a man has is to be interpreted as a command of the natural law; indeed, the purpose of both divine and human legislation is to assure peace against the tendencies men have that turn them away from what is good for them. (*ST* 1/2.95.1.) These

[1] For abbreviations in references, see appendix to this chapter, pp. 19ff., and list on p. x above.

"natural inclinations" are not unshakable, nor is "nature" simply a pattern of observed behaviour. Aquinas supplements elsewhere what he says in the passage to which we have just referred by saying that it is the good of *the whole man* which these inclinations concern, of man who is distinguished from the lower animals by *reason*. Man is a rational creature, and what is good for man is what completes and fulfils him as the kind of being he is—a rational social animal. (*ST* 1/2.54.3.) So the natural inclinations which Aquinas mentions are those which are according to reason, not simply any inclination which happens to affect man, independently of its accord or disaccord with that reason which marks him off from the rest of the world. We have no insight into the eternal law; that would involve seeing God. Our moral arguments deal with what is good for man as a rational creature, and Aquinas contends that our reason is able to tell us very generally what this is. For instance, temperance is a virtue by which we use according to reason whatever gives us sensible pleasure. To say that our nature inclines us towards these pleasures is not just a statement of fact, but rather an assertion that our rationality sets a standard for our enjoyment of them, and that being temperate means abiding by such a standard, even at the cost of great effort. (*ST* 2/2.141.1, 4.) Perhaps we can illustrate this by another passage, where Aquinas compares the opinion of the Stoics that all passions are bad, with that of the Peripatetics that moderated passions are good. (*ST* 1/2.24.2.) The difference is verbal rather than real, he suggests, for the former define "passion" as any inclination exceeding the bounds of reason; while the latter leave the word "passion" neutral, and hold those passions to be good which do not exceed the bounds of reason. In each case, it is *reason* which is the norm for saying that one such inclination is good and another bad.

Temperance with respect to sexual pleasure is chastity. (*ST* 2/2.146, Preface.) As food is licitly used for the conservation of the individual, so is sex licitly used for the conservation of the species (*ST* 2/2.153.2), and is abused when this purpose is frustrated. Any sexual action not itself ordered to the act of generation is wrong, being a sin against nature. (*ST* 2/2.154.11.) So are any actions opposed to the proper upbringing of children, such as fornication and adultery (*ST* 2/2.154.2, 8); all these actions are disordered in themselves as the genital parts are for the procreation and subsequent upbringing of offspring. (*DM* 15.1.) Incomplete sexual acts between the unmarried proceed from the same disordered inclination as intercourse between them, and so are also sinful. (*ST* 2/2.154.4.)

The views of Aquinas on sex will be examined in greater detail later on; for the moment, it is important to notice a point he makes about the unlawfulness of fornication. To say that extra-marital relations do not allow for the right upbringing of children is to make a general statement admitting of exceptions. Aquinas concedes this but contends that laws deal with the general run of things, not with the exceptional case. (*DM* 15.2 ad 12.) The answer seems to draw too close a parallel between the natural law, which is supposed to be the ordering reason of God, and man-made laws, which are the imperfect rules of thumb for human society. (cf. *ST* 1/2.96.2.) Certainly, the position is easier to defend if a direct revelation by God is supposed to have been made, with its consequent limitations on man's range of decision, than if "law" is taken simply to be the purpose of sexual action as measured by the standards of rational conduct and human society.[1] It is significant—and it is another point to which we shall return—that Aquinas concedes that fornication is not obviously wrong in the way that adultery is obviously wrong (*DM* 15.2 ad 3), so that its sinfulness needs inculcating by revelation or instruction.

At all events, he does provide another argument against fornication which is applicable to all forms of sexual abuse, and which reappears today in defences of the RP. The male seed is unlike any other human secretion in having a definite purpose, and its release has to be governed by that purpose, not merely by good manners. (*ST* 2/2.153.3 ad 1.) The seed is connected with the welfare, not of the individual alone, but of the whole human species, and to err in this matter is therefore grave. (*CG* 3.122.) The seed is closely connected with human life, being indeed potentially a man. (*DM* 15.2.) Nor can it be claimed that in using his sexual faculties without injuring another a man is but using what is his own: God is master of our bodies, and to abuse them is to infringe his rights. (*ST* 2/2.153.3 ad 2.) Having

[1] See below, pp. 37 f.

this dominion over them and their functions, he could make fornication lawful (as he did for the prophet Hosea), or permit theft (as he permitted the Jews to spoil the Egyptians) (*DM* 15.2 ad 8), or command the innocent to be slaughtered (as he ordered Abraham to sacrifice his son). (*ST* 2/2.64.6 ad 1.) Indeed, the virtue of chastity cannot exist at all without reference to God, to whom all virtuous actions must in some way be directed.[1] It can be seen that this line of argument moves away from the "political" objections to fornication based on children's need for paternal care, and considers the moral significance of the inseminatory act itself, independently of social or political setting. Again, instead of considering only the general consequences and exigences of human sexuality, it talks in terms of God's dominion over human reproduction.

This contrast between the two types of argument in Aquinas will reappear in the rational proofs of the RP to be examined in the next chapter. As for the appraisal of the arguments as found in Aquinas, this will be attempted in the sixth chapter, where a more general account will be given of what he says about sexual behaviour. For the moment, we ought to see what moral theologians have made of these theories of Aquinas in their own pronouncements on matters related to the RP.

3. "*Nature*" *and moral disagreement*

The Catholic theologians whose defences of the RP are going to be examined claim to share the philosophical principles found in the texts of Aquinas just quoted—indeed, they will often cite or elaborate these texts. For them, our perception of the pattern of reproduction is no mere factual datum; it can be developed into an insight into the divinely instituted order of things which man can infringe only at the cost of defying the Creator. It might be thought that theologians who claim to discern sexual morality in this way would agree about what they discerned. This is not the case, and a surprising lack of agreement obtains. To be sure, disagreement over moral issues is nothing new, but it seems curiously out of place for those for whom the norm of

[1] So the sexual abstinence of the Vestal Virgins was not chastity at all but sinful insensibility, as it was inspired by reverence for demons. (*DM* 15.2 ad 9.)

sexual behaviour is in the very structure of the generative organs themselves. (Hürth, *CAR* 255; cf. Marshall, *Ethics*, p. 79.) I am going to take three disputed questions among them, to show how the common criterion of "nature" allows a disconcerting variety of conclusions about what is natural. Having seen where theologians get in practice with this standard of theirs, we shall be able to consider in a more detached and cautious way their employment of it against contraception.

1. *Co-operation in frustrated coitus*

A problem frequently proposed for moral judgement is the case of the Catholic whose partner refuses to obey the Church's law and "frustrates the marriage act of its generative purpose". A husband practices *coitus interruptus* or onanism (spilling the seed by withdrawal), or uses a contraceptive (*coitus condomatus*) —what should the wife do? A wife uses a pessary or cap—what should the husband do? Consider first the wife's problem. Moral theologians, basing their answer on the need to preserve the natural pattern in intercourse, distinguish her obligations towards an onanizing husband from her obligations when he uses a contraceptive. With the former she may have intercourse (say all) and even attain the orgasm (say some)[1] as long as penetration lasts even though she is certain from past experience that he is going to withdraw and spill the seed. His action up to the moment of withdrawal is not intrinsically wrong, being indeed identical with the preliminaries for normal intercourse. So by co-operating with him what she is doing is not anything evil in itself. Of course, her enjoyment and consent to the pleasure must cease when he withdraws to inseminate *extra vaginam*, for by doing so he corrupts the sexual act.[2] On the other hand, if the husband practices *coitus condomatus*, the matter is different. Following a reply of the Sacred Penitentiary in 1916 (*D* 3638), moralists seem unanimous in declaring the husband's action

[1] Capello (§ 708) thought this a probable opinion.

[2] "Restraining assent to pleasure" would seem to consist in distracting one's attention from the pleasure automatically released by the sexual climax. (Sartre's *L'être et le néant*, in the section "Mauvaise Foi et Mensonge", describes a similar notion.) Clearly the practice is open to abuse —a mythical penitent is said to have confessed "fornicated three times, consented once"—and there is a grave obligation on married people to avoid acts that directly provoke the onset of the orgasm outside the natural context for it.

unnatural and frustrated from the start. (See, e.g., *CAR* 267.) For the wife to admit him would be joining in this unnatural act and so itself a grave sin. She must, says the Penitentiary, put up a positive physical resistance "as a maiden would to her ravisher". Only the fear of death or grave injury can justify her (purely passive) submission; quarrels, domestic strife and the rest are not sufficient reasons for tolerating the abuse. (*CR* November 1958, December 1959, February 1963.) It would be interesting to know how far wives are told by their confessors to adopt this uncompromising stand. Here I simply note that the reply in *CR* (February 1963) quotes Lanza as softening the confessors' obligation to remind wives of the extent of their duty; and that when a recent correspondent in that periodical asked for a candid statement of confessional practice in the matter (July 1963), no-one was willing to stand up and be counted. A much more significant obscurity surrounds the distinction drawn between the wife's obligations when her husband uses a contraceptive and her obligations when he onanizes. It is this distinction, based as it is supposed to be upon the norm of what is "natural", that I shall now examine.

That the male action in *coitus condomatus* can never be brought to a generative climax, while what the onanizing husband does is capable of such fulfilment, is undeniable, but how does this affect the morality of the action? Erotic actions incapable as such of culminating in natural insemination are not thereby wrong—if they were it would be sinful for husband and wife to touch each other's genital parts, and no moralist says this. The evil, the disorder, lies in the improper emission of seed. Taken as an isolated act, what the husband does both in onanizing and in contraceptive intercourse abandons the natural pattern at the moment the seed is deprived of its natural destination; up to that point it is not so deprived and what the husband does is not intrinsically evil. This is why the theologians allow the wife to join in the preliminaries of *coitus interruptus*, while forbidding her to continue doing so once the husband has withdrawn; for them, the moment of withdrawal is what changes the moral status of the sexual action, and what distinguishes the wife's licit co-operation from sinful sharing in her husband's guilt. Yet it is not hard to justify a similar distinction between preliminaries and climax in *coitus condomatus*.

Suppose the spouses wish to practise *coitus reservatus*,[1] but that one of them has venereal disease. The husband could here licitly use a condom to diminish the risk of infection, as there would be *ex hypothesi* no intention of emitting seed at all. Doubtlessly the example is improbable as well as grotesquely repellent. What matters, however, is that it is conceivable; the first stages of what the condomizing husband does are not irretrievably unnatural, for a legitimate employment can be assigned them. Of course, there is no moral parity between this hypothetical case and the practice of *coitus condomatus*. The condomizing husband has no intention of restraining himself from inseminating—he means to secure an orgasm, and in a way that will waste the seed. *But this is exactly what the onanizing husband means to do*. In each case the initial penetration *could* be done legitimately; in each case, it *is* in fact done by a husband who intends to corrupt the sexual union; in each case the wife is joining in the preliminaries of what is going to frustrate the seed of its natural destination; if she sins in one case, there seems no reason for denying that she sins in the other. The distinction commonly drawn by moral theologians is tenable only because they take "natural pattern" in two distinct and incompatible ways; they divorce ejaculation from penetration in *coitus interruptus* (so that the wife is not sharing in anything evil in itself), but treat them as one action in *coitus condomatus* (so that she is). The norm of "natural pattern" has been the guide to each conclusion, but it is hard to respect a guide which can be used to such opposed effects. To choose between these opposites does not concern us, but it seems worth pointing out that the condemnation is surely more plausible than the permission. The former can be justified for classifying the initial (and theoretically permissible) stages of *coitus condomatus* as "unnatural" because of the way in which the husband makes them end up. The permission, on the other hand, takes no account of what the husband means to do. It allows the wife to share in and enjoy the preliminaries of intercourse which she knows will be sinfully interrupted, and so violently isolates the

[1] *Coitus reservatus* is penetration without insemination, and is allowed more or less willingly by theologians as an "incomplete" act like kissing and embracing, as long as there is no proximate danger of the seed being lost.

moment of insemination from all the antecedents of which it is the normal climax and fulfilment. A confessor might as well on similar grounds allow a penitent to light the first few faggots when an innocent person is being burnt at the stake, on the grounds that the initial stages in the pyre's combustion afford the victim only a pleasant warmth.

So much for frustrations of the act by the husband. There are also inconsistencies in judging the case of the wife who does not receive the seed in the natural manner. If a woman intends before marriage never to have intercourse without a pessary, she refuses her husband the right over her body which allows him to perform an action naturally ordered to generation, and marriage is void for lack of consent. (Hürth, commenting in *Periodica* (1949) (*CD* 207) on a decision of the Rota to this affect.) Yet Lanza and Palazzini, writing four years afterwards, allow a husband who knows his wife uses a pessary still to have intercourse with her if he finds abstinence difficult, though what he is doing is, by Hürth's standards, not included in the rights he has over her, and so is sinful. Lanza–Palazzini (pp. 123–5) admit that a pessary substantially corrupts the vagina by stopping it from being a canal, but contend that the seed can still be *deposited* in its natural place. Their solution—which is given as provisional "until an authentic response"—does not apply if the wife uses a pseudo-vagina, that is presumably a receptacle for seed, not simply an intra-vaginal barrier in its normal path, a cup rather than a cap. But Healey allows an orifice to be constructed by plastic surgery for a woman born without any vagina, and permits her to marry and to have intercourse. (p. 136.) Although there is no communication between this "vagina" and the womb, although it is simply a man-made change in the woman's body without the other features present in a real vagina,[1] it can be used by the husband on the grounds that it occupies the natural place for the vagina and is of similar dimensions. Given this elasticity of the appeal to nature, it is difficult to see why Lanza and Palazzini draw the line where they do; or why Hürth—or anyone—does. And it is still harder to see how any "response", however authentic, could decide the issue on rational grounds.

[1] cf. Génicot, *Casus* 997 bis, for a condemnation on these grounds of the project.

For it is on supposedly rational grounds that the moralists have been arguing about these instances of frustrated intercourse. They claim to deduce their conclusions from "first principles", from an examination of the structure and purpose of human sexuality, and would not regard an arbitrary edict as resolving their disagreement. Of course, it might be possible to treat Roman decrees as "arbitrary" in the sense that a judge's rulings are arbitrary—that is, authoritative determinations, based on facts but not deducible from them, which affect simultaneously our view of the disputed case and our estimation of the law under (or outside) which it is authoritatively declared to fall. An allocution of Pius XII to the Cardinals in 1954 ("De Ecclesiae Potestate", 54) seemed to approach this view, but its exact sense remains obscure. I know of no moralist who has pursued this line of thought, to which I shall return in a later chapter.

2. *Artificial insemination*

That artificial insemination is condemned by theologians when performed outside marriage, or performed inside marriage with seed not obtained from the husband (AID), is not surprising, not only because of the traditional Christian background of the moralists, but because of the profound social disturbances bound up with the practices. It is only artificial insemination with the husband's seed (AIH) that we shall consider. It is at this stage that social and public considerations lose the relevance they had to the morality of AID; it is here that the appeal to nature ought to appear untouched by covert appeals of a consequential or utilitarian character. Yet it is at this very stage that dissension begins among moral theologians. They always forbade the husband to masturbate in order to obtain seed, but some (Vermeersch §241; Génicot II, 545 etc.) allowed seed to be procured without sexual pleasure by being extracted directly from the testicles, while other theologians allowed the siphoning out and re-injection of seed already deposited *intra vaginam*. Pius XII condemned testicular extraction and similar methods, on the ground that the rights of the spouses over each other's bodies are limited by the norms nature herself prescribes; in other words, the procreative right is limited to natural intercourse. If the husband furnishes seed in any other way, he is refusing to conform to the natural pattern of intercourse which limits the rights he and his wife enjoy over each other. No appeal can be made to the marital status of the spouses to warrant their taking this unnatural means of begetting a child. ("Fertility", 472–3.)

Unlike Vermeersch and Génicot, Pius XII refused to make the absence of pleasure into a criterion of lawfulness. The criterion "nature" for him means that a certain pattern of sexual contract must be preserved, without regard to the personal relations and married state of those between whom the contact takes place. This isolation of sexual intercourse from its human context is an essential part of the RP and we are going to meet it many times again; in fact it has already appeared in an argument Aquinas used against sexual abuse. (See pp. 8–9.) This isolation leads inevitably enough to the papal condemnation, but it weakens the claim made in the same allocution that these severe restrictions on artificial insemination make the sexual faculty intrinsically suitable for the upbringing as well as for the procreation of children. To prohibit AID may well safeguard these aspects of intercourse; it seems implausible to say that prohibiting AIH achieves the same end—and not only implausible but inconsistent with the assertion already noted that marital rights are not to parenthood but to certain patterns of sexual action.[1]

It might be thought that the method of re-injection would be acceptable since the seed is deposited to start with in a natural manner, and indeed Pius XII did specifically except from his condemnation artificial means used to facilitate the natural act, or to enable the completed act to reach its end. ("Doctors", 560.) Yet here again there is dissent among moralists. Some theologians allowed (allow?) the husband to practise *coitus condomatus*, immediately after which the seed would be removed from the condom and injected mechanically[2]. Others condemn

[1] Nor are matters clarified by the claim made in another speech of Pius XII that artificial insemination turns the family hearth into a biological laboratory. ("Midwives", 51.) The definition of the marriage act claimed to be bound up with this violation of the natural order ("a simple organic function for the transmission of seed") sounds uncomfortably like the impersonal and abstract appraisal of intercourse entailed by the papal condemnation of AIH!

[2] The 1922 edition of Génicot's *Casus Conscientiae* allows this, as did a

this as an abuse of the sexual faculty, and insist that the condom must first have a hole pricked in it, to let pass enough seed to satisfy the pattern of normal intercourse: what is left may then be removed and re-injected. (O'Donnell, 222; Healey, 149.) Others disallow any use of the condom as it entails depositing seed in an unnatural place. They permit only the removal and re-injection of seed previously deposited in the vagina—the sex act is achieved normally, the interference with the seed is only momentary, it is directly aimed at rendering intercourse fruitful and in no sense is a frustration of nature. (Healey, 154.) But for others again this removal is itself unacceptable and the syringe must not be withdrawn from the precincts of the vagina under penalty of interrupting the natural pattern of the action. (McFadden, 85, and others quoted by O'Donnell.) If the pattern of sexual relations is written into the very generative organs themselves—which is admitted by all the disputants—it is strange that what is written there can be read so differently. Could it be that the natural pattern of sexual union contains something more than the simple geography of those thus united?

3. *Parity of orgasms*

To show where the quest for "what is natural" may lead, consider the question of "incomplete acts" between the spouses—erotic activity not culminating in an orgasm for either party. Moralists permit activity of this kind as long as there is no immediate danger of husband or wife reaching a climax outside sexual union. The restriction affects the wife as well as the husband. That the female orgasm is neither a necessary nor a sufficient condition for generation does not, Hürth points out, excuse her from her sin if she deliberately reaches a climax in these circumstances—the lawful occasion of her doing so is the complete act of sexual intercourse and only that. (*CAR* 255.) But from this statement Hürth goes on in the same article to a conclusion bizarre enough to deserve separate attention.

The complete sexual functioning of one partner, he claims, necessarily involves the complete functioning of the other. There exists between them a transcendental and indestructible

Canon Tiberghien of the theological faculty at Lille. I owe these two references to N. St John Stevas's *Life, Death and the Law*, London 1961, 125.

relation. Given this relationship, it follows that for a woman to enjoy n orgasms during intercourse while her husband enjoys only one is for her to commit $n-1$ unnatural pollutions—her one lawful orgasm was that which morally coincided with her husband's. Thus alone can the natural structure of her sexual activity be preserved. (The mathematical terminology is my own but the doctrine is Hürth's [*CAR*]).

It is hard to know what to say of an opinion like this. The female climax is often less definitely located in time and in place than that of the male. How is the husband to decide which one is to count? Or the wife, come to that? Suppose the wife reaches a climax early in intercourse, must she "restrain her assent" for the rest of the union in case it leads to a second, illicit, orgasm? Or can she go ahead and enjoy it to the full, but then urge her husband towards a second climax, in order to make a retrospectively honest woman of her? And what of the husband? Although Hürth considers a plurality of female orgasms, his principles apply equally to the male climax. As he says, it is irrelevant that the female orgasm is not needed for procreation: what matters is the transcendental and indestructible relation between the two climaxes. Moralists allow a husband who reaches this climax before the wife to try to arouse an orgasm in her by subsequent caresses. But suppose he fails and she still wants sexual union with him? He knows that he is already one orgasm ahead; may he start again in the hope (culpable self-deception, perhaps) that his wife will have two orgasms to his one during the second encounter? Or, if it be objected that the second union is distinct from the first, may he embark upon it when experience suggests that there will not be a female orgasm this time either? Surely the questions need not be put in the first place. Hürth's transcendental relation, whatever it is, must be completely distinct from the personal relationship between husband and wife and from their activities during sexual union; indeed it is not they but their orgasms that it links. But is the sexual relationship between husband and wife to be so described? Is all that they do for each other, all the ways in which they show their love and closeness, to count for nothing except as triggering off a reflex where alone the transcendental relation obtains? Can "nature" be as abstract as this? By taking the quest for "natural structure" to so ruthless and impersonal a limit Hürth has at least shown the need for enquiry into what the structure is supposed to do. It is not so much that the conclusions reached are grotesque: the method of deducing them needs scrutiny.

This consideration of three specific moral cases of sexual conduct has shown that the divinely established order, supposedly deducible from the objective pattern of human sexuality, has given answers varying in plausibility and at times in conflict with each other. A question which remains is how we could ever go about solving such conflict; a further question is whether the objective order in human sexual relations is adequately described by the physical pattern of an act of intercourse taken in isolation. Let us keep these reservations about "nature" in mind, as we go on to examine the arguments against what are called "unnatural frustrations of the sexual act". Meanwhile, in the next chapter, the first of the rational arguments for the RP will be examined—the claim that it safeguards human values which contraception attacks.

Appendix. Account of sources consulted

1. Papal documents

Pius XI's Encyclical on Christian Marriage, 1930, cited as "Marriage". Addresses of Pius XII, with dates and methods of citation: to Catholic doctors, 1949 ("Doctors"); to midwives, 1951 ("Midwives"); to urologists, 1951 ("Urologists"); to the Congress on Fertility and Sterility, 1956 ("Fertility"); to the Congress on Haematology, 1958 ("Haematologists"). Numbers after "Midwives" will refer to the paragraphs of the CTS translation of it, which, as it is easily available, I shall use in quoting that pronouncement. Numbers after any other papal pronouncement will refer to the page in the official text in *Acta Apostolicae Sedis* for the appropriate year. However, any papal or official document found in the *Enchiridion* of Denzinger–Schönmetzer (1963) will be followed by "*D*" and the marginal number of that work.

Whether any of these papal utterances is an infallible pronouncement will be asked in due course; it is enough to recall for the moment that Catholics are supposed to obey their teaching whether they are infallible or not (see *Humani Generis*, *D* 3885), and they are in fact regarded as the norm of belief in this matter.

2. The writings of St Thomas Aquinas

Works quoted, and abbreviated forms of citation, are: *Summa Theologiae* ("*ST*"); *Summa Contra Gentiles* ("*CG*"); *Quaestio Disputata De Malo* ("*DM*"); *Commentarium in Libros Sententiarum* ("*Sent.*"). All references to these are made according to the usual conventions—part, question, article, answer, as the case may be. It will be noticed that I cite the Supplement to the *Summa Theologiae*, which was not composed by Aquinas. I have done this for two reasons. First, the Supplement is in fact cited by standard expositions of Catholic teaching on marriage; it has played its part in forming the tradition of rational speculation about these topics despite its non-Thomistic origin and contributed to what is—correctly or incorrectly—regarded as Thomistic teaching. As such, it deserves a mention, for I am less interested in its authenticity than its influence. The second reason is that the passages I refer to in the Supplement are in fact all taken from Aquinas's commentary on the Sentences, but it may be useful for readers to have a reference to the more easily obtainable work. The commentary on the Sentences is an early work, and the death of Aquinas robbed us of the mature treatment which the same topics would have received in the third part of the *Summa*. Yet the statements about marriage in the second part of it do not seem substantially different from what is to be found in the earlier commentary.

Although the doctrines of Aquinas are not imposed upon Roman Catholics, he is regarded as a guide for those whose faith seeks understanding, and his arguments about sexual morality are, as we shall see, appealed to in later works.

3. Patristic authors and classic writers on moral theology

I shall have occasion to quote the writings of St Augustine (d. 430), St Jerome (d. 420), St John Chrysostom (d. 407) and St Gregory the Great (d. 604). I shall also cite the opinions of medieval writers like Peter Lombard (d. 1159), Alexander of Hales (fl. c. 1240) and St Bonaventure (d. 1274); and those of later authorities like the sixteenth-century Cajetan, the seventeenth-century Sanchez and Reginaldus, and the eighteenth-century St Alphonsus Liguori.

It is obvious—and I shall make the point again in due course—that no generalizations about the standing of such diverse authorities would be of any value. What they teach will be evaluated at the appropriate time, and, where necessary, its place in Catholic tradition pointed out. I remark here that the Fathers quoted are among the most celebrated of early ecclesiastical writers; that the medievals have been accepted as authorities in later times; and that what the other moralists teach can (as will be seen) reappear in more recent works.

4. *Periodica*

A journal published in Latin by the Gregorian University, Rome, and devoted to moral theology and allied topics. Among the articles quoted are some by the Rev. F. Hürth, SJ, who was a well-known Roman theologian and a consultor at the Holy Office.

"De Finibus Matrimonii", *Periodica*, 33 (1944). (Anonymous, but the style is like Hurth's.) Notes on the decree of the Holy

Office (20 April 1944, *D* 3838) which condemned theories in *Sinn und Zweck ser Ehe*, by Herbert Doms. The decree from the Holy Office stressed the primacy of the generative purpose in marriage and the article examines this. Cited as *EOM* ("Ends of Marriage").

"Dubia Matrimonialia", *Periodica*, 38 (1949). A commentary by Hürth on a number of questions raised by recent decisions and articles on matrimonial matters. Cited as *CD* ("Commentary on 'Dubia' ").

"Adnotationes ad Allocutiones . . . ad obstetrices . . .", *Periodica* 40 (1951). A commentary on the speeches of Pius XII to the Midwives and to the organisation "Fronte della Famiglia". It may be noted that the CTS translation of "Midwives" adds a translation of the second speech. I cite this article of Hürth as *CM* (i.e., "Commentary on 'Midwives' ").

"Inquisitio critica in moralitatem 'Amplexus Reservati' ", *Periodica*, 41 (1952). The Holy Office issued in that year a warning about views expressed on the morality of *coitus reservatus*. (*D* 3907.) Hürth comments upon the statement, and raises more general moral issues. I cite this article as *CAR* (i.e., "Commentary on 'Amplexus Reservatus' ").

Other articles cited from *Periodica* are:

Furlong, F., SJ, "Tres Allocutiones Pii Papae XII ultimae de medecina" (1958). A commentary on speeches by Pius XII on medicine, including statements on steroid drugs.

Fuchs, J., SJ, "Amplexus Reservatus secundum principia ethicae sexualis S. Thomae" (1956). Considers not only *coitus reservatus* according to Thomistic principles, but the wider question of what those principles have to say about incomplete erotic acts between spouses.

Periodica is the forum for the views of Jesuit moralists in Rome, is often quoted in other publications, and seems to enjoy a good reputation among theologians.

5. *The Clergy Review*

This is the leading clerical monthly among English Catholics. "Questions and Answers" on moral problems is the work of the Rt Rev. L. L. McReavy, the chief canonist among Roman Catholics in England, and a *peritus* at the Vatican Council. All references to *The Clergy Review* will be to this feature of it unless otherwise stated: citations will be by *CR* followed by month and year of issue.

6. Manuals of moral theology

Out of the vast number of works used as textbooks in theological colleges or consulted by the clergy, I have chosen those well known and quoted by others: Capello, Davis, Génicot, Lanza–Palazzini, Noldin-Schmitt, Slater, Vermeersch. The arrangement of topics in them is almost invariable. Any reference I make to an author's teaching on sins against chastity outside marriage can be verified in his manual under the heading "De Luxuria" or "De Sexto Praecepto". References to the morality of sexual relations inside marriage will be under "De Sacramento Matrimonii" in the section "De Usu Matrimonii".

7. *Family Planning and Modern Problems*, by S. de Lestapis, SJ, trans. R. F. Trevett, Burns & Oates (1961)

This is a survey of views favourable to contraception and of the results of such techniques; a presentation of the Catholic view and of its spiritual, demographic and social consequences. Lestapis gives the fullest account known to me of the RP, and it is not surprising that his book has been so popular with Catholics. It gives much demographic and sociological information, and displays the author's wide reading on topics like population, statistics, and problems of food production throughout the world. Moreover, the author is obviously concerned to give something more than an abstract account of Catholic teaching. He wants to show this teaching as part of a wider approach to life and its problems, to point out the scale of values that goes with it and the consequences it entails, to show it as compatible both with the law of God and with human dignity. I quote his book as *L* followed by the page number.

8. Works on medical ethics and on marriage

Some of these deal with the moral issues of medical practice in general: A. Bonnar, *The Catholic Doctor*, London (1948); E. Healey, *Medical Ethics*, Chicago (1956); T. O'Donnell, *Morals in Medicine*, Westminster, Md (1956); C. McFadden, *Medical Ethics*, London (1962); J. Marshall, *The Ethics of Medical Practice*, London (1961). It appears that these are reputable works, though I do not (not only because I need not, but because I cannot) pronounce on the medical reliability of their content. What matters for me is the moral advice that they give.

Others are samples of the many recent works on the morality and practice of marriage from the Roman Catholic standpoint: J. R. Cavanagh, *Fundamental Marriage Counselling*, Mercier Press (1963); G. A. Kelly, *Catholic Marriage Manual*, London (1958); J. Marshall, *Preparing for Marriage*, London (1963); Léon-Joseph Cardinal Suenens, Archbishop of Malines, *Love and Control*, London (1961). The views expressed in these and similar works will be discussed later: I state here that they are often quoted by defenders of the RP, who seem to have a high opinion of them.

9. Pamphlets and booklets

These obviously lack the rigour possessed by (or at least claimed for) other works: but they display the RP in a popular form, and their enormous circulation makes them more influential, perhaps, than longer and weightier expositions. I quote from the CTS pamphlet *Birth Control* by G. P. Dwyer,[1] and from the *Family Handbook* by W. Lawson, SJ.

10. *The Time Has Come*, by J. Rock, London (1963)

This book has obtained a certain notoriety as it is an attack on the RP by a Catholic, and I shall examine its thesis in a later chapter. Until then I shall use it purely as a source-book for some statements made about contraception. Rock gives chapter and verse for these, and those I have checked are genuine.

11. Contenson, P. M. de, OP, "Fecondité, Bonheur, Morale", in *Revue des Sciences Philosophiques et Théologiques*, 1962, pp. 1 ff.

This is a most helpful review of a number of recent articles and pronouncements on this topic. It gives copious bibliographical information.

12. I mention two works which appeared after the com-

[1] Now Archbishop of Birmingham.

pletion of this book; I have already referred to them in the preface.

G. Grisez, *Contraception and the Natural Law*, Milwaukee, 1965. A philosophical defence of the RP which, although I do not accept its arguments, seemed too important to ignore. I consider it in Appendix B (pp. 224–34).

J. T. Noonan, *Contraception, a history of its treatment by the Catholic Theologians and canonists*. Harvard, 1965. An admirable account of how the tradition has developed. I summarize a number of its themes, and comment on them, in Appendix C (pp. 235–49).

All translations, unless otherwise stated, are my own.

2

Values

1. *The point of arguing*

As we proceed to this first of several lines of argument for the RP, we shall do well to ask what claim is going to be made for the provability of the position. The RP not only condemns contraception, it claims that to reverse the condemnation does not fall within the competence of the Church. The law on the point is no dispensable enactment like Friday abstinence; nor is it a divine revelation concerning human nature, like the New Testament commendation of virginity over marriage; it is an inevitable consequence of the very nature of the sexual act, and dispensations or licences make no sense where the natural law itself is involved. ("Midwives", 25; Dwyer, 3; Kelly, 54.) It is to be expected that those who believe this will hold that the evil of contraception can be rationally apprehended, and this is the view taken by standard authorities. The whole pattern of the sexual act clearly has procreation as its primary purpose ("Midwives", 47 and 62; Hürth, *CD*); the very structure of the genital organs shows that contraception is an abuse of them (Marshall, 79); it is not absolutely essential to be a Catholic to accept the Catholic position (*L* 98); right reason, arguing dispassionately from the pattern of nature, can in principle deduce the right and wrong uses of the sex function. (*CR* [February 1961], in a review by McReavy of a book by Trevett, p. 117.) But there are significant qualifications to this claim. McReavy, for example, goes on to say that the full significance of the function's divine purpose cannot be apprehended without reference to the order of divine grace. And while there are two chapters in *L* about the rational basis of the Church's position, the author says that the attitude of the Church is justified by reason enlightened by faith (*L* 147). He quotes Père Riquet's contrast of the atheist's world-picture with that of the theist: the latter cannot expect the former to share his vision of the world as revealing the divine purposes of a Creator, and must not be surprised if arguments which convince him do not convince the other. (*L* 217.)

Now, this will not do. True enough, theism is not irrelevant to moral beliefs. Ethical standards apprehended at the will of one's Creator have a peremptory absoluteness lacking in the personal and social values accepted by one for whom the concept of a lawgiving Creator does not make sense.[1] But it is the very perception of values which is at stake here, not the force or sanction to be attached to them. Talk of the Kingdom of God and of its exigencies is not relevant to our purpose. The Kingdom of God is to be attained by doing good and avoiding evil; if contraception is evil because of the very pattern of human sexuality, it is begging the question to explain this evil by appealing to the Kingdom of God, without giving a proof that a summons to the Kingdom affects the objective pattern of sexuality in the required way. Aquinas himself objects in a similar manner to the contention that fornication is wrong because it offends the rights of God. (*CG* 3.122.)

It would be very different if our summons to a heavenly destiny abrogated all conclusions to be drawn from rational inquiry into the objective fittingness of things—but to say this would be to concede that the RP cannot be rationally proved. Notice that such a concession would not be inconsistent with the contention that contraception is against the natural law. It is possible to hold that contraception does infringe the objective order of things but that this infringement cannot be proved. Natural law, on such a hypothesis, would still be a share in the ordering reason of God, but a share afforded us by revealed guidance, not by the unaided practical reason. To accept the RP in such a way would involve two acts of faith—one in the moral fact, another in its inevitability. But unless the step be taken (and defenders of the RP do not take it) this choice between resting the RP on Church teaching and resting it upon rational argument has to be faced, and the decision reached openly stated. To make the doctrine a matter of faith is not to abdicate any further use of reason; the coherence of the doctrine with the rest of revelation can still be examined, and attempts can be made to answer those objections that suggest that the RP is

[1] cf. G. E. M. Anscombe, "Modern Moral Philosophy", *Philosophy*, 1958, pp. 1 ff. We shall have more to say on this topic later, pp. 36 ff.

incompatible with the human condition as we face it. But to make the doctrine a matter of faith is also to remove it from a whole range of argument and objection to which it must otherwise be subjected. There can be no eking out of insufficient reasons in this matter with talk of the light of faith without a candid admission of such insufficiency; nor can there be any acceptance of those reasons without transforming into an article of faith what was supposed to be a conclusion reached on rational grounds. To think otherwise is to degrade faith into an apology for the inadequacy of arguments that good manners demand we believe to be effective.

A possible *via media* through the dilemma posed in the last paragraph can now be examined. Suppose it could be shown that rejection of the RP, for all its apparent convenience, leads to a loss of human dignity and values. And suppose that it can also be shown that the acceptance of the RP can, for all the attendant hardships, lead to an enhancement of those values. On such hypotheses, the ground would be prepared for an admission that God must really want human nature to work in this way; a design whose thwarting led to such impoverishment and whose pursuance led to such enrichment must have the authority of the Creator behind it. Whatever the cogency of this reasoning, it might at least turn a person towards a more favourable consideration of the RP. It is this line of reasoning which forms that "appeal to values" which we must now examine.

2. *The appeal to values*

This argument proceeds negatively, by displaying the consequences of contraceptive policies, and then positively, by describing the values that the RP safeguards through rejecting these policies. I consider the two approaches in turn, and shall refer to their exposition in Lestapis. In the second part of his book he mounts an attack against what he calls "contraceptive civilization". (*L* 44–96). This attack contains many demographic and sociological assertions. Population growth depends on large families to a greater extent than the number of such families would lead us to expect. Again, demographic changes themselves are complex and gradual. To embark on a massive reduction of the birthrate without considering the effects of this on manpower, for instance, is shortsighted: an increase in numbers can, in certain circumstances, be an asset to a country which needs to make a sudden advance into industrial activity and city life. (*L* 45.) On the other hand, some benefits supposed to follow from contraception have not in fact done so. Statistics from Japan show that the introduction there of contraceptive methods has not proved an effective means of reducing the number of abortions, while the availability of contraceptives is in all places and in itself an encouragement for premarital sexuality.

Whatever the justice of these claims, they are significant enough to deserve further investigation. If the illicitness of contraception were to be proved simply on social and "political" grounds, such bad results would (if proved) have to be balanced against the concomitant advantages. But he explicitly denies that social utility is an adequate norm for Christian behaviour, for Christians must consider the individual soul and its heavenly destiny. (*L* 97.) Given such a denial, the value and indeed the very relevance of all these data is severely lessened. If data cannot count against the RP, but only for it, their use here gives a misleading impression of an empirical proof for a thesis which must, on the author's own admission, elude it. It is further lessened by other counts on his indictment of contraception, accusations whose very vagueness seems to put confirmation or rebuttal out of the question. Contraception leads to instability in marriage (*L* 89), to a lessening of maternal love (*L* 84), to adolescent sexuality (*L* 83), to an attack on man's virility and woman's femininity (*L* 87), to a tolerance of homosexual practices. (*L* 88.)

Such vast claims—declared beliefs rather than verifiable assertions—may be taken as ways of interpreting the world's wickedness for those who already hold the RP on other grounds. And, given the amount of sexual laxity in the world and the disasters to which this can undoubtedly lead, evidence can be found to support almost any assertion of this kind. But such assertions can hardly be adduced as cogent reasons for accepting the exclusions of the RP without being provided with an empirical backing as vast as themselves. And this the author makes no attempt to give. Until he does so, they may be oratorical gestures, but they are not experimental confirmation.

But the RP is supposed to safeguard positive values in sexuality besides warding off negative influences. These positive values can now be briefly stated. Human sexuality is more than the appeasing of desire, more than selfish satisfaction; it involves mutual respect between the partners and a "dialogue" in which each partner is a person, not a mere object of pleasure. (*L* 103.) Again, married love must respect the will to create. The dialogue between the two partners must not remain closed, but must be transcended by the creation of a third, the new life which makes their love go beyond either of them. (*L* 105.) A society based on technological achievement like our own makes an adequate approach to sex difficult (*L* 111), but by clinging to this value we can preserve the sacral character of the family which is so precious and, today, so easily lost. (*L* 113.) Nor will our view of sex lead to economic difficulties, if international solidarity and love exploit the resources of the world to the full and seek to better the lot of those in need. (*L* 142 etc.)

These qualities of a complete marriage relationship are precious, and need safeguarding even at the cost of great sacrifices by each partner. Why they should be safeguarded only through the RP remains obscure. It is a platitude that human sexuality ought to be a personal relationship, involving more than the sedation of desire—though moral theologians might have mentioned the platitude oftener. But can the relationship be safeguarded only by an absolute ban on contraception? The ban certainly gives the couple a chance of showing that their love can survive the absence of sexual intercourse. Illness and separation can do the same; what needs proving is that the ban has to be imposed in the first place, and proof by appeal to the respect for the will to create is not enough. Certainly, contraception can make it all too easy for husbands and wives to turn their backs on the creation of new life, to let selfishness make them refuse the adventure of founding a family worthy of their means and abilities. But, as we learnt from Pius XII's pronouncement on artificial insemination already quoted (pp. 14 f), the natural pattern of married sexuality lies in performing a particular action in a particular way, not in producing a large family. It is no personal or parental consideration to which the RP appeals for support. Whether the offending couple have had one child or eleven is irrelevant to the vital question: is the sexual act being carried out by them now according to the natural pattern? Infringing the pattern is always wrong, whether inspired by a wish for children or by a wish for no more of them. Whatever we may think of this position, we cannot identify it with a slogan like "respect for the will to create". (Marshall, *Ethics*, p. 79, makes this point clearly.) This is an excellent motto for marriage, but it is not itself an adequate criterion for the morality of each and every act of intercourse, which is just what the RP demands. The values mentioned in *L* are indeed worth safeguarding, and are liable to be obscured by selfishness. To accept these values is to reject contraception when it is inspired by such unworthy motives, not to reject it as absolutely illicit.

Perhaps the use of the word "creation" and what he goes on to say about the difficulty of preserving the sacral character of the family in industrialized surroundings are bound up with that recurrent nostalgia of Roman Catholics for an agricultural, quasi-medieval society.[1] Put as crudely as this, the idea seems implausible. Yet is not the praise lavished by Catholic writers (especially priests) on large families bound up with a kind of cosmic toryism, a penchant for the haphazard, a distrust of planning and control (even by lawful means) in such fundamental matters? We have read so much about the rough and tumble of a large family, the cheerful trust in divine providence to see it round the next corner, the making do and contriving to keep so many warm and fed. At times, perhaps, some of us have been tempted to match these Second Nocturns of improvidence with other descriptions of large families, descriptions better suited to some we know ourselves. But there is no need to engage in such polemic; its terms are false from the start. No moral issue is being debated, only a matter of taste. Given the best will in the world, large families are not always advisable—it depends upon who have them, what they do for a living, what kind of children they have, and much else. To say this is not to discount the good qualities attributed to large families; it is to distinguish a legitimate personal preference from a moral ideal

[1] There were many symptoms of this nostalgia in the 1930s, and a recent exchange of views on the point can be seen in articles by Fitzsimons and Crane, *CR* (March and August 1959).

to be held up for universal imitation. To discount the wishes of parents for the education and professional formation of their children as insufficient reasons for limiting the size of their family is not only a crude oversimplification—it seeks to impose in the name of religion a private opinion that may be dictated by no more than social class or selective memories of childhood.

Lestapis has conceded that the RP demands an effort by all peoples to see that the riches of the world are used for the benefit of all, and he goes on to speak about the untapped supplies of food in the world, the wastage of resources, the obstacles to a more generous use of them. I cannot help noticing that these admittedly valid points hardly accord with the longing for pastoral peace and spontaneous ways of living which were encountered in the preceding paragraph; for does not a full-scale exploitation of the world's resources entail a merciless application of technology to agriculture—insecticides, artificial fertilizers, battery hens, and all the rest? Yet the argument breeds a deeper uneasiness. That the increased population of the world can in principle be fed seems likely enough; *homo sapiens* can conquer formidable obstacles if the incentives are right. But we are talking about the world as it is, not as it will be or might be. I do not venture to pronounce on the proportion of the world's population which is hungry, or undernourished, or monotonously nourished. I do venture the remark that unrealized potentialities cannot be eaten. It is immediate help that is needed, not the promise of abundance to come, and it is here and now (so the claim goes) that contraception can be of assistance. To dismiss the need for such measures by appealing to the world's unexploited resources is to commit the fallacy of identifying the refutation of "A can be produced only by B" with the refutation of "A can be produced by B". The falsity of "World hunger can be solved only by contraception" does not entail the falsity of "World hunger can be solved by contraception", still less the falsity of "Contraception can help to solve world hunger."[1] I am not competent to pronounce on the truth

[1] I make the distinction because it is too often supposed that to advocate contraception is to advocate it as a panacea. But moral questions apart, its use has to be considered in terms of the many and complex demographic and economic factors which decide the optimum growth for populations. For some idea of how complicated these facts are, see *L*, chapter 15; see

or falsity of either assertion, but this competency is not needed to detect bad logic. Nor is it needed to put such naive questions as: How densely populated a world do we want to live in? Is the possibility of physical sustenance an adequate guide to the answer? Are we to accept the ever-expanding city, the dwindling fields, the crowds, the noise? Whatever we do about distributing the world's resources, these are questions that deserve an answer; we need look no further than countries like England or Belgium to see why.

The real trouble with arguments against contraception on grounds of personal values, world economy and general utility is that they open the door to suggestions that the employment of contraceptive measures might be regulated by just these personal and social considerations. They might be used with this family here and not with that there, in one place as a temporary measure, in another for a five-year experiment, and so on. The RP can have nothing to do with all this; it is absolute in its prohibition, and even if the arguments we have examined were stronger than they are, they could never yield this required absoluteness. At most they might have been rebuttals of objections to the RP as we suggested earlier in this chapter (p. 27)—though if our critique is sound they have been failures here too. It is in the next chapter that we shall encounter an argument which claims to prove this absoluteness of the prohibition.

---

also (*L* 271) a quotation from Zuckermann as to the difficulty of introducing any kind of birth regulation into those parts of the world that need it most.

3

Nature

1. Principles of argument

The main weight of rational defence of the RP rests upon the argument to be examined in this chapter. Unlike those arguments which we have already considered, the appeal to nature would, if it were valid, furnish just that absoluteness and unchangeability which is characteristic of and required by the RP. Previous arguments have tried to confirm the position, to prove that the Church's law respects the essential values of sexuality, to show that there is no contradiction between her teaching and the conclusions of human reason. What we have here is something more. It is an attempt to show that, apart from any social or consequential consideration, and without regard to particular circumstances, interference with what is called the natural pattern of intercourse is wrong in itself. Once this is accepted, there can be no question of justifying contraception by circumstance or context, any more than, to use Aristotle's example, there can be talk of when, where, or how to commit adultery. It might be asked why, if so apodictic a proof exists, any other arguments should be needed. Indeed, if we accept the force of this appeal to nature, the presence of other arguments in accounts of the RP is an embarrassment rather than a confirmation. If the argument from nature is effective, talk about contingent facts is irrelevant—who would think of verifying the multiplication table with representative samples of pebbles and beads? On the other hand, if the argument from nature is not effective, we must remember that an apodictic argument which turns out to be faulty does not thereby become a persuasive argument which is sound. If the appeal to nature fails, we shall be back where we started—we shall be faced with arguments like those in the last chapter, arguments concerned with values in human life and sexuality. And, as we saw there, even if such arguments were admitted, they could not lead us to condemn contraception with that universality which the RP demands and which the appeal to nature claims to offer.

This argument against contraception needs to be understood, not as an isolated phenomenon, but as part of a wider process of rational apologetic for the Christian teaching on matters of sexual morality. Apologetic arguments in this field have to face certain difficulties. Some of these difficulties are common to all rational defences of Christian morals, others are peculiar to defences of the Christian virtue of chastity. The first section of this chapter will state these difficulties, and will try to show how they affect arguments in favour of the RP.

If we examine traditional Christian teaching on matters like the sanctity of human life, respect for property, and regard for sincerity in human relationships, we notice that the rules stating our obligations contain expressions which can call for a moral appraisal of cases in which we are actually confronted by these obligations. Thus, we must not *directly* take *innocent* human life; we must not deny the truth *where our audience enjoys the normal right to it*; we must not *unlawfully* take what belongs to another. These are all absolute commands, for it is never right to do any of these things. Yet in one sense their absoluteness is due to their being tautologous.[1] They display the form of our obligations without absolving us from the task of estimating the way in which these obligations present themselves to us on particular occasions. What is to count as murder, lying, stealing? Who are the innocent? When is life directly attacked? When is the right to truth forfeited, or when is the context such that the truth is not expected? When is it lawful to deprive another of his property? Notice that these questions of mine are not aimed against the absoluteness of moral standards and that they are not attempts to secure circumstantial toleration of what is conceded to be sinful. They are prefaces to a legitimate defining of what our obligations are here and now, they are enquiries as to whether or not what we propose to do really does fall under the admittedly absolute prohibition. That they are genuine questions does not mean that they are questions which always or even frequently arise. On the other hand, to ask such questions is not to commit oneself to a system of "situation ethics" in

[1] The point was made by D. J. B. Hawkins in his interesting article "Arguments in Sexual Ethics". *CR* (February 1962).

which cases of conscience are to be solved "by some internal light immune to rational discussion, and illuminating the case as something unique".[1] "Is this person innocent?", "Has he a right to the truth?" are questions which can be asked without expecting answers that are peculiar to one unrepeatable state of affairs here and now. On the contrary, the cases to be so judged are not isolated phenomena bearing some hallmark which separates the sheep from the goats for us. Hard work may be necessary to solve problems of conscience, and it is hard work which we may not refuse to undertake.

The Christian sexual code is neither more nor less absolute than the Christian stand on matters like murder, lying and robbery; but it can be specified far more *materially* than can those principles concerned with other moral topics. If we take the prohibition of sodomy, for example, we can give a definition of what is prohibited (*coitus per anum* between males) which contains none of that "moral" or "estimative" language present in the prohibitions already mentioned concerning murder, stealing and lying. In the prohibition of sodomy and of other sexual sins there will be what I shall call a *perspicuous concreteness* not present in the other prohibitions. Not, of course, that we may ever murder or steal or lie, any more than we may ever commit sodomy; but questions like "Is this murder?" "Is this theft?" or "Is this lying?" can raise perplexities in a way that "Is this sodomy?" "Is this adultery?" and "Is this fornication?" cannot. I say that the former group *can* raise perplexities; they need not. Baby-killing is obvious wrong, and to talk of estimating our obligations with respect to it is nonsense, if not worse. But "killing human beings" describes an action which may be justified or may not be—and the process of deciding whether it is justified is not the same as the process by which we decide whether a particular action is adultery or not. This may well take some deciding—the matrimonial life of some cinema actors has been suggested to me as a case where it would—but the decision is not bound up with moral evaluation and appraisal as is the decision over killing. Sodomy would furnish an even sharper contrast with actions like killing or depriving another of his property. To be sure, the whole pattern of chaste be-

[1] The quotation is from the condemnation of situation ethics by the Holy Office, 1956. (*D* 3918.)

haviour cannot be so perspicuously stated. If we define chastity as "the right use of sex" (as Aquinas does, cf. p. 7) then the presence of the words "the right" will call for that moral appraisal already associated with words like "innocent" and "unlawful". My point is simply that "Thou shalt not commit adultery" does immediately exclude a specific kind of situation to a degree that "Thou shalt not kill" (or "Thou shalt do no murder") does not.

We must distinguish this "perspicuous concreteness" of sexual prohibitions from the absoluteness of any prohibition of sin which is characteristic of theistic morals as a whole. It is a matter for philosophical debate as to how far a non-theistic system of ethics will admit prohibitions of an absoluteness which no considerations can circumvent; it may be that moral principles of such a system will be policies for the attainment of approved consequences rather than divine imperatives which, in some (perhaps exceptional) circumstances, must still be obeyed despite the consequences. At all events, a consequential or utilitarian ethic can never be an adequate guide for Christian behaviour. Not only is a Christian unable to assert without presumption that he is able to judge the ultimate usefulness of things, he has to estimate the merits of what he does, not just by consequences, but also in terms of some divinely decided moral antecedents of these actions. Feats of traditional casuistry which strike the unbeliever as a paltering with evil are sometimes due to the Christian's principle of never making an acknowledged sin into a step towards something else, however beneficial this something else may be. Whatever the Christian does must be shown to be at least morally indifferent, for there can be no question for him of letting consequences make up for doing what is wrong. The results of this casuistry may well be less offensive to non-pious ears than the casuistry itself, and the actual practice of the theistic and the non-theistic moralists can be similar enough. This does not mean that they use their moral principles in the same way.[1]

[1] If I may illustrate the point of what I have been saying by an example, belief in the absoluteness of God's law can commit us to a policy of *deliberate inaction*, where action, though unlawful, might produce a result less evil in some respects. To use an example offered me and others in debate, what would I do if some tyrant threatened to boil two babies alive unless I boiled one of them alive? Even if the choice were so stark, the

Sexual morality is where the Christian is most likely to part company with the unbeliever, for it is here that a consequential or utilitarian ethic finds it hardest to match its conclusions with those of religious tradition. It is not just that human instincts make right judgement impossible here—though fornication is more attractive than telling lies—but rather that Christian precepts on the point possess this perspicuous concreteness which excludes further moral appraisal. Certain actions, specifiable in non-moral terms, are prohibited without more ado. This does not mean that rational argument is out of place in these matters, or that abandoning the Christian code leads to sexual anarchy; but arguments from the nature of human love, the dignity of the human person, emotional involvement, social order, family stability, and the rest, will not be able to pass from general estimates of and directives about the sexual instinct to the unequivocal absoluteness of Christian practice. Of course, it may be that these considerations will lead the unbeliever to conclude that absolute rules in sexual matters are the only safeguard against disaster; it is more likely that they will not; and even if he does adopt absolute rules, they may not be identical with those of Christian tradition. This disagreement is not something at which we should be surprised. Even in the Bible there is enough variety in sexual traditions to show that Christian practice in this matter is not simply a divinely approved deduction from a dispassionate observation of the human condition. Christians subject themselves to divine commands which (like the whole doctrine of which they are a part) transcend the conclusions of reason, commands for whose content reason can furnish some analogy and offer some defence, commands whose execution will, so they hold, lead to the ultimate destiny of the human condition, which is the vision of God.

Christians who seek to defend their views about chastity on rational grounds are faced, then, with two difficulties. The first is not peculiar to discussions of sexual morality: their acceptance of moral obligations as commands from God prohibits

---

Christian would have to choose *to do nothing*; the consequences of his inaction could not justify his doing something in itself evil. (I am not of course claiming that silly examples like this are of any relevance to policy, let alone to morals. Why take the tyrant's word to begin with?)

them from issuing themselves with occasional dispensations and pragmatic sanctions, as they might venture to disregard a general policy of etiquette or literary taste in particular circumstances. So there is bound to be a limit to the appeals the Christian can make to personal and prudential considerations and the rest to vindicate his norms of behaviour. Nor is it hard to think of cases where the obligation of observing God's law will outstrip the prohibitive or persuasive effects of such considerations.[1] This in itself need not be a disadvantage: a good case can be made out for refusing to countenance any erosion of moral principles on the grounds of compassion or convenience, for refusing to allow the relief of present distress to obscure our view of the other and possibly disastrous results of derogating from fixed principles in moral matters. But the difficulty is there; and it is hard to believe that purely human considerations can always overcome it. The second difficulty for the apologist is peculiar to sexual matters and is due to what we have called the perspicuous concreteness of these items in the Christian code of behaviour. As orders from God, these edicts have the unequivocal directness of effective prohibitions; as principles to be rationally defended they will offer still more cases where only the sacrosanctity of a divine imperative will fully justify their observance, in the face of—not just transient emotion, but those very values which Christian marriage is supposed to safeguard.

This is a fact which needs honestly stating, not obscuring by going through the motions of reasoned polemic. To take over rational arguments against stealing or breaking contracts and to use them against adultery is misleading. If adultery were simply theft of another's partner or the breaking of a contract, it would be subject to the same moral appraisal as other kinds of stealing and unfaithfulness. We should call it unlawful taking of another's wife. We should be able to imagine cases where the matrimonial contract was declared to have lost its validity for the sake of the common good, cases where prescription would obtain, cases where we could apply the tag *nullius est primi capientis*. The whole point of adultery is that it is *not* just like

[1] It is possible to think of cases of suicide where something more is needed than talk of social consequence and the rest if we are to abstain from such a course of action.

unlawful taking of another's property, *not* just like breaking a contract. Adultery is determinable by a non-moral description to a degree that the others need not be. Rational judgement on the point is limited by this perspicuous concreteness of the prohibition, while the analogy with stealing is further weakened by other commandments which govern the Christian's use of marriage. The Christian prohibition of adultery has to be considered in terms of the whole Christian discipline of marriage, a discipline which (unlike the discipline of the Old Law) prohibits divorce and polygamy as well. What is rational argument supposed to do here—prove the absolute unlawfulness of divorce and polygamy? Surely the context of this prohibition of the Christian law gives it a severity which makes adaptations from arguments against stealing or breaking contracts palpably inadequate for its rational proof. Postulate a command from God—and our faith teaches that God has spoken in the matter—and we may use his authority to confirm moral decisions which by human standards are agonizing. Let us not insult those who make such decisions for God's sake by pretending that they are doing only what right reason dictates. Consider the deserted and wronged wife who wishes to begin marriage again with a good man who will care for her and for her children—it would not only be heartless to appeal to her on grounds of natural fittingness and the rest, it would be fallacious. After all, if it is proved next week that her absent husband was baptized with milk instead of with water, she could have their marriage dissolved and live happily ever after. And where does this leave our rational argument?[1]

If the Christian judgement on adultery raises difficulties for the apologist, the difficulties raised for him by the RP on contraception are greater still. Extramarital intercourse (and *a fortiori* homosexual relationships) fall outside that pattern of monogamous heterosexual union enjoined by faith, and the virtues of this divinely instituted state of life can be appealed to in arguments against aberrations from it—always within those limits of effectiveness which we have already mentioned. But

[1] *De facto*, the great majority of marriages are not sacramental and so, by Catholic law, dissoluble. The understandable but misleading reticence of popular teaching on this point gives a plausibility to rationalizations of these pieces of morality which would otherwise be seen as the divine revelations they really are.

can it be shown that contraception is opposed as such to the married state of Christians? It would of course be easy to prove such opposition between marriage and *some* ways of employing contraception in it. L's arguments about the safeguarding of matrimonial values do this, as we saw in the preceding chapter (see pp. 28–9): but to take arguments like this as excluding *all* forms of contraception *always* is to commit the venerable fallacy of passing *a dicto secundum quid ad dictum simpliciter*.

I am not concerned at the moment with Christian tradition about contraception, but I should like to point out an interesting difference that exists between official condemnations of contraception and similar condemnations of other sexual sins. Adultery, fornication, and sodomy have always been denounced in ways that put the absoluteness of the prohibition into the context of God's revealed word; contraception is usually condemned on grounds not specifically religious at all. Either (as we have already seen) the results and ideology of contraception are denounced as undesirable, or (as we are going to see) the nature of sexuality is invoked to prove that the practice is essentially wicked. It is strange (though of course not decisive for a Roman Catholic) that scripture contains no unequivocal prohibition of contraception, as it does of other offences against chastity.[1] It is inevitable—but just as strange—that those who defend the RP are obliged, so to speak, to leave Jerusalem and go to Athens for help.

The situation is like that faced by Aquinas in his argument for the unlawfulness of fornication (*DM* 15.2 ad 12, see above, p. 8), where he supplemented the inconclusiveness of social arguments with the principle that laws are to be estimated according to the general run of cases, not by the exception. Even allowing him this talk of generality (which itself seems bound up with a previous expectation of what sexual union should mean) we were still able to object that his answer drew too close an analogy between the divine norm for sexuality disclosed in its social setting and consequences, and the approximations of a merely human law. Not that Aquinas was unaware of this

[1] It is not clear whether Onan was condemned (Gen. 38) for spilling the seed, or for failing to raise up a family for his dead brother. (cf. Deut. 25). Significantly, the multitude of sexual regulations in the Mosaic code says nothing of a practice which must surely be the oldest form of preventing conception known to man.

difficulty—indeed, he appreciates the limitations of his argument in a way that many who claim to follow him do not. He admits that fornication is not obviously wrong in the sense that adultery is obviously wrong, and he links men's acceptance that it is wrong to fornicate with their being instructed by religious teachers commissioned from God. (*DM* 15.2 ad 3.) Once he has made this admission, his position is stronger. As we have already seen, he can now reject claims made for particular exceptions to the rule, by appealing to the divine will; and to the divine will, not as manifest in the humanly discernible pattern of sex (and so to be interpreted in terms of that varying pattern) but as proclaimed authoritatively by God.

Where the RP differs from the position reached by this argument of Aquinas is that it has to make do without a divine revelation. To say this is not simply to repeat what has just been said about the absence of a scriptural prohibition of contraception. The "has to" is logical, not factual; whether or not a revelation exists, the RP is committed to holding the intrinsic malice of contraception, a malice such that revelation from God would be only a confirmation of what is already determined by the nature of things. We saw that Aquinas offered another kind of argument against sexual abuse, an argument based upon the nature and purpose of the sexual union. (See above, pp. 8–9.) As we are now going to examine this "argument from nature" as it occurs later in defences of the RP, it might seem logical to begin by scrutinizing more carefully this argument of Aquinas. But it will be better to examine and to criticize the present-day use of the argument first—it is put forward often enough and elaborately enough for this to be possible. Only later will the position of Aquinas be reconsidered, when other aspects of his teaching can also be borne in mind.

The argument from nature submits that the sexual act may be clearly seen to be aimed at the transmission of life from its very structure. (Hürth, *CD* 217.) The first stages of it prepare the reproductive organs for union while encouraging the partners to bring about this union. The union itself becomes ever closer as the climax approaches, and culminates in what is at once the pleasurable relief of sexual tension and the placing of the man's seed within the woman in such a way that further, automatic processes of hers may lead to her being fertilized by it. The sexual satisfaction and loving intimacy attained in intercourse are part of a process which is achieved in this generative union of man and woman. "The Creator has arranged that the husband and wife find pleasure and happiness of mind and body in the performance of this function. Consequently the husband and wife do no wrong in seeking out and enjoying this pleasure. They are accepting what the Creator intended for them." ("Midwives", 59.) But to separate this satisfaction from its context, or to attempt to rob the union of its generative effect, is to go against the order of things ordained by the author of nature and founder of marriage. (Hürth, *CD* 219; *EOM* 225.) The personal enrichment and greater closeness brought about by intercourse are natural effects of it intended by God, and are praiseworthy; but they are secondary effects, subordinate to the primary generative purpose and may not be attained if that primary generative purpose is thwarted. "As things are, the marriage act is of its very nature destined for the procreation of children; so those who perform it while robbing it of its natural force act against nature and do something essentially shameful and wicked. Not even the gravest reasons can make such an intrinsically unnatural act into something good and in accord with nature." ("Marriage", *D* 3716.) This seems a fair summary of the argument from nature, and has the advantage of being based on papal pronouncements and upon a respected theologian's commentaries on them. More, of course, remains to be said of what exactly is involved in this argument, and there are, needless to say, many other expositions of it.[1]

I intend to deploy three lines of objection against this argument. Perhaps "objection" is an inadequate word—my purpose is to disclose as clearly as I can exactly what the argument is trying to prove and how it sets about proving it. This may be of service, I hope, even to those who cannot agree with my final, adverse verdict.

2. *The first objection*

A first and understandable reaction to the argument from nature is to say that it proves too much. If the whole pattern of

[1] The textbooks of moral theology we have mentioned may be consulted (usually under the heading "De Onanismo"); and the works on medical ethics always have a chapter on it.

coitus is aimed at procreation, how can coitus be justified when procreation is impossible, either temporarily or permanently? The prohibition of intercourse when procreation is either not intended or not possible (due to existing pregnancy, age, and so on), a view admired by Montaigne (*De la modération*), seems to have been taught in our own day by Gandhi. One of his followers, describing the Mahatma's thought, says, "What should we think of a husband who sowed the best grain in his possession on stony soil, or of a landowner who would stand by and see his field (whose soil is good) sown with grain that was certainly beyond all criticism, but under conditions that make it impossible for it to germinate?" (Quoted in *L* 40.) These words might be taken as a picturesquely forcible version of the Roman argument from nature. But of course Gandhi was in fact wanting to limit intercourse to occasions when procreation was intended, and it cannot be denied that the obvious force of the agricultural image favours his interpretation of it rather than the Roman view. Defenders of the RP who use the argument from nature escape what seems to be a natural enough consequence of their position by declaring the essential subordination of the secondary effects of intercourse to be independent of the actual achieving of the primary procreative effect of it. The relation between the effects is "transcendental"; that is, it derives from the essential structure of sexual union. The subordination of secondary to primary purpose is still present, even when the primary effect is not and cannot be realized. (Hürth, *CD.*) In other words, the purpose of intercourse is generative even when it cannot lead to generation, "just as it can be said that all eyes are intended and constructed to see, even though in abnormal cases, because of particular internal or external conditions, they can never be capable of giving sight". ("Midwives", 47; and cf. *EOM* 226.)

This pronouncement about the indestructibility of the relationship between the secondary and primary effects of intercourse is of a piece with what was said about the unlawfulness of AIH in another allocution of Pius XII (see above, p. 15), and it significantly modifies the view of coition involved in the "argument from nature" as originally stated. Initially, the whole pattern of intercourse was said to be apt and destined for the procreation of children, to reach its climax in the generative act.

Now it is admitted that this pattern may be followed even when it is quite certain that there will be no procreative effect. Conversely, departures from the pattern cannot be justified by appeals to the generative purpose of sexual relations. The condemnation of artificial insemination by the husband made "nature" to be determined, not by any generative finality, but by a particular anatomical pattern of conjunction. Just so, the real point of the RP is now not that a generative action must be performed, but that a particular type of union must be achieved. This pattern of coitus has been given a moral significance independent of the generative function which, according to the original form of the appeal to nature, was supposed to be its raison d'être. The change in emphasis is substantial, and cannot be bridged by talk about the innate purpose of eyes which *de facto* cannot see. Nelson could not have justified putting his telescope to his blind eye on the grounds of that organ's innate purpose. His job was not to posit an action essentially ordered to sight and only accidentally impeded from achieving sight—his job was to *see*. And if permanently or temporarily sterile couples may have intercourse without being guilty of shirking their duty, then their duty must be just to unite in a certain way, without regard to what follows. The objective order for them, as for all couples, turns out to be decided, not by generative finality, but by a temporally and locally delimited pattern of genital behaviour.

3. *The second objection*

This line of objection to the argument from nature is perhaps the commonest of all. Does not human activity, from shaving to dam-building, consist in mastering and thwarting nature? Does not the RP logically entail the condemnation of smoking for putting the lungs to an unnatural use, and of chewing-gum for producing gustatory pleasure without nutrition? Would it not have deplored the invention of aircraft, on the ground that nature had not equipped men with wings? There is no need to continue the examples as the line of attack is well known and, put in so crude a form, is not very cogent. Undoubtedly, the very concept of human activity involves an interference with the *status quo* of the world—man is an animal that can adapt its environment to a degree shared by no other, and "natural" for him cannot mean what it does for the rest. If the objection said no more than this, it would prove only that "nature" is far too ambiguous a concept to be used without qualification in moral argument; a trite enough conclusion, but worth drawing, perhaps.[1] For the theory of natural law described earlier, "nature" is the norm of human conduct not in the sense of the *status quo*, but inasmuch as it means the divinely ordained and not-to-be-transgressed order of creation which forms the basic guide of the practical reason; this is what Aquinas meant by his "share in the ordering reason of God". (See above, p. 6.)

And it is here that this apparently naive objection can be developed so that it begins to pinch. The illicitness of obtaining sexual relief outside a generative context was supposed to be perceptible from an inspection of the physiological pattern of intercourse. Yet an examination of intercourse among beasts reveals a similar physiological pattern; are similar moral obligations to be deduced, if not for the beasts, then for men who rule them? Presumably not—for I know of no moral theologian who questions the licitness of submitting livestock to artificial insemination, sterilization, and the rest. To quote only one authority, Pius XII said that for man, unlike other animals, the procreative right is limited to the natural act performed within the bonds of a valid marriage. ("Fertility", 472.) Understandably, there can be no talk of making marriage a necessary preliminary to the couplings of beasts, but it is not so clear why the natural pattern of the sexual act should not have to be respected there as well. Lestapis makes some attempt to distinguish the human situation from the situation of other animals; the rest of creation can be regarded as subject to man's God-given dominion, but man must respect God's dominion over himself (*L* 126) (he invokes Heidegger's terminology to support the distinction, but without explicative effect). Two questions remain unanswered. The first is why man's dominion over the beasts should include just those biological processes which in the human species are sacrosanct. It is not enough to reply that man has rights of life and death over beasts: there are occasions

[1] For an idea of the assortment of uses that "nature" has at the hands of philosophers, see, for example, Basil Willey's *The Eighteenth-Century Background* (1962).

when he has the right to kill his fellow men, but none when the RP lets him practise artificial insemination on them. The second question—complementary to the first—is why these particular biological processes in man should have been removed from human control. Once more, it is not enough to say that God alone has power over human life and death. Theologians traditionally allow human life to be directly taken in certain circumstances—are the processes for the transmission of life to be regarded as "invincibly innocent" and so immune from any such attack?

The questions would not arise if the RP amounted to a simple respect for humanity (for then the distinction between human beings and the rest would follow naturally enough), nor if it taught a general reverence for the order of nature (for then it would be loath to meddle with the reproductive apparatus of any living creature). Neither of these views adequately represents the RP. "Respect for humanity" cannot as such entail the rigorous and absolute preservation of the "natural pattern" demanded by the RP; while "reverence for the order of nature" connotes a policy of respect towards all animals where the RP is concerned only with the sexual actions of the human species. The contrast brings home to us that it is not fair to say, with Lestapis, that man has been given permission to go against the order of nature in other species (*L* 126). Rather, the whole idea of an objective pattern of sex is confined to the species Man. Which shows more precisely what has already been noticed: that the terms "objective" and "natural" are misleadingly generic; it is not an overall observance of the pattern of creation that is being taught, but the untouchability of particular human functions.

"Private individuals have only that control over their bodily organs which is concerned with their natural purposes." ("Marriage", *D* 3723.) These words of Pius XI get nearer to the heart of the RP than any talk of deducing the purpose of sex from observation. Observation and deduction cannot be an adequate approach to the RP. From observation we may conclude—innocuously conclude—that reproduction is the primary purpose of intercourse. But of course this is not what "primary" has to mean for the RP—it has to mean a good deal more. Our examination has shown that "primary" here means more than "ordinary" or "original" or "principal". It does not refer to the intentions of those who have intercourse (*finis operantis*) but to the *finis operis*, the built-in purpose of intercourse itself. And this purpose we have seen to be still further restricted to the structure of each act of intercourse considered in isolation. Perhaps *finis operationis* would be a better term for a relationship which dictates, not a general "life-respecting" policy for sexual relations in marriage, but an unswerving adherence to a particular form of sexual contact irrespective of further consequences.

Observations of human sexuality and deductions from observation cannot be enough for the RP. What must also be taken into account is the privileged position of man in the divinely constituted order of things, a position which marks him off from other animals and makes him subject in some respects to God alone: and we have seen that he does this. (*L* 126.) Yet to acknowledge the privileged position of man does not itself provide a rational basis for accepting the inviolability of the reproductive functions demanded by the RP. To talk of man's special place in the world cannot be enough; it remains to be shown how these important limitations of man's power are to be deduced from his position in creation. Even if reason demonstrates the existence of God and man's subjection to him, the form taken by this subjection has still to be traced; and it is not easy to see how the form called for by the RP could be traced by reason alone. A divine pronouncement would settle the matter, but the whole point of the argument from nature is that it claims to need no such act of revelation. That "the divinely ordained pattern of nature may not be transgressed" is a truism. That this divine order includes what the argument from nature says it does is not a truism at all, and needs proving.

If the RP openly started by postulating this inviolability, it would be able to point to various facts about human beings and human sexuality which were aided by the postulate, and which provided in consequence, not a proof, but rather a suggestion that the postulate was not wholly at variance with human needs. Once proclaim the inviolability of the sexual pattern on the grounds of divine revelation, or simply decide that it is inviolable because of tradition or personal inclination, and human life and sexuality are surely complex enough to make us free to discern the fittingness of this inviolability in the structure of sexual intercourse. Our proclamation and our decision enable us to appraise the structure in a new way, to recognize significance in it which others do not. If we do this we must be quite honest and clearheaded about the nature of our decision. It is only in virtue of previously accepting the inviolability that we can recognize this significance; we are not deducing inviolability from an independently and dispassionately observed structure. What comes first is the acceptance; only then can the phenomena of human sexuality be shaped by us into a form reflecting this accepted inviolability. The phenomena themselves do not furnish compelling grounds for being so shaped, or proof that this shape should be imposed. We must not confuse decision with observation. Thinking of our friend may help us to see his face in the tea-leaves: but we did not learn to recognize him by gazing into a cup.

Perhaps this account of the second line of objection to the argument from nature has shown the crucial importance of Pius XI's pronouncement already quoted. What matters for the RP is not a general following of nature but rather the inviolability of certain human biological functions. Yet if this immunity of certain human biological functions has not been so far rationally demonstrated, the area of debate has been more accurately marked out. In the next section we begin the third line of objection, which continues the debate at a deeper level.

4. *The third objection: exposition*

Two lines of objection to the argument from nature have been considered so far. I first disclosed an ambiguity in the contention that sexual intercourse has reproduction for its purpose, and suggested that the argument takes the natural norm as a special pattern of anatomical contact rather than as the generative finality of sexual relations. The second line of objection considered this "natural norm", and tried to show that "nature" here is too generic a term; it is the privileged position of certain human functions that is central to the RP, and the argument from nature does not furnish adequate grounds for knowing what functions are so privileged, or that their sacrosanctity is absolute. The third line of objection goes further, and attacks the whole philosophical method which underlies the argument from nature. It is this line of objection which is going to be considered in the next two sections. Unfortunately, to reject the argument from nature on philosophical grounds is, nowadays at least, to court the accusation of teaching "situation ethics". So it might be useful, before going any further, to quote part of the description of the system offered by the Holy Office in a denunciation of 2 February 1956 (*D* 3918): "Those who follow this system hold that the final norm of action is not the objective order, determined by the law of nature, and known for certain from that law, but some inner decision and light in each individual's mind from which he gathers what he must do here and now . . . this decision, in many cases at least, is not measured by any objective independent norm; nor can it or ought it to be so measured, for it is wholly self-sufficient." I am not concerned with the justice of this description, only with stating what it is that the Holy Office was out to condemn. At the end of this chapter, when the reader has had a chance of seeing how my views tally with this description, I will return to this accusation. But here and now I should like to state that I am not setting out to teach any situational system of morality. On the contrary, this third and last objection of mine to the argument from nature might be accused of reaction rather than of innovation. I am going to submit that this appeal to nature, this main rational argument for the RP, far from being an instance of that doctrine of natural law so bound up with Christian tradition, is a travesty and impoverishment of that doctrine, and vitiated by a philosophical error associated with empiricists like Locke and Hume. To justify this apparently strange contention will take some time, and will have to begin with a digression into the history of philosophy.[1]

One of the commonplaces of traditional British empiricism is the belief that philosophy consists in an examination and inventory of certain mental objects called "ideas" or "impressions". The inventory may be a long one, and the examination may call for subtlety and discernment, but its objects are already given. What remains for the philosopher is to catalogue them and to

[1] Reference in the next paragraphs are to Locke's *Essay Concerning the Human Understanding* and to Hume's *Treatise of Human Nature*; references to each are given in the usual way.

distinguish them one from another. Philosophy, in other words, is a scrutiny of mental operations: its job is to see what activity in the mind is involved in memory, causality, universal concepts, and the rest.

Consider Locke's account of memory. For him it is a storehouse of ideas, by which we can conceive heat, light, and so on, even when not confronted by them. Ideas are nothing but actual perceptions; and what we call memory is the ability the mind has to revive perceptions it received in the past. (2.10.2.) Or take his account of universal terms. That we have general terms like "man" or "animal" is because we are able to make general ideas by *abstraction*. There would be no end to naming if we could not do so, for names are the outward sign of ideas, and our ideas initially stand for particular things. (2.11.9.) By abstraction we frame an idea in which a number of particular objects agree, not thereby creating anything new but only omitting from the particular ideas that which is peculiar to each (3.3.7), and the same process may be applied to abstract ideas themselves, to reach an idea still more comprehensive. (3.3.8.) The artificiality of abstract ideas makes them appear not a little obscure to philosophical reflection—for instance, the abstract idea of a triangle has to be both equilateral and scalene, and neither of them, all at once. (4.7.9.)

Hume follows the same method, more drastically. When he wants to distinguish memory from imagination, it is on the grounds of its superior force and vivacity that he does so. Nothing in the simple ideas which compose both alike, he says, is an adequate distinction; all that marks off one from another is an accompanying feeling. (1.1.3; 1.3.5.) As for the analysis of causality, it must amount to a search among the two objects called "cause" and "effect", for the impression which produces such an idea. It cannot be any particular qualities of these two objects which do so, for the causal relationship can exist between other objects where these particular qualities are missing. Nor are spatial contiguity and temporal order, though present where causality is present, enough of themselves to ensure the presence of causality; there must also be an idea of a necessary connection between a cause and what it causes. And a search among the qualities of any one cause and its effect seems to offer no impression or impressions from which this idea could be derived. (1.3.2.) Further examination shows that the constant conjunction of the two ideas is required, as well as spatio-temporal relationship; there is, however, no demonstrative argument from past to future instances. (1.3.6). It is, Hume decides, custom or a principle of association that leads us from the impression A to the idea or *belief* of B with which A has been in the past both constantly conjoined and spatio-temporally related. The belief of B is the idea of it conceived as a matter of fact; there is a superior force or steadiness to it which distinguishes it from a fictitious idea that fancy alone presents to us. (1.3.7.)

Much has been written of late against this view of philosophy as an inspection of mental contents.[1] It will be enough for us to attack those things and presuppositions in it which we believe can be traced in the argument from nature as well. Notice first of all the restricted sense of memory which interests Locke. There are certainly occasions when a sudden flood of recollections is released by a taste or odour—Proust with his *madeleine* is the paradigm of all such cases—but they are the exception rather than the rule, nor are they a sure guide to what we mean by memory. That I remember how to use a safety-razor, how to tell when a kettle is boiling, or how to get to the bus-stop, means simply that I have learnt these things in the past and do not need to relearn them each morning. Memory in the sense of learnt abilities is not adequately describable in terms of a revival here and now of impressions perceived in the past, as if the fact that we remember how to do something were to be judged by the contents of our mind at a particular moment, rather than by a successful performance of a previously learned action. Nor, to take what Hume says, is memory stamped with some hallmark, perceptible here and now and distinguishing it from imagination. I may be mistaken about my friend's telephone number on Monday and right about it on Tuesday without my "ideas" on the point appropriately differing in vividness. It is not an on-the-spot inspection which decides the issue between imagining and

[1] L. Wittgenstein's *Philosophical Investigations* (1953) and G. Ryle's *The Concept of Mind* (1949) are only two of the best known. For a related denunciation, which includes a defence of Aquinas from the charge, see P. T. Geach's *Mental Acts* (1960). In a very different tradition, E. Husserl's *Logische Untersuchungen* (1900 ff.) also attacks the methodology of empiricism.

remembering. Other things have to be considered, among which is the question whether our judgement tallies with the facts or does not tally with them.

Locke's account of general terms is of a piece with his views on memory. An idea for him is initially a label for a particular object, it is always something *there*, something from which bits can be omitted by abstraction, as if selective bleaches were being successively applied to a coloured fabric. What is left after these omissions is itself still there, still as much a mental object as ever. If it is the abstract idea of a triangle, we can still ask, "Is it scalene?", just as much as we could ask the question of a triangle drawn on a piece of paper. The answer we get—that the abstract idea of a triangle has to be both equilateral and scalene at the same time—can be avoided only by abandoning the philosophical technique which sets us the task of examining meaning, universality, memory, and the rest, as particular isolated phenomena, whose presence, absence and content can be detected by examination, just as a microscope can here and now disclose the presence or absence of organisms in a solution. Berkeley's attack on Locke (in *A Treatise concerning the Principles of Human Knowledge*, preface, sections 11 ff.) showed a way out of the impasse. It is in the *use made* of signs and words that their generality lies, not in the progressive dilution of a mental object. If a theorem is proved with an isosceles triangle for the diagram but is valid for all triangles, it is so valid because the deduction applied to the diagram does not appeal to the fact that two of its sides are equal, but only to the fact that it has three sides and that they are straight. The theorem is not valid because we have managed to produce a mysterious mental artefact called the abstract idea of a triangle, by contemplating which we can arrive at a conclusion which applies to triangles universally. "Looking", "contemplating" and the rest put us on a false trail from the start, lead us to believe that universality, memory, and so on are to be explained in terms of a scrutiny of our minds' furniture.

It would be impertinent to dismiss in a paragraph anything so formidable as Hume's analysis of causality, but we can at least notice what sort of investigation he claims to be conducting—it is of a piece with the kind of philosophical activity already noticed in Locke and in himself. That we say "A is the cause of B" is supposed by Hume from the start to be due to some trait of experience, to some flavour or modality in it. Indeed, the conclusion he eventually reaches is that, over and above contiguity, succession, and constant conjunction, there is some—as he puts it—added zest or "je-ne-sais-quoi" which gives us the idea of B's necessarily following from A. It is not unfair to set this highly idiosyncratic picture of causality, with its technique of recognition redolent of detecting blindfold a favourite whisky, against the variety of ways in which we actually do seek explanations. Why did Hitler not invade England after Dunkirk? What brings on inflation? Why is jazz popular in so many countries?—in the presence of these and other real questions, it is idle to pretend that they are answered by sampling the vivacity of ideas or by a scrutiny of mental contents.

We might call this technique of Locke and Hume the "peep-show" theory of philosophy,[1] as it sets out to detect significance in terms of what can here and now be glimpsed or described or catalogued among our mental furniture of ideas and impressions. To condemn this method of the empiricists is not to reject the concept of a private mental life, or the possibility of self-scrutiny. It is only to reject the identification of these activities with philosophy. Introspection as such is not idle—it is one way of self-knowledge at which some people are better than others. It is precisely because it is not idle that it is wholly distinct from the mental inventories proposed by Locke and Hume, for these *are* idle; the task they try to perform is not amenable to such techniques. Some people have a rich inner life, some do not: this is a matter of personal disposition, and doubtlessly the world needs both its Joyces and its Robbe-Grillets, but—and the but is all-important—it is not a matter relevant to the philosophical investigation of topics like memory, universality or the causal relationship. We are not lacking in mental vision if we disagree with Locke and Hume here—we are simply denying that there is anything to be viewed in the way they suggest.

To detect this peep-show fallacy in the argument from nature may seem a tall order. It will be clearer (and more persuasive, I hope) to proceed in two stages. For the rest of this section I shall

[1] I do not know whether the phrase is original: if it is not, I cannot now remember where I encountered it.

try to trace the fallacy in neo-scholasticism, the system of philosophy followed by the majority of those who defend the RP. Only then, in the next section, will an attempt be made to show the presence of the fallacy in the argument from nature they use against contraception.

It might seem the height of perverseness to look for a mistake of the empiricists in that scholastic tradition for which they are anathema. I do not suggest, of course, that there is any basic agreement between the two lines of thought. However, there is a surprising convergence between them in philosophical method. Let us examine some passages from C. Boyer's *Cursus Philosophiae ad Usum Seminariorum*. This is a reputable textbook of neo-scholasticism, and is a fair sample of the works which have provided the philosophical formation for so many priests who have undertaken to explain and to defend the RP. It is not difficult to find in Boyer's book much the same kind of mental inventories as those made by the empiricists he so vigorously opposes. That we know the mind to be capable of attaining truth can be shown by analysing *what is experienced when we are certain* (vol. 1, p. 178) and *when* we make proximate deductions from first principles, we are *aware* that our mind is directed to reality. (vol. 1, p. 181.) That we have universal ideas means that the mind *perceives in its direct act* the nature of a particular object *without perceiving* what contracts that nature to particularity. (1, 236.) The infallible criterion for truth is the presence of *objective evidence;* if what seemed evident turns out not to be the case, objective evidence was not really present after all (2, 216–7). Other texts could be quoted, but the very baldness of these reveals their resemblance to the more sophisticated fallacies of Locke and Hume. Consider the equivocation between truth and certainty, or between "evidence" as logically bound up with truth and "evidence" as obviousness, usually but not always so bound up. Do not these testify to the reappearance in a neo-scholastic of the empiricists' belief that a philosopher is not doing his job if, here and now, he cannot point to some mental object as the goal of his search? There must be some special flavour to phenomena which makes them *objective* evidence as opposed to *apparent* evidence, so that to err in the matter is rather like confounding two scents or flavours. If we think universally, there must be some object for the mind to grasp in one way while not perceiving it in another. If we can make *true statements*, this must appear from some facet of our experience when we are *certain*.

It is the peep-show of the empiricists all over again; the philosopher's task is to *look*, to see "what happens inside him when he thinks." Locke and Hume wanted to reduce logical distinctions like those between memory and imagination to psychological events like feelings of vividness. Boyer sets himself the same objective and wants to interpret truth in terms of what we feel when we are certain, evidence in terms of some infallible concomitant to true statements, and conceptual thinking in terms of selective perception. Needless to say, the scholastic's inventory of phenomena is much longer than the empiricist's; he refuses to be confined within the subjectivism of Locke and Hume, and claims that his mental scrutinies yield an objective account of reality. For Boyer, universal concepts truly express the natures of things (1, 219), causality is not to be reduced to Hume's "belief" (1, 359), there is to be no truce with scepticism. (1, 194.) Yet whatever his conclusions may be, the method by which they are obtained is surely uncomfortably like that which Locke and Hume followed, though to such different results. Debates between the two camps become essays in competitive introspection. For the scholastic, the empiricist sees too little, he is philosophically myopic; for the empiricist, the scholastic sees too much, he is the victim of metaphysical *muscae volitantes*. Both agree that it is a matter of what can be inspected, both agree that there is a peep-show to peer into, and differ only as to what can be descried in it.

It is in this basic agreement that both philosophical traditions come to grief. Significance, evidence, causality—these are not to be investigated as if they were particular and isolated phenomena. It is not that they are special, elusive phenomena, by which other phenomena which they accompany achieve meaning, objectivity, or the causal relationship. They are not phenomena at all. Consider the topic of "meaning" or "significance". An isolated phenomenon, however special or elusive, is exactly what significance is not. Simple scrutiny of a playing card will not disclose the force it enjoys as a trump; the use of money cannot be taught by putting a shilling under a microscope; the meaning of words is not some occult event which accompanies their utterance. These are errors which go with the peep-show view of philosophy, and are bound up with the presupposition of this view—that significance and meaning can be traced or depicted as objects are traced or depicted. The way out of these errors is not to say that the tracing or depicting of significance is a very subtle kind of tracing, and a very spiritual kind of depicting—it is to refuse the pictorial terminology altogether. If the meaning of a last will and testament cannot be explained simply by painting a picture of somebody signing one, this is not because of any grossness in our paint brushes or colours. The impossibility is a matter of logic: significance cannot be explained in terms of what can be seen or depicted at one particular moment. Meaning and significance presuppose some system, or a background of capacities and needs, of agreement and of common assumptions. These phrases are generalities because they are trying to illuminate something which is equally general—"verum vagatur per omnes categorias". The background to a sign is neither physically present in it nor actually asserted by it, yet it is indispensable for the sign's function. To lead a trump is not the same as describing the game of cards being played; but "trump" would have no significance if there were no rules about play and about the value of the different suits. The significance or purpose of something human is to be understood against a background of human needs, obligations, and destiny. Without such needs, its sense and point can be seen to disintegrate. For instance, imagine a race of men who have never enjoyed the sense of hearing. What would it be like to say that (without the benefit of any mechanical aids) they used speech as we do? We can see in this simple example how meaning begins to crumble without an appropriate context of use and capability. We are not puzzled as to *how* these men would talk, as we might wonder how two ordinary men encased in diving suits could converse with each other. Rather, we cannot attach the concept of speech to this peculiar race of men at all—their condition seems to offer it no foothold.[1] Or consider what has to be presupposed in social, economic and political matters for a shilling to mean what it does for us. To give someone a shilling is not to read him a lecture on the monetary system—but if there were no such

[1] cf. Wittgenstein, *Philosophical Investigations*, 1, 284.

system there would be no giving away shillings at all. Propositions about purpose and nature which confine themselves to criteria open to inspection at any one moment cannot but be defective, for they offer no proper ground for the content claimed for them. It is my intention to show in the next section how this defective theory of significance invalidates the appeal to nature found in rational apologetic for the RP.

5. *The third objection: application*

To show that the RP is driven to adopt the empiricist criterion of meaning in its argument from nature, we must realize what problem the argument is intended to solve. On the one hand it has to establish that contraception is something evil in itself, not anything which is made evil by excess, or by unregulated use, or by lack of sufficient reason, or by circumstances. The practice has to be excluded absolutely, and as with all prohibitions of sexual sins, the exclusions will be "perspicuously concrete", to use the phrase explained in the first section of this chapter. But on the other hand, the malice of contraception cannot be said to lie simply in failure to procreate, or simply in a lack of respect for the natural order of things; the first two objections have shown that neither formulation is adequate. Not procreation, or the lack of it, but the observance of a particular anatomical pattern is what counts; and what is to be respected is not just "nature" but a particular biological function in human beings. So an absolute illicitness is to be proved; and the illicitness is to be concerned with the abandoning of a pattern of sexual conjunction, and not immediately with anything else.

Faced with this task, the argument from nature must start from the pattern of intercourse and from its disturbance when contraception takes place. For let us get the admission clearly and immediately made that there *is* then a disturbance—frustration if you like—of the seed's natural purpose. Seminal emission by the man in intercourse is only the first part of a process whose further steps we extinguish, either by preventing the seed, with a condom, from entering the woman at all, or by keeping it away, with a pessary, from where it can fertilize her. All this interference with the pattern of fertilization is observable fact. But if we are to proceed from this physiological assertion to the conclusion of condemning those who practise this interference, something more is obviously needed. It will have to be shown that the physiological pattern of human intercourse is more than just one of the many patterns man may adapt for his own purposes; it must be a divinely constituted order which he is not free to treat in this fashion. Moreover, since the argument from nature is a rational argument, this extra premise must itself be attainable without recourse to revelation. For the RP, in other words, human reason must be able to "recognize the moral significance of an objective biological pattern". (McReavy, in a review of P. Chauchard's *Biologie et morale*, *CR* (February 1961), p. 117.) The phrase neatly expresses the basis of the argument from nature. Yet, if the real aim of that argument is to be displayed, some elaboration is needed. It would have been better to place the word "individual" in front of the word "objective". For it is the individual act of intercourse that must be shown to be inviolable, not just the overall generative purpose of sexual intercourse. For the argument from nature, there can be no appeal to anything apart from what is going on here and now in this act of intercourse: a wider appeal would open the door to taking the whole matrimonial union of husband and wife into account, and to the consequent tempering of the RP.

But under such conditions, the biological pattern of a particular act of intercourse can give us an adequate basis for the absolute exclusion of contraception only at the cost of adopting the impoverished theory of meaning which we found in Locke and in Hume. If significance and purpose can be detected here and now as isolated phenomena, can be picked out as much as elements in a picture or design might be picked out, then the meaning and point of sexual intercourse can and must be judged by what goes on in the individual act of coition, without regard for anything else. And, since the undisturbed coital act reaches its climax in the placing of seed in a position where in favourable circumstances further processes may cause it to fertilize, such placing of the seed must be the purpose and object of intercourse. On the other hand, if meaning and purpose are not to be estimated in this restricted way, we shall not be able to pass from the fact that a husband and wife deprive this particular act of intercourse of its undisturbed structure to the conclusion that they are acting against the sense and point of their sexual faculties. It will first have to be shown that this disturbance of the individual act is part of a refusal to accept the fullness of what sex ought to mean and to entail for them.

To estimate the purpose of human sexuality in terms of the structure of each act of intercourse is to think in terms of a philosophical theory which takes account of only those phenomena which can be inspected at any one time. It is also to ignore many factors which an estimate of what sexuality ought to mean for human beings could plausibly take into consideration. There will be many occasions in this essay for me to point out the complexity of the human sexual relationship, its varied effects, and the need for it to be integrated into the whole framework of shared life together. Let it be enough for the moment to point out that such a view of sex is not only platitudinously obvious, but inextricably bound up with the Christian doctrine which restricts the use of the sexual faculty to the state of marriage. The effects and the obligations of such activity cannot be adequately discussed in terms of what goes on in each act of intercourse taken in isolation: it is the activity specific and proper to a whole state of life, and its use must be a worthy part of this state of life, not a recurrent but unconnected biological phenomenon in it. Indeed, some defenders of the RP seem aware of this as they express their position sometimes by saying that the primary purpose of *marriage* (not just of intercourse) is the procreation and upbringing of children. (See *L* 130; also the Code of Canon Law, can. 1013, §1.) By talking in terms of marriage, they give an appearance of wanting to take the whole state of life and marital vocation of the spouses into account; and by adding "upbringing" to "procreation" they seem to admit that the obligations imposed upon husband and wife by the structure of sexuality are more than purely biological. (*L* 164.)

The move is to no purpose. Saying that the procreation and upbringing of children is the primary purpose of marriage does not of itself commit one to the RP; in fact it excludes it. Either the statement says too much, and leads to Gandhi's limitation of intercourse to the occasions when procreation is intended; or it says too little, and simply condemns spouses who culpably fail to produce a good and well-brought-up family worthy of their means and abilities. "Primary purpose" is of itself quite compatible with this interpretation. That the primary purpose of marriage (or of intercourse) is to procreate children can be admitted by anyone who holds, first that in man (as in other species) the sexual relationship can culminate in procreation, and secondly that the greater complexity, joy and closeness of the human relationship does not destroy its generative finality, or allow this generative finality to be ignored and obstructed by human beings for their own selfish desires. Those who say this are not bound to accept the RP, for they are concerned with how a husband and wife use their sexual abilities in their whole life together, not how each and every act of sex between them is carried on. In other words, they are still free to seek the meaning of human sexuality in the way in which husbands and wives face up to their generative obligations, not just in the anatomical structure of isolated acts of intercourse.

Let me put this point another way by anticipating a little and talking about the method of preventing conception through confining intercourse to those times when the woman is less likely to conceive—the method known as the "Safe Period" or "Rhythm". The method will be discussed in the next chapter, but what needs noticing here is a pronouncement Pius XII made about its lawfulness. He stated that the method was not wrong in itself, but that family limitation was not automatically justified because not effected by means which interfered with the natural structure of intercourse. By entering the married state, husband and wife take on its obligations, and unreasonable restriction of intercourse to the sterile periods is a shirking of these obligations. ("Midwives", 33–35.) The appeal to the obligations of a state of life, which had not previously appeared in a papal document (Hürth, *CM* 119), constituted an admission that the morality of family limitation cannot be assessed on purely physiological grounds, but must take personal responsibility and obligations into account as well. Needless to say, Pius XII had no intention of opening the door to a theory in which the physiological considerations would lose their central place; for him, their observance was a necessary condition for the goodness of the sexual act, and he was concerned only with denying that it was a sufficient condition. Nonetheless, his pronouncement did shake the identification of the objective order of morality in this matter with something purely corporeal. And whether or not other steps follow, his pronouncement makes rational apologetic for the RP more forced than ever. Apologias for it can no longer talk of marital responsibility, self-control, the good of the species, the generative vocation of married people, and the rest, as if these excluded contraception and could be safeguarded only by this exclusion. Exactly the same considerations can govern and must govern the use of another procedure for preventing conception, which Catholics contend can be just as efficient, and which, when these considerations are observed, is allowed by the Church. In other words, what the argument from nature must seize on for the "significance" and "purpose" in sexual intercourse cannot be any of these considerations. It must—logically must—be nothing more than the anatomical pattern of single sexual contacts. If the argument from nature appeals to anything more, it will become acceptable to those who want sex to be used in terms of the generative vocation of the spouses, but who would evaluate their use of contraceptives just as Catholics evaluate their use of the Safe Period—that is to say, in terms which are themselves vocational and not anatomical. If the argument from nature is to avoid this unacceptable conclusion, it must ignore all the wider context of married sexuality and work only on the pattern of individual acts. Here, and nowhere else, is where the purpose of intercourse must be detected. The married state of which sex forms part, the human species it serves to multiply, the personal obligations and needs of those who perform it—these are factors that can be examined only *post factum*, when the question of purpose has been already answered, and answered anatomically. As far as purpose and meaning and finality are concerned, these other considerations are no more than ornamental trappings; the substance of the thing lies and must lie elsewhere.

The criteria for the right use of the Safe Period show how different the condemnation of contraception is from the moral judgements passed upon other aspects of family life. Parents, and those who evaluate the conduct of parents, will know how many moral problems are posed by topics like discipline, household economy, education, and behaviour towards neighbours. They will also know that such problems are not solved by an inspection of some physiological pattern without regard to anything else; questions have to be asked about the characters of parents and children, their resources and capabilities, and the various obligations to which members of the family are subject. The problems are concerned with how one ought to live, and they cannot be answered without reference to life. It is questions like these that have to be asked about the right of spouses to use rhythm, and the extent of their right: their sexual activity has to be judged in terms of their powers and their obligations, as human beings and as Christians. That the questions cannot be asked about contraception must mean that the purpose and significance of human sexuality is already thwarted and destroyed when the physiological pattern of contact in any one act of intercourse is disturbed.

Needless to say, I admit unreservedly that this *may* be the case. If God has made each separate act of human sex inviolable, just as he has made each consummated sacramental marriage indissoluble, then there is no more to be said. The prohibition will be just as "perspicuously concrete" as other prohibitions about sex, and there will be no room left for further judgements about condoms, pessaries, and the rest. None of this is in question; what is in question—and what I do not admit—is the rational demonstrability of the RP by the argument from nature. This proof is, as we have already seen, unlike proofs offered for the unlawfulness of murder, lying, or stealing, for it is not conceived—as they are—in terms of individual or social rights and dignity, but in terms of biological contact. It is also unlike proofs for the illicitness of sexual behaviour like sodomy, adultery, and fornication. These are excluded once we accept the Christian institution of marriage, for they are all in their different ways incompatible with it. But contraception not only lacks a scriptural condemnation as unequivocal as those which excluded unfaithfulness, promiscuity, and unnatural vice, it is not *prima facie* incompatible with the Christian married state. That it is not incompatible will be understood if we recall what was said in the second section of this chapter (pp. 44): the moral norm laid down by the RP is not in itself concerned with the generative finality of marriage, but only with the pattern of sexual contact. The foregoing investigations into the precise force of the prohibition of contraception showed that the purpose and structure which matters for the view of sexuality bound up with the RP cannot be sought outside the order of biology. If the argument from nature had taken *the married state* for its starting point, then proposals to permit contraception would have had to face at least an initial objection that they were robbing that state of its meaning and purpose. As it is, there is no such objection to be faced. Consideration of what marriage means will certainly force us to put just those restrictions on contraception that the RP places on the safe period: I cannot see how it can force us to exclude it totally. For a rational proof of *that*, we shall have to limit our idea of what "meaning" and "purpose" are to the narrow confines demanded by the empiricist or peep-show theory of significance. It is one thing to accept as revealed by God that the quantum of moral significance rests in the pattern of the individual act of sex—it is quite another to locate moral significance just by looking at such individual acts, as if this was how their purpose could be rationally apprehended. What I am objecting to is not a divinely revealed imperative, but the identification of the absoluteness of God's commands with the strait-jacket of a fallacious piece of philosophy.

6. *Fundamental defects*

Underlying the appeal to nature, and going with its empiricist approach to philosophy, there seems to be an implicitly drawn analogy between the sexual function and a machine. A typewriter is for typing, a saw for cutting, a corkscrew for opening bottles; their respective purposes can be understood from an examination of them, and not to use them as they are meant to be used leads to trouble. Just so, intercourse is for procreation, and to interfere with its intended function is to thwart God's handiwork and so is ultimately disastrous. The analogy is perhaps more plausible if left unsaid, as it can then give colour and force to talk about purpose and aim when these are expressed in purely physiological terms; stated as openly as we have put it, it is very threadbare indeed. First of all, the use of machines is perceptible only against a wider background of usage and experience. It seems obvious to us what saws and typewriters are for because of what we have learnt; they do not bear their uses on themselves like labels. Again, machines may be ruthlessly put to new uses as human ingenuity dictates, or even smashed in emergencies—is the same to be said of the sexual function? Lastly, and perhaps most significantly, the analogy is drawn with the wrong kind of machine. Sex is something richer and far more variable than a "univocal" machine, like a typewriter or a saw. An electric motor or an atomic reactor would be less deficient analogues, for their uses are many, not one, and their right employment has to be judged by criteria that are not observable in any inspection of the machines alone. This unspoken comparison with suitably simple machines seems to underlie much that is said about the primary and secondary purposes of intercourse. As we have already seen, the distinction amounts to making the single sexual contact into a *sine qua non* for any acceptable use of human sexuality. (See above, p. 47.) Of course the distinction will do this only if the criteria of purpose are limited in the way just described: and it is here that the mechanical analogy is attractive. People not of an inventive turn of mind readily take machines as having a preordained purpose which must be respected if they are not to be misused—it is just so with human sexuality. It is hard to know of what this betrays the greater misunderstanding—sex or machines.

If the analogy with machines is implied rather than expressed, there is another analogy which is explicitly stated, and indeed forms a popular expression of the argument from nature. A parallel is drawn between sexuality and eating. Both are physiological functions which pleasure accompanies and so encourages the attaining of their respective purposes, reproduction and nutrition. To divorce the natural consequence of eating from the pleasure of it was what the Romans did in the vomitorium. We condemn their practice as disgusting—why should we not condemn contraception? And if we permit contraception, why do we blench at reintroducing vomitoria? (Dwyer, 6.)

The argument is a hardy annual, but even on its proponents' own terms it can be given a simple answer. If the analogy is just, why may a doctor provoke a vomit in order to examine it, but not an orgasm in order to perform a semen test? (Decree of Holy Office, 2 August 1929; *D* 3684.) Why is it lawful to vomit if we feel queasy, but sinful to masturbate in order to relieve sexual tension? Talk of pleasure-seeking is irrelevant; we have already seen that Pius XII made the biological pattern, not pleasure, the moral norm for using the generative faculties.

(p. 15.) The pattern may not be abandoned in sexual behaviour; why may it be abandoned in nutrition? That is, why is it lawful to feed patients *per rectum* but not lawful to practise AIH on them? This much is an effective rejoinder, but a closer examination of the argument's defects will show the presence of the empiricist fallacy once again. The most obvious ambiguity in the *argumentum ad vomitorium* lies in taking a restricted example of the prime analogate (*disreputable* vomiting) while considering the secondary analogue without qualification (contraception *as such*). Asked the simple question, "Is it ever lawful to procure a vomit?" we should not hesitate to say that it was, because we automatically take into account the setting of the act—it matters for us whether the scene is Trimalchio's supper-room or a doctor's surgery. If the analogy between vomiting and contraception were to be taken seriously, we should be able to judge the morality of the latter as we judge the morality of the former—from its purpose and its setting. Just as we condemn the vomitorium because of the context of its employment, the gluttony that inspired it, so we should condemn contraception if practised with analogous self-indulgence. Which would not be the RP: nor should we be using the defective criterion of meaning involved in its proof.

The analogy is surely grossly misleading from the start. Suppose we had not already condemned contraception, should we be likely to condemn it on grounds that it is like vomiting? Using the vomitorium meant being dissatisfied with the ordinary pleasure of the table, meant forcing oneself to repeat the whole process by indulging in an aesthetically repellent practice disgusting to bystanders. Can this reasonably be compared with contraceptive intercourse? Is blocking the seed's passage comparable, physically speaking, with spewing out one's dinner? Are the husband and wife supposed to be doing something like this? Remember, there is no suggestion that, dissatisfied with the ordinary pleasures of sex, they are urging themselves on to ever new excesses by aphrodisiacs and monstrous perversions. On the contrary, it is precisely the ordinary pleasures of sex that they want. Close the vomitoria and the Romans can still enjoy their dinner; can a similar consolation be offered to those who are to be dissuaded from practising contraception?

The analogy does nothing but give a specious dress to a phrase so often used before: the couple who practise contraception are interfering with the physiological pattern of this particular act. Which we do not deny—we deny only the proof offered that the inviolable purpose of intercourse is to be gauged from the physiological pattern alone. And I suggest that the inviolability could hardly be proved in any case from an analogy with eating, a physiological process confessedly not so inviolable.

The greatest weakness in the analogy could be summed up in the phrase "another physiological process"; the comparison ignores differences far more important than resemblances. Hunger and sexual desire are powerful and recurrent drives in human beings, but what further proportion is there between them? Sexuality needs to be worked into a whole pattern of shared life, it ought to be part of the commitment of one human being to another and to whatever new life may come from this commitment, it is part of a much wider relationship. This is exactly what eating is not. For all the fellowship that may go with it, it is essentially a self-directed activity, whose purpose can be achieved in an impersonal and purely physiological manner, and which inevitably lacks the profound social and legal consequences of sexual behaviour. Again, the desire for nourishment recurs regularly and the activity of eating must take place repeatedly in order that each exercise of it may attain its limited and temporary result. What proportion has this with the sexual drive in marriage, which is equally recurring, but whose procreative result is so immeasurably more lasting, and where so much else is involved besides procreation? Indeed, that so lame a comparison is so popular throws a dismal light on the level of argument in this matter. One author, for instance, after giving the *argumentum ad vomitorium*, says that there is no essential difference between contraception and homosexuality.[1] If he can bring himself to believe this, why stop at homosexuality? Why not say bestiality? Or intercourse with *succubi*?

We can sum up by saying that there is a common ground to these analogies with machinery and with eating. They both attempt to compare sexual intercourse with something less complicated, something of which it seems less implausible to say that its meaning can be gathered by inspection. After all, a machine is by definition a device with a set purpose, even

[1] See Lawson, *A Family Handbook*, 40, and others.

though this purpose may be later extended. Given suitable surroundings and conventions, we can take the background of usage for granted and say, "This machine is obviously for doing so-and-so with." The empiricist criterion of meaning seems justified in this instance. Why should it not be applicable to sexuality? But this determined finality of a machine is a standing tribute to the independence and freedom of man, not a suitable analogue to human destiny. Copper, glass and germanium do not if left to themselves perform the tasks they perform in valves and transistors; it is the ingenuity and adaptiveness of man which builds on their original qualities to get results from them that would be otherwise unobtainable. The finality of a machine is essentially parasitic upon human intelligence and planning; it is inverted reasoning to use such derived finality as a proof that man's intelligence and planning are out of place in his management of the biological pattern in the sexual function. Again, eating is a plausible analogy with sexuality because it is physiological; but the analogy is no more than plausible because the significance of human eating is so much simpler than that of human sexuality. There is a far wider gap between man and other animals in mating than in feeding. Indeed, to point out the obvious, fertilization varies far more in the animal kingdom than does nutrition. Salmon, seals, cats, pigeons, chimpanzees and men are far more alike when eating than when perpetuating their species. Again—and this too is an obvious point—the biological pattern of fertilization in animals is necessarily extravagant, for chance and destruction leave only the luckier or fitter few to survive. In man, there can be no direct attack on innocent life, born or unborn; the sexual urge is more constant than in other species; it is part of a life-long monogamous union; and the consequences of procreation are far greater and far lengthier. Must the generative activity of spouses be judged in terms of particular biological acts, rather than by the fulfilment of their vocation according to their abilities and obligations? Why must the phrase "sexuality apart from procreation" be interpreted in terms of each sexual contact, and not in terms of the whole of married life, into which human sexuality has to be integrated? Is it not extremely bizarre to single out this least purely biological sexuality and to judge its purpose by a purely biological norm, while the sexuality of other animals, where such a criterion would be more plausible, is exempted from it? To limit the moral significance of intercourse between husband and wife in the human species to a biological pattern is to *abstract* (in an eminently Lockean sense of the word) the idea of a certain physiological union from the whole complex of love and intelligence that makes that union distinctively human. But the abstraction, impoverishing as it is, seems unavoidable if the RP is to be proved by the argument from nature.

Defenders of the RP seem aware of this impoverishment, as they are ready to assert that sexuality is for the good of the species, for peopling the world, not just for the benefit of individuals. (Dwyer, p. 8; and compare *DM* 15.2 ad 12 and *CR* [December 1961].) The assertion is, perhaps, an attempt to take into account the multiplicity of purposes in sexual intercourse, and as such it is welcome. The mechanistic tone of the purely biological argument, reminiscent of a pilot's harbour-chart showing what channels are navigable, or of an electrician's wiring-diagram showing what plug goes where, is apparently tempered by less limited considerations. In fact, the assertion turns out to be a means of barring the door against tampering with the sexual act for *personal* reasons. But in doing so it promptly opens another door to modifications on *public* grounds. If the statement that human sexuality is for the welfare of the human species has any meaning, it must follow that needs of the species like over-population or genetic defect can justify interference with the pattern of human sexuality—which is incompatible with the RP, whose defenders seem now to have reached an inescapable dilemma. Either the biological, "sub-human" pattern is stressed, or wider considerations are admitted. On the first hypothesis, only the empiricist theory of meaning can see significance in an isolated biological pattern, while the very impersonality of the criterion makes the unique position of man among other animals all the harder to understand. On the second hypothesis the norm is indeed less implausible, but it can avoid unwelcome weakenings of the RP and yield the appropriate answers, only by covertly appealing to the former, biological standard.

I suggest that these anomalies in expositions of the RP are due to its resting on something like what logicians call an *inconsistent triad.* In its strict sense, this is a set of three statements which cannot be simultaneously held without a contradiction following, yet any two of which can be consistently affirmed. Here the three elements of the triad are presuppositions of the RP:

(1) The empiricist's view of philosophical proof.
(2) The natural pattern as the norm for sexual behaviour.
(3) Human sexuality as unique, because of man's unique position.

(1) and (2) together make up the assertion that no change in the physiological pattern of sexual contact is ever lawful, and that abandoning it by artificially obstructing the seed is blameworthy. By (1), the pattern referred to by (2) must be "photographically" perceptible here and now; to use the phrase of Hume's there must be "some *je-ne-sçais-quoi*" to mark off the lawful from the unlawful. To introduce considerations other than the immediately perceptible facts of physiology would be against the empiricist criterion in (1). Unfortunately, the conjunction of (1) and (2) would demand the prohibition of interference with the genital functions of livestock, so (3) has to be introduced to give man a place apart in our moral reckoning. Yet (3) cannot be allowed its full force, or the ambiguous "natural pattern" in (2) would have to be given a non-empiricist meaning, in contradiction to the already asserted conjunction of (1) and (2). Against the background of the conjunction, (3) can be asserted only momentarily, dampening the unwanted conclusion about livestock without compromising the conclusion about man.

Yet (3) can be held along with (1) as long as we are prepared to stomach the implausible results. If (1) and (3) are to provide a proof for the wrongfulness of contraception, then the wrongfulness must, by (3), be distinctively human, and, by (1), be perceptible according to the empiricist criterion. That is, it must be possible to detect in the activity of contraception certain phenomena which show that the purpose of human life—a purpose derived from what man is—is being violated. Faced with this problem of detection, defenders of the RP take two courses. They quote bad results which may follow from uses of contraception, or bad reasons which can inspire its practice (see above, p. 28, and below pp. 91–2), applying words like "self-indulgence", "sterility" and "revulsion" to the practice as such. Not only is all this a brash confusion of *some* uses with *all*, it leaves the apologists faced with the task of rescuing the "rhythmic" method of preventing conception from this roll-call of accusations, while at the same time claiming as great an efficiency for it as for contraception (see pp. 26–9; and see below, p. 89.) Alternatively, defenders of the RP try to make this conjunction of (1) and (3) less implausible by drawing defective analogies to sexual intercourse like eating or machinery and even deliberately limited instances of these analogies (*gluttonous* vomiting, *wanton* machine wrecking). They can hope that the oversimplification in the analogies can obscure the complexity of human sexuality; they can hope that the very limitations in the analogies can provide a vivid enough picture which can apparently be adequately assessed by empiricist criteria, paving the way for a similar assessment of contraception. I have tried to show that the hope is vain.[1]

The conjunctions of (1) with (2) and of (1) with (3) (and of (1) with (2) and a dash of (3)) have led to consequences unacceptable in themselves and inconsistent with each other. It is in (1) that the trouble starts; an empiricist criterion of significance cannot do justice to the meaning and purpose of human sexuality, for the excellent reason that it cannot do justice to meaning and purpose at all. If (1) is jettisoned, then the conjunction of (2) and (3) will demand that we approve the prevention and encouragement of conception according to the status of man, both supernatural and natural, according to the obligations of husband and wife towards God and their neighbours, according to their needs and resources, and according to the society in which they live. It will mean that we shall have to judge the fulfilment of married obligations with reference to the marriage itself and to those who make the marriage, not by appealing to the unobstructedness of every single act of intercourse they perform. In short, the conjunction of (2) and (3) will

[1] I do not claim, of course, that these ingenious tactics have been consciously planned by defenders of the RP, but I should like to point out a fact about clerical education which may have something to do with the defects of the argument from nature. In seminaries and clerical universities it seems to be nobody's job to expound this argument. The course in moral philosophy does not include it, and the course in moral theology mentions it only as something presumed to be already familiar.

have husbands and wives appraise their control of conception by the very criteria Pius XII said must govern the use of the infertile period. (See p. 60.)

It ought to be obvious by now that my attack on the argument from nature has not been a *plaidoyer* for situation ethics. I do not like labouring the obvious, but the accusation of falling into *Situationsethik* is modish, vague enough to be elusive, and endowed with strong emotional associations. For the sake of getting things clear (not to mention for my own sake) it will be necessary to spell out my meaning. In one perfectly innocuous sense all ethics is situational, for human acts are never performed in the abstract. In a more significant sense, Christian morals cannot be situational in the way that a morality based on consequences or utility can be. If God's law has once been ascertained by faith or reason, man cannot take on himself the task of refashioning it or of derogating from it. Sexual morals for the Christian are bound to be more distinctive than Christian principles for other types of conduct, for the commands are concretely perspicuous in a way that other precepts are not. "Thou shalt not commit adultery" presents us, we might say, with a *fait accompli* in a way that "Thou shalt not steal" does not. It is no accident that situation ethics always embark on a rethinking of Christian teaching about sex. I confess myself unable to see how a situational view of sexual behaviour can get round the clarity of the biblical pronouncements in the matter without falling into platitude or heterodoxy.

I am not proposing any such break with God's word. I have been dealing in this chapter with arguments that claim to offer a rational justification for the absolute prohibition of contraception taught to Catholics and have tried to show that these arguments are either inadequate or fallacious. There are other arguments that try to give this rational basis—I am going to treat them in the same way. If absoluteness is to be attached to the prohibition, it will have to be shown to be part of revelation, whether in Scripture or in the infallible teaching of the Church. Whether this can be shown is a question also to be discussed. But what I am not saying, and what I will not say, is that the morality of contraception is to be decided by some "inner light or intuition", to quote the official condemnation. (See above, p. 35.) The long and perhaps tedious digression on empiricism ought to have proved at least that I have no sympathy for such intuitive procedures.

It is more likely that the accusation of teaching situation ethics would be motivated by a fear that my proposal to abandon the empiricist criterion would introduce anarchy in so important a matter. The fear is groundless. To begin with, there is no way of ensuring ourselves in advance against all moral perplexity, just as there is no way of making a sign which is proof against all ambiguities of interpretation. Commerce, war and the upbringing of children often bring us face to face with problems from which there is no answer to be pulled like a plum from a pie, yet does it follow that there are no standards in business, in battle, or at home? If it be asked how a husband and wife would, on our hypothesis, determine their right to regulate births by contraception, let it be asked how they are now in the present state of affairs to determine their right to regulate births by the safe period. Their motives can be good or bad, their judgements of the case fair or blinded by self-interest; what is here that is not found in any acute moral problem? To think that moral perplexities are removed by the adoption of "nature's objective order" in the Roman sense of the phrase is to forget what was amply demonstrated in Chapter 1—that acute disagreements exist among moral theologians who all accept this norm for right action. (See above, pp. 10 ff.)

Nor, of course, does abandoning the RP mean tolerating evil in a good cause. "Tolerating evil" does not come into the matter. Murdering baby boys was Herod's way of preserving his throne, and we condemn him because we condemn the direct killing of the innocent, however pressing the political situation. But in our case, the point at issue is precisely whether contraception is like this, is something wrong in itself, and not rather something whose morality depends upon how and why it is used. It is certainly not being suggested that we should admit that it is evil but practise it on the grounds that its consequences are beneficial! As I stated early in this essay (see p. 3), I am concerned only with purely contraceptive procedures, not with any kind of feticidal interference after conception has taken place. It is a sad commentary on arguments for the RP that the platitudinous distinction still needs to be explicitly made between the contraceptive control of the generative faculty and the taking of life, born or unborn, innocent or otherwise.

I should like to end this long analysis of the argument from nature with a brief postscript of a more positive sort. There is one defence of the RP that I do find persuasive although not convincing, this is based on what might be called the dangers of power. Do not the technological achievements of our own day tempt us to think that we can control human sexuality and human life at will, without reverence for humanity? Is there not enough in the history of the last thirty years to show what hideous results can follow when technical prowess is allied with moral depravity? Are we not embarking on a Gadarene slope unless "mechanically verifiable" limits are set to what is permitted us? The argument has something to commend it, for the danger of power without humility is very real. To think that all problems are problems of method, to want to cut the world down to our own meanness, to lose sight of people in dealing with objects, to forget what really matters in our concern over so many things—all these have always been temptations, and the technical power we have today makes them more attractive and more ruinous than ever. Yet does it follow that the RP alone preserves us from these temptations? As I understand it, what is being said in this argument amounts to a refusal to make decisions. Here, we are invited to agree, the moral weakness of men cannot be trusted, here a norm of conduct is needed which by its very subhumanness and materiality will give them as little room as possible for manoeuvre in a matter where they cannot be expected to decide objectively. If this line of argument were frankly adopted by any moralist, one could at least respect the stand he had chosen to take; there would be little more to say, as argument would *ex hypothesi* be ineffective. Argument might, of course, be used to dissuade someone from adopting the position: but the position once adopted, its adherents cannot consistently debate a matter they regard as too dangerous for human wit and decision. Of course those who hold the RP cannot very well use this argument in so undiluted a form, as it would void their claim to deduce their views from the natural order. Instead, a covert appeal seems to be made to this argument in debate, when they speak of the strength of sexual temptation in order to play down the powers of reason in this matter. Not only is this inconsistent with the whole point of the RP, it has the offensive corollary that to disagree with it must be a symptom of bad faith. In fact, of course, the argument does something with which we are familiar enough by now—it makes statements which we can accept, but which are not an adequate base for conclusions by no means as obvious.

Yet though it does not convince, I think the argument more persuasive and valuable than many others, perhaps because it is frankly an admonition or appeal rather than a supposedly objective piece of deduction. While rejecting it, I can accept the spirit in which it was proposed. It urges caution and reverence—who would disagree? In an age of technological power, the value of the individual and the family, and reverence for human life, need stressing as never before. At the same time there is surely a good deal which makes it hard for us to preserve this reverence. Yet do not the very dangers contain within themselves the possibility of an antidote? Cannot technological achievements be used to safeguard these values as well as to attack them? And whether we reject contraception or not, are not just as great dangers of technological power without principle still to be faced in other matters? If this particular danger can be countered only by adopting the RP, this has not been proved. The argument can be retained as a warning against real dangers; it is ineffective if taken as a proof that the RP is their only antidote.

4

Sterility

1. Artificial sterility

The lengthy examination of the argument from nature in the preceding chapter ought to have shown that the heart of the RP, the essence of its talk about "nature", lies in the claim that certain human biological functions are sacrosanct. The inseminatory pattern of intercourse must not be disturbed; nor may the results at which the inseminatory pattern is directed be obtained outside it. This limitation of man's power over his generative faculties includes those operations which directly attack the very possibility of reproduction. Here it is not merely the individual act that is being deprived of its inherent force, but the entire organism itself is being deprived of the faculty of procreating new life. (cf. "Midwives", 24 and 27.) The power we enjoy over bodily organs is circumscribed by their natural purposes. ("Marriage", *D* 3723.) Actions, whether temporary or permanent in effect, performed for such purposes on men or women are an unwarranted usurpation of dominion over the human body beyond the limits set by its Creator. (*CR* [December 1960].) However, we also saw in the last chapter that the condemnation of interference with the pattern of intercourse was not held by theologians to entail an abstention from conduct which would in fact rob intercourse of its generative effect. (See p. 43.) Just so here, from the prohibition of direct sterilization, whether permanent or temporary, it does not follow that actions must be prohibited if they have sterilization among their results. Distinctions have to be drawn; and the drawing of them is relevant to the use of the infertile period as a means of preventing conception, and to more recent debates over the use of drugs that temporarily suspend ovulation. I shall begin with a brief account of the moral principle to which appeal is made in these questions.

Many actions in life have undesirable side effects, and the morality of performing actions like this is judged by moralists according to what they call the principle of double effect. According to this principle, it is permissible to set in motion a cause, in spite of its evil effect, provided (1) that the act producing this effect is not itself wrong; (2) that a good effect issues from this act at least as immediately as the evil effect; (3) that the agent has a reason for so acting proportionate to the foreseen and permitted evil effect. (cf. Davis, 1, 52.) I am not concerned here with investigating the principle, but with stating it as moral theologians have actually expressed it. Clearly, apart from any more fundamental reservations, a full account of it would have to safeguard it from abuses—especially those which can follow from an improper use of its first condition. For us, it will be enough to give two complementary examples. Consider a woman whose Fallopian tubes are affected by cancer. An operation to remove them renders her permanently sterile (an evil result), but the operation is followed just as directly by her being saved from cancer (a good result) and this good result is of sufficient value to permit the tolerance of the evil concomitant effect. So, by the principle of double effect, such an operation is lawful. Contrast with this a case of a woman who undergoes a similar mutilation in order that she may not give birth to defective offspring, or undergo a dangerous pregnancy at some future date. Here the sterilization is *direct*; that is, the immediate purpose of the act is to attack the woman's reproductive powers. The attack on her reproductive system is a stepping-stone towards the praiseworthy aim of defending her from danger, it is not simply an effect which (inevitably perhaps) accompanies some other effect. The effects here of sparing her life, or sparing her from defective offspring—good in themselves—are obtained as a result of this attack, not concomitantly with it. So, as a direct attack on her reproductive system is not lawful, and evil may not be done in a good cause, the principle of double effect leads to the conclusion that this operation may not be performed.

It is important to realize that the application of this moral principle to direct sterilization is of a piece with the condemnation of contraception that we have already seen. More is being asserted than just the illicitness of direct attack on a bodily function. Actions whose direct purpose is to attack the body or interfere with its powers cannot be inevitably wrong, or mortifying practices would be wrong; what matters is that a mutilation is directly inflicted on a function over which man has no absolute dominion. (*CR*, December 1960).) The reproductive system enjoys this privileged status. Just as the process of sexual union was declared to be sacrosanct, so that any direct interference was unlawful and any attempt to achieve its generative purpose by other means equally illicit, so the generative apparatus itself is to be held immune from any direct attack, however beneficial the results may be. Both condemnations throw into relief that the essence of the RP for both contraception and sterilization lies, not in any simple appeal to nature or respect for what is natural, but rather in a decision that certain human functions are beyond direct human control.

What criticisms were made of the former condemnation can be made of the latter, and of the arguments advanced in its favour. Direct sterilization is an attack on the reproductive system; as such, like any other physiological mutilation, it is (tautologously) an evil. But to assert that it is always a *moral* evil means attaching a special moral significance to the physiological pattern of reproduction. "Special" because the attachment of moral significance is not enough in itself to warrant the RP; it is inviolability that must be attributed, not merely importance, worthiness, and the rest. Conversely, to reject the RP is not to advocate evil in a good cause, but rather to say that the moral significance of direct sterilization must be judged, like the morality of contraception, not by scrutinizing a physiological pattern in isolation, but in terms of the married state, in terms of human dignity and of human needs. The particular moral significance demanded by the RP must, of course, be attached to the pattern of reproduction if it can be shown that God has reserved such dominion over the reproductive faculty to himself. (cf. "Marriage", *D* 3723.) But this is a conclusion to be reached by rational argument, if the RP is capable of being proved by reason; it is not a premise from which the desired conclusion can be triumphantly deduced. There is perhaps an unexpressed analogy in attacks on direct sterilization which we encountered as a background to attacks on contraception (see above, p. 72); the unconditional prohibition of direct attacks on innocent human life is extended to exclude direct attacks on human reproduction. The analogy is just as defective as before. It is no human creature that is being killed, it is a human function that is being controlled. Why should the sexual function be set wholly apart from other human processes? Why should external considerations be irrelevant to attacks on it? Obviously, sterilization can be performed for the basest of motives; this does not of itself prove its intrinsic immorality, and that the faculty must be proclaimed to be untouchable. For the RP motives and needs cannot be considered. If they were considered, it would be absurd to pretend that the condemnation of Nazi racial policies commits us to condemning the sterilization of a mother who has already born six children, and for whom a seventh pregnancy is likely to be fatal.

It is perhaps not surprising that a number of celibate writers have shown a curious insensitivity to the burdens placed by the RP on married men and women. Some either bluntly dismiss these problems by saying curtly that "the health of such a mother can be safeguarded in other ways" (Kelly, p. 56), or combine adjurations to continence with scepticism as to the danger of lapsing from it. (Bonnar, pp. 70–1.) A useful antidote to these bluff insensibilities can be quoted from Dwyer: "There are plenty of cases where the doctors have been proved wrong [in their warnings]. But no one can blame parents who take a doctor's word when he is speaking in all honesty in a matter in which he is, after all, an authority." (Dwyer, p. 13.)

A matter of greater importance is the shift in emphasis between pronouncements on this topic by Pius XI and by Pius XII. For the former, a mutilation of a bodily organ was justified if the good of the whole body could not be otherwise obtained ("Marriage", *D* 3723). The latter, realizing perhaps that this principle might be taken as a justification of sterilization when subsequent pregnancy might be dangerous, distinguished cases when the organ *itself* was a source of trouble (the cancerous tubes whose removal will incidentally cause sterility) from cases where it is the *use* of the organ, or of other related organs, not the organ itself, which leads to danger (the weakened organs of the woman which could be damaged by processes following fertilization). In the former case, the operation is licit, but not in the latter; here, it is the *exercise* of the sexual organs which can lead to danger, and the woman may avoid fertilization by abstaining from intercourse. ("Urologists", 675.) The distinction between organ and use of organ seems to do little but rephrase the assertion that direct attacks on the generative functions are intrinsically wrong, nor does it elude the obvious objection that if an organ cannot be safely used it is *ipso facto* a danger to the whole body, and so may be sacrificed. Indeed, the distinction seems so tailor-made to the point at issue as to be uninformative. If it were meant as a general principle, one could imagine a case where a cancer of the hand was aggravated only by movements of the fingers, and where the moralist would have to forbid amputation on the grounds that abstention from digital movement would do the job. He would, of course, not give this advice—because the finger movements are not sacrosanct in the way the reproductive actions are. Once more, the distinction is operative only if this sacrosanctity is previously conceded. If the concession is not made, we must either forbid the operation on the fingers, or allow that personal danger justifies interference with a bodily function to permit sexual activity without dangerous consequences.[1]

It might be objected that the RP, for all its severity, is at least saved from inconsequences inherent in the view we have suggested. Might we not, the objection goes, allow prematrimonial sterilization on the grounds of genetic defect? And would not this substantially vitiate that generative finality which we have admitted to be part of the pattern of marriage? Is it not safer to preserve this finality even at the cost of the unyielding absoluteness of the RP? The objection is worth answering, because its solution shows yet again that the ban on direct sterilization and the ban on contraception are bound up with a defective theory of significance. To begin with, acceptance of the RP by a couple in these tragic circumstances need not entail any difference between their feelings about the procreation of children and the

[1] As things stand, theologians have to try to show that the reproductive organs are defective "in themselves", not just "in their use", in order to allow their removal. For instance, is a womb after repeated Caesarean sections in a pathological condition that will permit a hysterectomy, for the good of a whole body? (cf. O'Donnell, 110.) These efforts are praiseworthy, even if doubtfully consistent with the distinction itself (after all, need such a womb be dangerous if not fertilized?). We need notice only that the search for the pathological as something perceptible *here and now* is yet another instance of the empiricist criterion of significance being used to give support to the RP. The topic is discussed in a later chapter (pp. 202 ff.).

feelings of those who practise sterilization. The eugenic danger would be a sufficient reason for permanently confining intercourse to the infertile period ("Midwives", 36); the successful operation of this method would not be held to vitiate the generative finality of their sexual activities, even though every care was taken by them to ensure that those activities had no generative effects. The view seems paradoxical only because "generative finality" has been defined so narrowly by the RP. It would be better to transcend the empiricist approach to finality and frankly admit that this restricted union was generative only in a marginal or "parasitic" sense, in the sense that the situation could not be acknowledged as generative without the support of the conceptual framework of normal sexuality.[1] If we accept this move, sterilization will not diminish the "generative" character of intercourse in a marriage like this, any more or any less than the policy of infertile intercourse. The mutilation itself, severe though it is, will be also accepted as part of an essentially exceptional union. That is to say, neither from the case of the couple who practise sterilization nor from the case of the couple who systematically confine their intercourse to the infertile period can a full notion of marriage and sexuality be obtained. Indeed, the very act of sterilization or the exclusive use of the sterile period can show forth in its own way the respect that these afflicted spouses have for life, in not wanting to procreate defective offspring. It may be urged that human offspring are procreated in the first place for heaven, not for earth. (cf. "Marriage", *D* 3722.) But a distinction has to be drawn between loyal acceptance and love of defective offspring, and the deliberate procreation of them. The former is bound up with the respect for the individual human being basic to Christianity; the latter is a policy within the rights of the parents ("Haematology", 739), but not a policy which can be used to impugn the prudence of other parents in refusing to have children under such conditions. ("Midwives", 36.)

The RP finds cases like this awkward. On the one hand, its

[1] We use expressions "parasitically" when we stretch an accepted meaning to cover the awkward case. In doing so, we rely on the normal sense to give substance to this exceptional usage. Thus, we might tell a blind man that scarlet is like the sound of a trumpet and blue like the sound of a clarinet. But we did not learn to use colour words by hearing musical instruments played.

declaration that the generative function is immune from direct attack makes any appeal to other considerations beside the point. On the other hand, its defenders naturally like to make such appeals, even though secretly, to give greater plausibility to their thesis. The same technique is used in their attacks on contraception, and has been analysed in the preceding chapter. (See pp. 69–70). The obvious and hideous abuses to which sterilization can be put can be effectively quoted in support of the RP—as long as the "restricted diet of examples" is not enriched by facts that tell a different story. It would be more candid to stick to asserting the immunity from direct attack of the reproductive organs. Unfortunately, this could bring once more into embarrassing prominence the problem of demonstrating this immunity on rational grounds.

The sterility discussed so far was supposed to be permanent: but temporary direct sterilization is also forbidden by the RP. A decree of the Holy Office of 21 February 1940 (*D* 3788) forbade temporary as well as permanent direct sterilization. Commenting on this, McReavy defined direct sterilization as an act directed either of its nature or by the intention of the agent to the end of sterilization as to its proper and immediate term, whether for its own sake or as a means to something else; and traced its unlawfulness, like the unlawfulness of direct permanent sterilization, to an unwarranted usurpation, to interference with human faculties over which man has no direct dominion. (*CR*, December 1960.) Recent controversies give a special point to examining the temporary sterilization of the woman by drugs that inhibit ovulation—drugs whose apparently swift and simple solution of the problem of controlling conception has earned them the affectionate sobriquet of the Pill. It would seem to be clear that taking the Pill for contraceptive purposes is an unwarranted interference with the generative apparatus, and so gravely sinful. Matters do not turn out to be quite as clear as this. First of all, drugs like this may be taken to cure pathological conditions—dysmenorrhoea is cited as an example (*CR*, December 1961)—and in such circumstances the incidental consequence of temporary sterilization may be allowed by the principle of double effect. This in itself is not very novel, but it introduces the term "pathological condition", which opens the door to further and less expected results. Just where does the "pathological" start? Or stop? According to the Louvain moralist Janssens (quoted in *L* 211), for ovulation not to stop during lactation is pathological, and may be cured by steroid drugs. Though not medically competent, I confess myself surprised at this use of "pathological". Because of this inhibition of ovulation, some authorities recommend breast feeding as a method of preventing conception. The survey on contraception conducted by *Which?* did not find it efficient. Were the failures pathological—or were the successes lucky? Whatever the merits of employing the term "pathological" like this, its usefulness cannot be denied. It is even more useful—and even more surprising—to class irregularities in ovulation as pathological, and so as lawful occasions for taking the Pill. (*CR* (December 1961).)[1] Certainly, since the safe period is calculated with reference to the date of ovulation, irregularities in the cycle each month or its more fundamental disorder in the months after birth can have unwelcome consequences: but can these inconveniences be classed as pathological? The word, surely, is used here morally, not medically. No verifiable claim is being made. "Pathological" is simply "what lies outside the untouchable order of nature", and in this case "nature" is presumed to include a precisely calculable cycle of ovulation, any deviations from which may consequently be corrected without sin. It is an understandable presumption, but not one that would be easy to justify.

Indeed, the presumption leads to a curious situation that I offer for the consideration of moralists. It is conceded by defenders of the RP that a pathological condition gives the individual a right to cure it for the sake of the whole body by proportionate means, and to permit the occurrence of bad side effects, according to the principle of double effect. Expositions of this principle seem to assume that the agent will lament the occurrence of the side effect. Yet all that is essentially required by the principle is that what he does should not in itself be wrong. To put it differently, if he were told, *per possibile vel per impossibile* that he could attain the good effect in a way that would not entail the evil side effects, he would have to choose

[1] McReavy himself expressed some doubts about it, and from my own different point of view I respect them. But the general opinion of moralists seems to allow such a use.

this other way instead. It is only in this sense that he must "lament" and "only tolerate" the evil result of what he does. In another sense, he may welcome it. Thus, a cancerous finger may be amputated for the sake of the whole body—but the bad side effect of losing a finger may even be welcomed, as it will save me from military service. This does not stop me from having the operation, what matters is that the bad effect should not be the means of obtaining the good effect, and that the benefit obtained should be proportioned to the permitted evil. Now let a woman whose ovulatory cycle is not regular take the Pill for some days each month, as moralists permit, to correct her "pathological situation". Having taken it, however, she chooses to have intercourse only while its sterilizing effect lasts; is she within her rights? If it be objected that her intention vitiates her act, I reply that what matters here is not the intention but the presence of a pathological condition, for this is what justifies the use of the drug.[1] A pathological condition is one which by definition needs curing. The curing of an organ may entail a permitted bad side effect. As theologians have already admitted that the benefit of curing a pathological condition of irregular ovulation compensates the evil of incidental sterilization, how can they condemn the woman's conduct? Remember the question is not how many children she has had already—she may have had none, she may have had twenty. We are not talking about such human or vocational considerations here, we are concerned about her right to cure a pathological condition. In what sense must she "abhor the evil side effect"? Must this "abhorrence" show itself in abstaining from intercourse until the sterilizing effect of the drug is past? If so, would the man with the cancerous finger have to wait until the war was over to have it off? Or work himself up into a state of martial enthusiasm before going on to the operating table? True enough, cancer is serious and irregular ovulation is not—which brings us back to the oddness of calling it pathological.[2]

Moralists may be able to fault my reasoning here, but there are other instances of using the Pill admitted by some of them

[1] I return to the question of intention later. (See pp. 208 ff.)

[2] Since the writing of this chapter I have heard a talk, "Intention", given in the Third Programme by Professor H. L. A. Hart. I was interested to notice a similar observation by him on what I have called the "abhorrence" involved in the principle of double effect.

to be lawful where the application of the principle of double effect begins to creak audibly. According to some authorities, ovulation may be suppressed altogether for a number of months in order that the woman may afterwards more easily conceive. (See the authorities mentioned in Furlong.) Here the desired effect of pregnancy is obtained *by means of* an interference with the genetic apparatus which is supposed to be immune from any direct attack. The woman becomes more fertile *by being temporarily sterilized*—one is a step to the other. True enough, the purpose is good, but is it supposed to justify the means? Can future fertility affect the morality of direct sterilization here and now? The temporary character of direct sterilization is irrelevant, according to the RP (see p. 81) it is the *directness* of the attack that matters. Once make temporariness a criterion of lawfulness, and the door is open to an appraisal of direct sterilization in terms of its time and duration in a marriage. This could not be reconciled with the RP as taught at present.

A second example goes further. A Jesuit moralist, Lynch, holds (and in accordance, he believes, with a view of most theologians) that the Pill may be similarly used for three or four months by a woman with an irregular cycle. The aim is that when the cycle is resumed it will be resumed in a predictable fashion and the method of rhythm can be successfully employed. (Rock, 103.) Such a usage does not just delay the onset of ovulation in a cycle; it suppresses the cycle altogether for some months. Nor is fertility the aim of this suppression, but rather the introduction of a method of preventing it. The desired result of cyclical regularity is reached by a direct mutilation of what is supposed to be immune from such attacks. Moreover, if this were not enough, a third use is purely contraceptive in its aim.

For according to the cautiously and tentatively expressed view of Hürth, a woman in danger of rape may take the Pill to ward off the chance of pregnancy.[1] Against the obvious objection that her aim, laudable though it be, is achieved through direct sterilization, Hürth replies by introducing a further dis-

[1] In a symposium with Palazzini and Lambruschini, "Una donna domanda—come negarsi alla violenza?", *Studi Cattolici* (November and December 1961), Rome. The three are agreed that the Pill may be taken in such emergencies: I consider Hürth's argument alone, for it seems to me the most cogently reasoned of them.

tinction. Direct sterilization, he says, can be *absolute* or *relative*. Absolute sterilization simply causes sterility, prescinding from anything else, and as such is not intrinsically evil. What is evil is relative sterilization, which is the inducing of sterility with a view to performing the sexual act willingly while frustrating its generative capacity. For instance, a woman experimenter takes a drug inhibiting ovulation to test its efficacy: assuming that she has no intercourse before or after, what she does is not wrong, as it is only absolute sterilization. Again, the woman fearing rape has *ex hypothesi* no intention of accepting her ravisher's embraces, she only suffers the violence of one who has no right to her. Neither, says Hürth, performs relative sterilization, neither is trying to cheat nature.

There is much more in Hürth's answer than this,[1] but he seems to have abandoned the principle, explicitly stated by so many authorities, that no direct attack on the reproductive system is ever lawful. For the woman in question to block the passage of the seed with a pessary would presumably be allowed by moralists, for they permit her to use douches to expel the seed when rape has occurred: such seed is an "unjust aggressor", it has no right to be there. (cf. Génicot and others.)[2] To use a douche or a pessary certainly corrupts the natural pattern of intercourse: but it corrupts it by expelling or obstructing seed that has no right to be there in the first place. That is, the corruption begins only when the initial injustice is committed by the aggressor, to which the victim gives no consent. Hürth's solution is radically different. More than a barrier is placed in the path of the seed which has no right to be there, for he allows a direct attack upon the woman's reproductive system. For him, sterilization is a means to an end, not a tolerated concomitant to a desired good effect. But the novelty of what he says seems to undermine the distinction he draws to support it. For if the reproductive pattern is not sacrosanct in its functioning (that is,

[1] Including a picaresque example of what he thinks is licit self-defence: a farmer may mine the ditch round his orchard and set up automatic machine-guns to keep out intruders . . . trespassers will be persecuted?

[2] But I learn from O'Donnell, 222, that the moralist Merkelbach (like Liguori, 6, §955) forbade the use of douches by a woman who had been raped: for him, man has "no control over semen". I mention this extraordinary opinion because it seems more in accord with the RP's "postulate of inviolability" than more normal views.

if it can be directly attacked without sin), why should it be sacrosanct in its use? (That is, why make absolute restrictions on the reasons for directly attacking it?) It cannot be suggested that what matters is that sexual pleasure is not sought by the woman who takes the Pill in an emergency or as a scientific experiment; this avenue has already been blocked by what Pius XII said about artificial insemination (see above, p. 15); the Pope condemned even unpleasurable violations of the objective order in sex. ("Doctors", 560; "Fertility", 472.) It is the pattern that counts, not the pleasure, and it is the pattern that Hürth's direct sterilization attacks for its own sake, however understandable the motives may be for doing so. Indeed, after Hürth's admission that temporary direct sterilization can be lawful, it should not be impossible to devise situations where permanent direct sterilization would also be licit. The possibility cannot be excluded from the start—unless he wants to accept duration as a criterion for lawfulness. Nor does Hürth give any reason beside his distinction for the lawfulness of suspending ovulation for experimental purposes. He would condemn with other moralists the procuring of seed by self-abuse for examination; each practice directly attacks the natural course of the reproductive system, and where is the difference except in the pleasure?

I hope that my criticism of Hürth's solution will not be taken as showing any lack of sympathy for those faced with the agonizing problem he is trying to solve; but I do suggest that such contortions are necessary only because the RP has chosen to consider the morality of reproduction according to the physiological pattern taken by each act of intercourse. The reconciliation of this empiricist view with the considerations that normally govern moral decisions cannot but be difficult. All we have here is yet another reason for abandoning these endeavours to patch up a defective criterion, in favour of a general rethinking of philosophical foundations.[1]

2. *Natural sterility*

As is well known, the monthly period of infertility in the

[1] The whole question of sterilizing drugs is considered in greater detail below, pp. 185ff.

woman's cycle is the one method of preventing conception allowed by the Roman Church apart from complete continence. An examination of the principles which govern its use will complement what we have said so far about her teaching on sterility in relation to the control of conception. The exposition will form a natural introduction to the next chapter, which considers the final rational claim made in favour of the RP—that it proclaims the positive value of chastity.

The most cursory examination of Roman Catholic writing on marriage today shows the attention which is being given to this method of preventing (or encouraging) conception. The theory and practice of it are expounded in talks and books; research is going on to make the calculation of the fertility cycle ever more accurate and the regularizing of it ever more efficient. Simple but accurate accounts of the method are being provided for the illiterate—it is here, we are told, that a solution to problems of population and marital relations is to be found. Let me say at once that I have not the medical competency to make a first-hand assessment of the efficiency of this method of birth control, or the other competencies necessary to give opinions about the feasibility of using the method to control the population increase, or the effects of such a limiting. But I can offer some comments on current propaganda for the method, and on questions raised by the propaganda and by the method itself.

These claims made for the safe period might be taken more seriously if it were not for a curious reticence which pervades even so full a treatment of the theme as that in Lestapis' book. For instance, the slow rate of population growth in developed countries is favourably contrasted by him with the embarrassingly high rate in more primitive lands, where there are social and psychological obstacles to any form of population control. (*L* 241 ff.) The rate of increase in these places shows the effect of a sudden and drastic drop in the death rate, and it can hinder the efforts being made to help the inhabitants achieve the industrialization and organization necessary for modern society. Once get such primitive societies "over the hump", as Lord Snow would put it, and the population pattern will not be so adverse to progress and human dignity. The sentiments are praiseworthy, but much seems left unsaid. *Why* is population growth in advanced countries so slow? Must not the change be partly due to a deliberate limitation of conception? And has this limitation been achieved only by the use of the safe period? No proof is offered that it has been, and indeed the facts Lestapis quotes seem to suggest that it has not. Thus (as we might expect) Sweden is attacked when Lestapis talks about contraceptive civilization (*L* 29); but it appears among the countries with the optimum rate of growth in the chapter on population increase. (cf. *L* 242–4.) He really cannot have it both ways. Again, it is not enough to say that the Church leaves the population problem to the civil authorities. (*L* 141.) Not enough, that is, if the RP is to admit of a rational apologetic to back its acceptance. It is one thing to proclaim a policy as God's law, cost what it may; it is quite another to claim that unprejudiced reason obliges us to accept that policy. If the position is one for which a rational basis can be offered (and Lestapis devotes two chapters to doing so), then the safe period cannot be proposed as the solution for population problems, while whatever effective population control exists depends largely on other methods. It seems a confession of defeat to admit that much time may pass before the RP is accepted (*L* 287), for the population is with us already, and clamours for a solution here and now. And it is an abuse of language to call "solution" a process to be adopted only in the indefinite future, when the brunt of the problem will have been borne *de facto* by the contraceptive practices the solution rejects as immoral.

Most strangely of all, Lestapis' commendation of the method is tempered with little about the complications involved in calculating the cycle, about its variability and at times unpredictability, about the sheer impossibility of using it at all in some cases.[1] To see how varied and how conflicting these are we need go no further than the correspondence columns of the Catholic press. One week we are told—told almost with menaces—that the method works, next week we are warned with equal vehemence that it does not. It might be different things that are being discussed, to go by what is claimed for and against the method; it is as good as contraception, it is better, it is far worse, it is reliable, it is unreliable, it is easily calculated,

[1] I say "little" out of caution; I have searched his book without finding any such concessions at all.

it is hard to calculate, taking basal temperatures is simple, taking them is difficult.[1] I note with interest that Lestapis himself provides contradictory accounts; at one place, the woman is supposed to be fertile for a few days only each month (*L* 187), at another she is fertile for all except the 8–10 days following ovulation (*L* 138). It was the best of methods, it was the worst of methods. . . .

In this confusion there seems to lurk the same tension which we encountered in the "argument from nature". On the one hand, a claim was made on grounds that admit of no human or contextual consideration, and those who make the claim are understandably anxious to give it flesh and blood by adopting more tangible reasons. Yet only those original and purely physiological grounds can furnish the conclusion required by the RP. True enough, as we saw in the preceding chapter, there are good reasons for not accepting these grounds in the first place, but at least they did make a semblance of offering apodictic proof. The more perceptible and colourful reasons cannot even do this. The same dilemma has to be faced by advocates of the safe period. If it is the only way short of complete continence in which Catholics can control conception, well and good. But if this is a conclusion whose proof rests on the moral significance of a physiological pattern, it cannot depend for its truth on the ability of medical men to plot the fertility cycle. This tension is most acute when the safe period is recommended in cases where those who reject the RP would counsel, not contraceptives, but sterilization. In such crises of conscience there can be no gainsaying the essential difference between the two positions, and yet the temptation to offer "palpable" reasons here is obviously greater than ever. The result is that praise of the safeness of the safe period (even if justified) stumbles over a simple but momentous point of logic—a failure rate of one in a hundred does not diminish the unpleasantness of any one failure by 99 per cent. A revolver may have five of its six chambers empty. Yet if I play

[1] The recent increase in arguments over the RP has brought with it an increase in testimonies for and against the safe period; what I say in the text applies with even greater force to this latest stage in the polemic. I venture to recommend Q. de la Bedoyère's "Eight Years of Rhythm" (*CR*, January 1965) as a brief but significant (and, may I add, courageous) piece of testimony.

Russian roulette with it, I am not risking only one-sixth of my life.[1]

This tension between the isolated but supposedly apodictic reasoning from biology, and the more attractive but only persuasive considerations from human capacities and values, is greater for present advocates of the safe period than it was for earlier moralists. To defend the use of the infertile period is to defend a method of preventing conception, a method of birth control, a way of having sexual satisfaction without some of the consequences at which sexual activity is aimed, a separation of pleasure from procreation. Sure enough, the infertile period can be a lawful way of doing all this—can be, that is, if those wider considerations mentioned by Pius XII (see above, p. 60) are respected—but the fact remains that what inspires the use of the method is a desire to prevent conception. Husbands and wives who use the safe period do so because they do not want to conceive a child. The jibe that the infertile period is just like contraception because its purposes are identical is, of course, ineffective as it stands; a common purpose by no means guarantees that all means taken to secure it have the same moral value. But the jibe does give an admittedly botched expression to a genuine problem—that admitting the use of the safe period means weakening all arguments against contraception apart from those concerned with what distinguishes it from this other and approved method of achieving the same anticonceptional purpose. And of the arguments which we have encountered so far, none passes this test except the appeal to biological structure. The same genuine difficulty is concealed in another fallacious objection—that Rome sanctions the safe period only because it is less safe than contraception. Obviously, as it stands the objection does not hold. Effectiveness is morally irrelevant. What matters for the RP is that no direct interference be made with the generative apparatus (remembering the

[1] This point of logic seems to have escaped Sutherland (whose *Laws of Life* (1935) gave one of the first popular accounts in English of the safe period). In his *Control of Life* (1947) he states that a calculation given earlier by him of the infertile period gave results almost directly contrary to the facts. In other words, those who followed his advice would in fact be having intercourse near the time of maximum fertility. His comment on this blunder is only "Nevertheless, and notwithstanding the times in which we live, I offer no apology to anyone who owes his or her existence to that error." (p. 229.)

emendations made to this principle by Hürth and other theologians), that the corporeal geography of the sexual act be undisturbed, and that the couple harmonize their use of natural sterility with their procreative vocation. Yet once more the same difficulty emerges. Defenders of the RP are in the awkward position of having to distinguish one method from another on grounds that must logically be remote and colourless, because they can no longer appeal to any considerations except those which apply to contraception and not to the use of the safe period.

On the other hand, moralists who did not favour the safe period were not so hampered in their apologetic. For them, rhetoric about "self-indulgence", "passion" and "sterility" could be deployed against the limitation of conception *as such*, the virtues of large families and trust in providence could be extolled without reserve, and separation of sexual pleasure from procreation could be denounced without qualification. The doctrine of these moralists might well be attacked, but it could not be accused of inconsistency. Their grudging toleration of a method of controlling conception which did not involve complete abstinence treated it as something exceptional, as outside the normal course of married life, as a matter on which the less said the better. Canon Mahoney, McReavy's predecessor in the *Clergy Review*, held that although the use of the infertile period was not in itself illicit, information about it was not to be made public. (*Priests' Problems*, p. 322.)[1]

As I shall later be drawing conclusions from this contrast in attitudes, I should like to point out the debt that progress here owes to the (admittedly guarded) commendation of the safe period by Pius XII already mentioned (p. 41). The Pope's pronouncement gave a lead that has yet to be followed by some authors, for the older attitude is by no means dead. In his *Marriage and Rhythm* (1957), J. L. Thomas is on the defensive against unnamed adversaries of the method for whom it is "evil-sounding" and "an unhappy compromise" (136) and one of the commendations on the book's cover is equally apologetic. The well-known American authority Kelly gives an account of the

[1] For similar reservations on the part of other writers, and for much evidence about the attitude towards limitation of conception twenty and more years ago, Sutherland's *Control of Life* repays examination.

lawfulness of the method which bristles with a whole hedge of conditions and qualifications. For him, parenthood is the business of marriage, control of births is never normal, and it is appropriate to think of the safe period (which is neither sponsored nor endorsed by the Church, but merely permitted) when five children have been born in ten years (Kelly, p. 51): how the conceptions are to be so neatly spaced he does not explain. For another American moralist there is no limit to the obligation of fecundity (*CR*, May 1960), while even Marshall, whose *Preparing for Marriage* (1962) has been justly praised, prefixes his chapter on regulating conception[1] with "it is a pity that we have to discuss such a negative subject at all in a book which aims at a positive view of marriage". No centre for advice on the method has been allowed in the whole of Southern Ireland until very recently, as the Irish bishops thought it might be abused.[2] And, just as recently, but more picturesquely, a university chaplain recommended complete abstinence for birth regulation, as contraception was not only sinful, but difficult and dangerous, while the safe period lacked sufficient certainty. Men were asked if they wished to impose on their wives "the filth and risk of contraceptive prophylaxy", women if they were marrying "lively satyrs you dare not thwart". If the answers were "Yes", then the author would say "*ennur si*, meaning I do not believe you".[3]

I have mentioned all these opinions to show that contemporary research into the human fertility cycle, and the foundation of approved centres where advice on it can be got, are events whose novelty we ought not to forget. It is not from any desire to embarrass the advocates of the safe period that we should keep these matters in mind. Our difficulties raise the question rather as to how far the novelty of their position entails new opinions about the purpose of marriage. This is a

[1] Significantly entitled "Contraception".

[2] *Catholic Herald* (10 October 1963). It will be remembered that the Irish bishops also successfully opposed a State welfare scheme for mothers and babies in 1951.

[3] I know of the author's views only through extracts from his pamphlet printed in the *Catholic Herald* of 19 May 1963 (under the caption "A husband or a satyr?"), and through subsequent correspondence in that paper. "*Ennur si*" is presumably a compositor's blunder for "Eppur si muove": it refers, tactlessly perhaps, to Galileo's ordeal before the Holy Roman Inquisition.

topic which will be considered in the sixth chapter. What we have seen of the safe period may now be complemented in the fifth chapter by an examination of something in which, argues Lestapis, it essentially differs from contraception—its proclamation of the positive value of chastity in marriage.

5

Chastity

1. Chastity and family limitation

In the preceding chapter I tried to show that the distinctions drawn by defenders of the RP between natural and artificial sterility were either restatements of an unproved assertion about the untouchability of the human reproductive apparatus, or that they lacked probative force and raised difficulties rather than solved them. We detected there, just as we had detected in the fourth chapter, a gap between an absolute condemnation and the reasons offered for it; we saw paradoxical exceptions made to the prohibition of sterilization for its own sake; and the chapter ended by contrasting the attitudes and problems of those defenders of the RP who favour the use of the infertile period with the attitudes of those who do not.

This contrast is a symptom of a general growth in theological esteem of the married state and of married sexuality. Although it would not be denied that such a growth has marked Catholic thought and activity in recent times, I am going to attempt in due course to draw consequences from the change that may not be so readily admitted. The first step in my deduction will be to examine a claim for the RP found in *L* and in many other works: that it protects and proclaims the value of chastity in marriage. In other words, it is not a mere prohibition that is being taught by the RP, but a way of advancing in the spiritual life in the state of marriage.

For Lestapis (and he is only giving eloquent expression to sentiments shared by many others) the method of periodic abstinence implies, as contraception does not, the practice of continence in marriage. The use of the safe period is an art, presupposing a whole pattern of life, to which the couple are to be educated. Contraception is a technique and an artifice, and can easily sink the marriage relationship into a technique of satisfaction. One integrates the flesh with the spirit in chastity, intensifying the spiritual aspect of bodily union, the other asks for no effort and gives nothing beyond sensual pleasure. Contraception remains closed in on itself, it cannot rise to a higher level. The use of the safe period can so rise, as it unites desire with reason, and helps the couple to overcome those obscure forces which humiliatingly exploit their liberty. Unlike contraception, it calls for absolute faith in Christ, in whose truth we are trying to live, and in our partner, whom we seek to safeguard in soul and body. (*L* 181–94). Let us examine this argument, to see something of what it suggests and what it takes for granted.

The case put by Lestapis seems weighted against contraception from the start by terminology. In a perfectly proper sense of the words, contraception and rhythm are both "techniques", both "artifices". Indeed, the care and calculation required for the successful employment of the infertile period make it a far more elaborate technique than a contraceptive method as simple as the use of a sheath. "Technique" would seem to be used by Lestapis more as an evaluative than a descriptive term—we are to interpret it as something subhuman and mechanical, fixed and outside man, whose employment leaves man unaltered. But if "technique" is to be given this evaluative meaning, the evaluation must take into account the motives of those who use the various methods of preventing conception, and their whole marital situation as affected by the methods; and by these criteria, both contraception and rhythm can turn out to be "techniques". The only way to avoid this objection is to show that contraception is bound to be practised "mechanically" and for unworthy motives, bound to lead to spiritual impoverishment; and that rhythm must always be used for the best of reasons and with the best of results. Lestapis makes no attempt in this chapter to prove the former contention, the nearest he gets to doing so is in the second chapter of his work, where he discusses the values bound up with contraception. I have already stated and examined what he has said there (p. 28); no further analysis would turn his evidence into the universal indictment he needs here. The second assertion is not proved either, and indeed it would be hard to see how Lestapis could submit that the motives for using rhythm must always be good. If the infertile period is always virtuously employed, why did Pius XII have to attack abuses of it? (See p. 60.) It would be fairer to say that both contraception and rhythm are methods capable of being used or misused—as methods usually are, in fact. It is no discredit to a technique that it can be used with evil as well as good results, unless we identify its own moral indifference with its users' indifference to morality.

Lestapis and other defenders of the RP might seem on stronger ground when they commend rhythm for involving the married couple in a pattern of life together in a way that contraception does not. The monthly period in which complete sexual relations must be suspended provides husband and wife with an opportunity of transcending the physical expression of their love by subordinating the flesh to the spirit (*L* 184, 186). Their common abstinence is performed for Christ's sake, in faith and love, and can lead to their ever closer union and to a heightened joy when complete sexual relations are assumed. (*L* 190 ff.) Contraceptive techniques, on the other hand, are bound by definition to separate pleasure from all responsibility; their use does not call for any spiritual effort, as does the practice of continence; they act automatically, and in defiance of nature's wishes, dynamic forces, and structures. (*L* 185.) Rhythm can protect and proclaim the value of married chastity and of faith in Christ in a way that contraception is unable to do.

The argument is persuasive, precisely because it is so unlike the appeal to nature. It displays no references to the biological structure of intercourse, no examination of particular anatomical facts in isolation from everything else. Instead, it talks in terms of the vocation and the way of life followed by Christians, and addresses them as persons, not just as potential fertilizers. In preceding chapters I spoke of the difference between the way in which Christians hold moral principles and the way in which they are held by those who do not accept a law-giving God. Let me now complete what I have said by pointing to another difference, which is just as important. There is an essential discontinuity between the demands made on us as political and rational animals, and the demands made on us by our vocation to be God's children. It is not just that moral principles are held with a special absoluteness because they are God's commands; the principles on which a Christian bases his life cannot be adequately expressed in terms of human and rational goodness.

The Aristotelian holding of the mean can never be an adequate yardstick for the conduct of those who think they have been called to a destiny immeasurably above their nature, and whose summons to be perfect as their heavenly Father is perfect commits them to holding their ground in a desperate struggle where victory lies, not with their power, but with God. Nor does the summons just commit us to a struggle; it removes us from the area of social and personal duties to something more wonderful and more terrible altogether. A Christian is by his baptism a witness to God, and he can never be sure that being a witness will not mean being a martyr. His life as a believer can never be a closed list of duties, but must remain open to demands that would be outrageous if anyone but God made them. Given all this, a Christian cannot expect his life to be adequately governed by rational benevolence, or his obligations to be adequately described in terms of it. He will accept the standards of Christ's teaching, will realize that they impose upon him a view of life which is higher than that of socially acceptable common sense, and will ask for the help without which he cannot live up to them. He will admit that the meaning of his life and the duties of his state necessarily involve a reference to something outside the order of the here and now altogether. For all his love for the world, a world he believes God made and saw to be good, he cannot forget that he has here no abiding city. It is a fallen world in which he lives, and the grace of his baptism does not remove all the disabilities of this fallen condition. If his destiny is to live in a way above his state as a man, his inclinations can only too easily lead him to live in a way below this state; rational moderation can never exclude for him the need to do battle for his salvation. Temperance and mortification in his life will not be simple demonstrations of his self-control and reasonableness, but will be acts of self-denial and atonement motivated by love, moments in the struggle by a fallen man to serve the God he loves and fears to lose. And the struggle may cost him more than he dreamt: the road to heaven admits of no exhaustive map-making, its hazards are known only to God.

Sexual matters can be no exception to this rule of life. The Christian commendation of continence for God's sake is not an isolated precept that matters only for the few; in another way it concerns each Christian marriage. Reason by itself shows how necessary it is to make the sexual relationship between husband and wife into something which unites them and forms part of a common life and affection, something more than an occasional entertainment which leaves everything just as it was. Christian belief accepts all this, and adds that the love between husband and wife should direct them both towards the love of God. By the sacrament of matrimony their love is made a sign of his love; and the procreation of children to which their love leads makes them instruments of his creative power. Sex, like everything else in their lives, is to be put at his service. Like everything else, it can bring them nearer to him or separate them from him. Like everything else, it will not be used as it should unless they master it for God's sake and for their own. Otherwise, it will master them, and their common life as spouses and Christians will have to be lived on its terms instead of on God's. The mastery of sex for his sake is not only a difficult task for which divine grace is needed, it is a task which lasts as long as their marriage. It involves tenderness and consideration for each other; faithfulness in the face of temptations; a place for God in their minds and hearts; a love which is generous and grows deeper as time goes by. How can such a task be achieved unless the practice of abstinence is woven into the fabric of their sexual relationship from the start? This much would be true if the problem was only one of inculcating habits of self-control. But the Christian, who places the human situation within the wider setting of God's providence, and of the fall and the redemption of man, sees in sex (as in any gift of God) something which must be made part of the deeper union to which God calls all of us through Christ. The exceptional vocation to continence for the Kingdom of Heaven's sake is a witness to the Christian belief that all human love ought eventually to find its fulfilment in the love of God. Such continence would not have been needed in an unfallen world, for there would have been then no struggle to make love reach this fulfilment. As things are, the few renounce sexual love that they may have the chance of giving more to God and so more to their fellow creatures; the many who accept this love accept thereby the vocation of making it a means to God and to each other, not an end in itself.

As I said, the argument is persuasive. But it is not a proof of the RP. What it persuades us to accept is the Christian pattern of life and marriage which I have sketched tritely enough in the two preceding paragraphs. That the sexual relationship should lead to the procreation of a family worthy of the abilities and responsibilities of husband and wife is an obvious enough truth, a truth ignored at the cost of ignoring what marriage and sexuality are for; it is not a truth which needs a distinctively Christian context for its assertion. Christian belief will inculcate (as other religions do) the need for the control of sex in marriage, the need for its integration into a whole complex of love between husband, wife, and God, which is destined ultimately to transcend its distinctively sexual modality. Christian belief will say all this and much more; there is no need to labour the obvious. Unfortunately, it does seem necessary to labour something else that should be just as obvious. These values, so easily forgotten and so often rejected, cannot be identified with the prohibition of contraception, without an adequate proof of the identification. Certainly, the proof offered by Lestapis is quite inadequate. Taken as a proof of the RP, what he says is only a specialized form of the preceding argument, and like that argument, is effective only if a restricted significance is given to contraception and an extended significance to rhythm. That contraceptives do not as such involve abstinence and that rhythm does, is more than obvious, it is tautological. But it is not possible to pass from the tautology to the conclusion Lestapis makes without showing two things, analogous to those which had to be proved to vindicate the former argument. (See p. 95.) It must first be shown that the abstinence enjoined by rhythm is necessarily of spiritual profit. It must then be shown that contraception necessarily excludes the practice of abstinence. Can these two propositions be proved?

Consider the first of them. What plausibility it has comes, as so much else comes in apologetic for the RP, from a defective criterion of significance. If X is having contraceptive intercourse, what he is doing is here and now perceptibly different from intercourse without contraceptives, and is here and now perceptibly directed against conception. If X is now having "rhythmic" intercourse, there is no perceptible difference here and now between what he is doing and what he would be doing in non-rhythmic intercourse, nor is there any perceptible orientation of it here and now against conception. Yet this is not and cannot be the whole story. "What X is doing here and now" is not a matter of what we might photograph here and now.[1] How X is using rhythm, and whether he is being unselfish or selfish, cannot be decided by "photographic inspection". But apart from this defective criterion, what other reason is there for proving the spiritualizing effect of rhythm from the abstinence it imposes? Abstinence can be enforced by rhythm, just as it can be enforced by absence or by imprisonment or sickness. Abstinence as such is not virtuous (see *ST* 2/2.141.1)—what matters is how the abstinence is accepted, and how it is integrated into the whole married life of the spouses. That it can be so integrated, and with spiritual profit, is undeniable; it is just as undeniable that the opportunity may be lost and the deprivation grudgingly tolerated. Rhythm can be and is practised by people of no religious persuasion at all—for some, it will be the cheapest and simplest method of limiting conception. Rhythm can be and is practised by those who reject contraception, yet practised by them with the very selfishness that inspires some users of contraceptives. That rhythm provides an occasion for virtuous self-denial does not mean that it ensures virtuous self-denial, nor that self-denial in married sexuality implies the practice of rhythm.

The second presupposition of Lestapis' argument (that contraception necessarily excludes the practice of abstinence) is no more plausible—it seeks our acceptance by confusing a moral with a logical truth. Certainly, contraception does not involve abstinence in the way that rhythm does; this is a piece of logic, not a piece of morals. But it is also a piece of logic that we cannot pass from the statement "Contraceptive intercourse does not involve abstinence" immediately to the statement "Contraceptive intercourse excludes abstinence". If A is compatible with not-B it need not be incompatible with B, it can be com-

[1] To adopt an example of Professor Austin's, suppose X stands at the altar and says, "I will." What is he doing? Is he getting married or not? We can imagine a host of different reasons why we should say he is *not* getting married—he's doing it at gun-point, he's drugged, he has a wife already, the clergyman is unauthorized to perform weddings, it's only a rehearsal . . . See the variety of grounds on which these reasons are based, and see how impoverished the empiricist's "instantaneous" criterion seems when confronted by such variety.

patible with them both. Lestapis gets near to admitting this objection when he writes that "contraceptive techniques are bound *by definition* to separate pleasure from all responsibility". (*L* 185. Italics mine.) This certainly removes his condemnation of them from being verified or falsified; but it does this only at the cost of turning his assertion into a matter of words. Lestapis is now using "contraception" simply in the sense of "anti-conceptional methods which separate pleasure from responsibility". But this is precisely that "human" and "vocational" estimate of such practices which the RP is bound to reject. On the other hand, if he wishes to retain the normal meaning of "contraception", his remark is an unproved assertion, and it still has to be shown that contraception is incompatible with abstinence freely chosen for God's sake. Intercourse, like any other pleasurable activity, ought to be subject to the Christian practice of renunciation for the love of God and for man's strengthening in the fight against sin. If the RP only reminded us of this duty, or even insisted upon its practice, there would be nothing extraordinary in what it said. Abstinence would be practised according to the type of intercourse—contraceptive or rhythmic—that was being used by husbands and wives. Some would not be able to use rhythm effectively; some would; some would be permanently sterile; each would have to understand the obligation of abstinence and carry out that obligation in his own way. But this is just what the RP cannot be saying. We are back to a familiar situation. The RP is supported by an elaborate appeal to natural or supernatural values, while the position itself cannot but depend upon a physiological criterion to which questions of value are irrelevant.

We may go to a document already quoted for an instance of this ambiguity. "Here too, the husband and wife ought to know how to keep within the bounds of moderation. As in eating and drinking they ought not to give themselves over completely to the promptings of their senses, so neither ought they to subject themselves unrestrainedly to their sensual appetite." Here is an unexceptionable appeal for temperance and moderation: but what is the conclusion immediately drawn? "This therefore is the rule to be followed: the use of the natural generative instinct and function is lawful in the married state only, and in the services of the purposes for which marriage exists." ("Midwives", 60.) An appeal for moderation turns out to be the inculcation of the observance of a purely physiological "natural" criterion. The same tension is found in an adverse but not unsympathetic review by Marshall of Rock's *The Time Has Come*. (*The Tablet* 12 October 1963.) Marshall admits that Catholics have neglected in the past to proclaim the responsibility needed in parenthood in favour of "an exclusive concern for the physical integrity of marriage relations".[1] He speaks of the "indicated design in man" as not being discerned "solely from physical structure". Man has been given reason and will and in consequence "responsibility for the exercise of all his powers". So far so good; but then he takes everything back again by claiming that this means that the man will not "truncate his powers in order to avoid responsibility for each and every act", and that he will not (i.e., by steroid drugs) take from his wife "something which is fundamental to her being a woman, so that he shall not have to decide about the meaning and construction of each act of love". What is this but the old physiological criterion? His talk of responsibility, so welcome after the praises of fecklessness in some books, turns out to be quite distinct from that "reasonable service" to God which would use sex and procreation in a way worthy of a Christian and a rational being. What he says has to be just a decorative flourish and emotional suasion to the old insistence on the inviolability of every single act of intercourse—in fact, to just that concern for the physical integrity of marriage relations of which he has already spoken. True enough, the concern is no longer exclusive —but the concern is still all-important, for the integrity is a *sine qua non* for lawful use of sex.[2]

I am reminded of some imposing piece of Victorian machinery, with its array of well-polished brass levers and elaborately calibrated gauges, but its interior gutted and replaced by an inelegant but efficient electric motor that reduces the apparent controls to idle appendages. Here, after all the talk of abstinence and selfishness, it is only the old anatomical pattern that really counts. But if so, why talk in spiritual terms? Conversely, if we

[1] He mentions a delightful Americanism for this: "inspecting the plumbing".

[2] Marshall denies *en passant* that an appeal to physiological criteria represents the thought of Aquinas: this is a question I shall deal with later (pp. 130 ff.).

are going to talk in spiritual terms and speak of the need for the practice of abstinence in sexual relations, why must the abstinence be dictated by the safe period? What unique virtue is attached to abstinence which is governed by physiological considerations? Especially when the considerations differ from case to case. For some, rhythm means a sizeable abstention, for others it means only a brief interruption in married relations: is the spiritualizing coefficient of the procedure to depend upon menstrual vagaries?

What makes the appeal to chastity so elusive is the lack of standards of comparison. Whereas debates over family discipline, for instance, can be solved (or at least investigated) by the various experiences of those that have tried different methods of bringing up their children, there can be no comparing the marriages of Catholics who use rhythm with those of Catholics who use contraception. The latter are doing something they know has been condemned in official pronouncements which they ought to obey. Their position is false from the start, and the falseness of it can produce an equally false conscience, can lead them to drift away from religion altogether. From this undoubted fact we must not jump to the unwarranted conclusion that contraception could never be practised without spiritual damage. To draw this conclusion we should first have to prove that the damage came from an action which inevitably offended against chastity, and not just from an action which was a breach of obedience. Contraception is in fact a great rock on which the married life of Catholics can come to grief. It is also something taken for granted by those who do not share the Christian view of marriage, and whose opinions of the married state may include attitudes to divorce and promiscuity that will seem impoverished and deficient to Christians. Most of all, it has played its part in the divorce, not just between sexuality and procreation, but between sexuality and love, which disfigures our time. As a result, the associations of the practice are so unfavourable that we need to make a real effort to distinguish the present situation of contraception among Catholics from the results of contraception as such. But hard as it is to make, the distinction is worth making. Perhaps matters could not be otherwise than they are—if so, we must still acknowledge the part that association and training play in the attitude of Catholics towards contraceptive practices. We must make the distinction for honesty's sake and for the sake of clear discussion. Defenders of the RP object to the testimonies of Catholics who disobey the Church's law here being used as evidence in favour of its abrogation. ("For Members", *Catholic Gazette* [April 1964].) Their objection is justified; in the face of such explicit commands of the Church, appeals to private judgement by members of the Church cannot but be suspect. "Personal conscience" has justified too much evil conduct in the past for it to be a final court of appeal in matters like this. But if it is wrong to excuse disobedience to this law on the grounds of individual opinion, it is just as indefensible to cite the experience of Catholics who have resorted to contraceptive devices and have then returned to the practice of rhythm because of the psychological disturbance they felt. It would surely be very surprising if, conditioned as they have been to regard contraception as grievously sinful, they did not feel some such disturbance. Two confusions lie behind this kind of argument against contraception. An aesthetic repugnance is identified with moral turpitude (thus leaving the door open to contraception when the offensive element is removed). And a situation in which Catholics, in a state of grace and in full accord with the Church, would use contraceptives according to the same norms as they are now supposed to use rhythm, is presupposed to be incapable of actualization. Perhaps it is so incapable; but psychological arguments for its impossibility cannot take their conclusion for granted.[1] This is why appeals to the self-indulgence which can undoubtedly inspire the use of contraceptives, or to the defective attitudes of some of their users, and so on, are bound to be ineffective. As they stand, they cannot but be open to the obvious objection: "Contraception has not been tried and found wanting by the Church; it has not been tried." We have, of course, no similar excuse for a biassed attitude towards rhythm—its openness to both use and misuse ought to be obvious enough. I am sure that Lestapis and the rest would not deny this; my complaint is rather that their repeated and almost lyrical commendations of the spiritual values in rhythm suggest that no other way of preventing conception can possibly have

[1] The "aesthetic" argument against contraception will be examined at greater length on pp. 196 f.

these values; while the values themselves serve to create such strongly favourable associations for rhythm in the reader's mind as to distract his attention, not only from the method's drawbacks but from its basic moral indifference.

2. *Chastity in married life*

But there is a deeper misconception concealed in the contention that rhythm proclaims the value of chastity in a way that contraception cannot. Lestapis' argument, like so many other defences of the RP, seems to assume that sex is an unrestrained animal passion aroused without difficulty to a climax by husband and wife, and knowing no barriers but those imposed upon it by periodic continence. If sex in marriage were like this, rhythm could be commended for enforcing a temporary curbing of this emotional torrent that would otherwise know no checking or control. But is sex like this? And is marriage? Must things really be in such a plight unless rhythm is used? Surely married sexuality has built-in needs and opportunities for self-mastery. It is an act for two people, needing the efforts and understanding of both if it is to be worthy of their state, not a reaction which can be triggered off at will, like tickling or the knee-jerk reflex. What sexuality is, and what human beings are, mean that there will be in any marriage countless occasions for restraint and consideration, countless occasions when desire is conquered and sublimated in the name of tenderness. Surely exertions in such uncontrived and natural contexts—and how real these exertions can be—will be more deeply involved in the growth of husband and wife together than will any abstinence dictated by adventitious considerations like the day of the month. Advocates of rhythm see in the periodic abstinence it imposes that reasoned control over appetite which is truly human and truly Christian. Thus for Lestapis the use of the infertile period means that the vehement movements of the flesh come under the control of the spirit, and by chastity the flesh no longer speaks out of its turn. (*L* 184.) The regimentation of the sexual impulses by this method of preventing conception does not go counter to spontaneity, for love is at home with reason, and is degraded when caprice rules it (187), while, by rhythm, the couple triumph over humiliating exploitations of their liberty. (*L* 183.) "Reason" and "impulse" are oddly used here. Is it not more reasonable—that is, more truly human (cf. *ST* 2/2.141.1)—to weave the practice of abstinence into the whole fabric of married life, to let it colour the whole variety of affections and emotions and situations which can lead to intercourse? Perhaps we must reject this suggestion. But if we reject it, let us do so because we loyally accept the consequences of a divine command, not because we have so stilted a conception of reason and so poor an opinion of sexuality, that we talk as if this infra-rational, effortless urge could be made human only by the physiologically dictated abstentions of rhythm. This is not only bad theology, it is bad psychology as well, and a psychology that betrays its badness in phrases like "humiliating exploitations of liberty". Sexual desire certainly can be this—equally certainly, it need not be. What room do such slanted descriptions leave for distinguishing a hated enslavement to a despised object of lust from the intense longing to unite with a beloved partner?[1] Yet not to distinguish them disqualifies us from saying anything about marriage worthy of respect. Does Lestapis' *plaidoyer* for the "rationality" of rhythm give a worthy place to the spontaneity and variability of human love, which may arouse the desire for intercourse at one time and not at another (and so lead to self-denial prompted by consideration, not by the calendar)? As for Lestapis' submission that love is degraded when caprice rules it, I can only protest at this use of "caprice".

[1] Compare, for instance:
"O Dii, si vostrum est misereri, aut si quibus unquam
extrema jam ipsa in morte tulistis opem;
me miserum adspicite; et, si vitam puriter egi,
eripite hanc pestem, perniciemque mihi.
Heu mihi subrepens imos, ut corpore, in artus,
expulit ex omni pectore laetitias!
Non jam illud quaero, contra ut me diligat illa,
aut, quod non potis est, esse pudica velit.
Ipse valere opto, et tetrum hunc deponere morbum.
O Dii, reddite mi hoc pro pietate mea." (Catullus, 70.)
with this:
"Mutuis animis amant, amantur:
unam Septimius misellus Acmen
mavolt quam Syrias, Britanniasque;
uno in Septimio fidelis Acme
facit delicias libidinesque.
Quis ullos homines beatiores
vidit? Quis Venerem auspicatiorem?" (Catullus, 42.)

Suppose a sudden tenderness, provoked by a chance word or look, or a sudden need to reaffirm unity in the face of difficulty, invite husband and wife to a closeness that will involve intercourse, is it reasonable—or fair—to talk of capriciousness? Is it irrational to want to let the sexual act, and voluntary abstinence from it, arise from the whole range of affection and regard between the spouses? Or must reason here consist in behaving like Mr Shandy and his grandfather clock?

The restricted sense given by Lestapis to marital chastity is curiously illustrated by his commendation of *coitus reservatus*—penetration without insemination (like most moralists, Lestapis calls it *amplexus reservatus*). The practice was recommended some years ago in some Catholic marriage manuals as a help against temptations to use contraceptives, and in a manner unqualified enough to bring about this warning from the Holy Office: "Priests, whether engaged in the cure of souls or in the direction of consciences, must never, asked or unasked, presume to talk as if no objection could be made from Christian law against *coitus reservatus*". (*D* 3907.) These reservations expressed in the official pronouncement were partly concerned with the possible loss of seed; for the practice itself is, like any other incomplete act, subject to the qualification that there must be no proximate danger of this happening. They were also partly concerned with the divorce implied by the practice between sexual activity and procreation (for this see *CAR*). Thus, a writer in the *Clergy Review* at the time described the practice as "an extreme and dangerous application of the principle permitting incomplete actions to the married" (*CR* (December 1952).) Hürth's article itself is very cautious and reserved, and he will go no further than "it is not established that *coitus reservatus* can never be practised without sin". (*CAR*.)[1] It is, then, surprising to find the practice enthusiastically commended by Lestapis as being a way of reducing the intensity of sexual desire to the dictates of reason (*L* 169). It is still more surprising to find that one of its benefits is supposed to be a hormonal interchange between husband and wife. I have not the medical competence to weigh the testimony

[1] For views against the medical advisability of the practice, see *Marriage* by Keenan and Ryan, 200. For a favourable view of the practice on these grounds, see K. Walker's *Love, Marriage and the Family*, ch. 9.

Lestapis adduces in support of *coitus reservatus* against the explicit condemnation of the practice by other professionals. I can only suppose that this interchange of hormones is brought about by the absorption into each partner's body of substances secreted by the other in the first stages of sexual excitement—what moral theologians would call *distillationes.* To procure these deliberately seems sailing very close to the wind for one who, like Lestapis, is so concerned to preserve the physical integrity of the sexual act. (Besides—according to Keenan and Ryan—the practice could very well lead to fertilization.) Again, that the husband should have enough control over his reflexes to put the automatism of the sexual act at the service of his wife and himself is certainly desirable, and is part of the right use of sex in marriage. But to commend the incomplete sexual activity of *coitus reservatus* on the grounds of its greater rationality and calmness seems very like identifying marital chastity with a particular emotional mode in copulation that may be suitable at one time and not at another. Or is there something essentially subhuman in the orgasm, whenever it takes place? Lestapis offers a quotation from Chauchard, a neurophysiologist, that suggests he thinks so. For Chauchard, *coitus reservatus* is an ascesis which, by ridding the sexual act of its animal automatism and so giving it a fully human dimension at the cost of renouncing the extremes of pleasure, brings in its train both peace and joy. (*L* 169.) Surely, whatever one's opinion of Chauchard's contention, and whatever one thinks of *coitus reservatus*, nothing is gained by confusing this issue with the question of marital chastity as such. But there is something else which needs saying about the practice. While agreeing with Lestapis that no ecclesiastical pronouncement has definitely condemned *coitus reservatus*, I find it a little cavalier of him to say that "the first purpose of the Monitum from the Holy Office was to insist that the questions remains an open one". (*L* 169.)[1]

There is a related argument for rhythm which must be considered now, as it contains a dangerous ambiguity. Appeals to the virtue of chastity in support of this method speak of the

[1] According to the monitum itself, the occasion of its publication was that "certain authors have described, praised and recommended a certain act called *amplexus reservatus*."

need for trust in Christ as the centre of the way of life it enjoins. (*L* 190 etc.) "Trust in Christ" can be taken here as asserting what any Christian must believe—that to live in the state of marriage as God wishes can be done only by faith in him through his Son, who has made marriage a sign of his own love for the Church. To put it differently, chastity in marriage—that is, the right use of sex between husband and wife—cannot be practised without God's help, nor can any other virtue. But "trust in Christ" taken in this sense licenses no deduction that contraception shows mistrust of him, unless the unlawfulness of the practice has already been proved. Then indeed there can be talk of mistrust—that mistrust of God's providence which characterizes all sin, makes all sin an attempt to remould the world to our own desire rather than to his. Until this be shown, to call contraception mistrust in God is just as gratuitous as to call any other act of foresight mistrust in God without proving that the foresight employs evil means. But "trust in Christ" can be taken in another way, a way peculiarly undesirable when rhythm is being compared with contraception. As is well known, rhythm is often accused of being less reliable than other anti-conceptional methods.[1] The accusation, justified or not, occurs often enough to make talk here of trust in Christ sound something very like an excuse for using a defective method when better means are available. Such an interpretation would be wholly unseemly. It would surely be unworthy and irreverent to try to shuffle off accusations of inefficiency by appeals to divine providence, instead of openly admitting that the RP was not, when it came to the pinch, concerned with efficiency at all.

Even the word "chastity" itself is put to a use which is confusing. Abstinence from sexual activity is called continence by Aquinas (*ST* 2/2.155.1); unlike abstinence, chastity is compatible with sexual activity, for it consists in the moderate use of sex according to right reason. (*ST* 2/2.151.1 ad 1.) Lestapis, however, prefers to call the monthly abstinence "chastity", so that the couple during that time are "attempting to live chastely". (*L* 167; cf. *L* 208.) It seems strange that they cannot attempt to live chastely at other times—stranger still that what Aquinas called the right use of sex now refers to abstaining

[1] Whence the riddle—Q: "What name is given to those who use the safe period?" A: "Parents."

from it. I admit, of course, that many others have used "chaste" to mean "abstaining". But Lestapis is writing as a theologian and is aware of what he is doing. Why then should he fall in with the practice of turning chastity into continence?[1]

3. *Chastity and tradition*

My remarks about the terminology of Lestapis bring to a head the other exceptions taken to the argument from chastity. If the argument only inculcates the need for temperance, it makes valid points but is insufficient for the RP. If it is to be sufficient, it has to rely covertly on the principle that no interference may be made with the sexual act. By this, all talk of temperance becomes superfluous, and we are back to the "appeal to nature". An attempt is made to mask this superfluity by comparing contraception and rhythm, to the detriment of the former. Yet even here the conclusion to be proved has to be smuggled into the descriptions given of the two methods. In doing so, the argument commits its users to statements about reason and instinct in married sexuality that stand in as much need of proof as the conclusion of which they are supposed to be premises. At the last, chastity, which started by being the due employment of a bodily activity, ends up by being abstinence from it.

All this seems to give colour to a most popular accusation used by opponents of the RP—that it is only a symptom of the hatred and distrust of sex to be found in Christianity, and more especially in the Roman Church, whose celibate clergy confuse sexual activity with sin. There is no need to elaborate the charge, for it has been made often enough, and is so vague in its object and its accusations that we should be at a loss to know how to set about its confirmation or refutation. The moves in the game have been over-rehearsed by both sides. Councils are quoted against the view that sex is wicked, Fathers of the Church to the effect that it is; religious celibacy shows that the spiritual life is incompatible with sexuality, the Church's defence of the marriage bond shows the value she attaches to the act of

[1] Extremes meet, and the tireless Mellors agrees with him. He writes to Lady Chatterley, admittedly among other things: "I love being chaste now. . . . Now is the time to be chaste, it is so good to be chaste, like a river of cool water in my soul . . . it is like fresh water and rain." (*Lady Chatterley's Lover*, Penguin ed., p. 317.)

marriage; the Catholic Irish are hag-ridden with neuroses about sex, the equally Catholic Italians show all too healthy an inclination to indulge in its pleasures. And so the wrangle can go on—indefinitely, if we please. The accusation is in fact one of those many beliefs which, even if false, will hardly be eradicated by rational argument. It is an attitude to evidence, a reflex conditioned by experience or upbringing, rather than a coherent opinion open to evidence for or against.

Yet the topic is not one which we can altogether avoid. The burden of much written in the preceding pages has been that the rejection of contraceptive procedures will have to be on the basis of a divine command, a manifestation of God's will and purpose for men, not on the basis of a dispassionate inspection of human sexuality. As a complement to this critique of rational arguments, the distinction has been drawn more than once between accepting a command and accepting the reasons advanced for its justification. But at the same time, the prohibition of contraception has been distinguished from the prohibition of other sexual offences. The latter were obviously opposed to the monogamous union proposed by the New Testament, and were clearly condemned in Scripture. Contraception was not so obviously opposed and had no such clear condemnation —the one text adduced against it was ambiguous, and the topic does not recur among the many sexual regulations elsewhere in the Bible. For Roman Catholics, of course, this does not settle the matter. However the relation between "Scripture" and "Tradition" be expressed, there can be articles of faith which are not overtly contained in the written word of God, even though theologians may attempt to derive them from the general direction and pattern of that word—certain Marian dogmas come at once to mind. If contraception is to be condemned because of divine revelation, that revelation will have to be discerned in the authoritative teaching of the Church, it will not be a doctrine which can be read from Scripture without more ado.

A question is thus raised which is of another order to any discussed so far: Does the infallible teaching of the Church condemn contraception? In other words, is her present condemnation of it irrevocable? This is a theological question, and this essay has been up to now a philosophical study of certain arguments used by theologians, not itself a piece of theology. Yet it is a question which I feel obliged to try to answer, having repeatedly thrown back the prohibition of contraception from the realm of moral philosophy to that of religious belief. "If contraception is condemned by God, there can be no more argument, and no exceptions made; but the absoluteness must come from his revelation, not from a defective piece of philosophical reasoning": I have said this often enough to feel under some debt to the reader to ask the obvious question—*has* it been condemned by God? That is, given what Roman Catholics believe about Scripture and Tradition, has the Church infallibly and so irreversibly committed itself against contraception? With a certain trepidation, I am going to leave the firmer ground of philosophy and attempt an answer to this question in the next chapter.

6

Tradition

1. The appeal to tradition

In the decree of its fourth session, the Council of Trent described the place of Scripture and tradition in the Church as follows:

> The Council sees that this truth and guidance [of Christ's gospel] is contained in the written books and unwritten traditions which the Apostles received from Christ's own mouth, or which have, as it were, been handed down by the Apostles at the command of the Holy Spirit and so have reached us. Following the example of the orthodox Fathers of the Church, it accepts and venerates with equal affection and reverence (1) all the books of the Old and New Testament, for the one God is the author of both, (2) the traditions themselves concerning faith or morals as received from the lips of Christ or dictated by the Holy Spirit and preserved in an unbroken succession in the Catholic Church. [*D*, 1501.]

I complement this with an extract from a recent account of what tradition means for the Catholic theologian who looks at past theological development:

> For the Catholics tradition is not a mere appeal to history; it is a strictly theological conception. As Catholics see it, tradition is the teaching of the Church. The same Church always teaches the same doctrine through the power of the indwelling Spirit in the Church. The magisterium under that power formulates the doctrine adequately for the moment of its teaching. Such formulation is dogma, which is the normative expression of the truth of revelation. Truth does not evolve, because there is only one truth which the Church communicates and that is the total revelation of Christ. The Church grows in awareness of the revealed truth and in that sense there is an evolution. . . . The point to be stressed is that

the new dogma does not deny the old one. . . . This process takes place in history but is not an historical process. It is strictly ecclesiological. [G. Weigel, SJ, *Where Do we Differ? Catholic Theology in Dialogue*. London (1962), p. 16.][1]

The precise placing of tradition in theology is a matter for fruitful debate nowadays in the Church, but this much should be clear: a Catholic cannot approach the historical witness of the past to the faith with a spirit of detached curiosity. He will of course strive to be as unprejudiced and as accurate as he can in describing and evaluating what was said, but he is dealing with something more significant for him than a simple discovery about the history of religion. The Councils, papal decrees, liturgical and pastoral practice, the teaching of the Fathers and theologians—for him these are all part of the progress of the Church towards an understanding of Christ, and if he wants to understand Christ himself, he cannot ignore them. Obviously, not all elements in this heritage are of equal value and force, nor is its content unambiguous. Nor is the theologian's job simply to shuffle and to rearrange what is already given once for all. But he cannot approach his subject timelessly, approach it without preconceptions, start with a clean slate. Catholic theology, though it talks much of what is eternal, is essentially conditioned by time, it cannot but have a past. The theologian is himself a member of the Church; and what the Church teaches and has taught he believes to be true to what was first proclaimed by the Apostles.

This is why the argument from tradition against contraception is by far the strongest we have yet encountered. In one sense, of course, it is not really commensurable with the arguments considered in previous chapters. They claimed to deduce the RP from an examination of certain facts—facts about human values, about biology, about sterility and about chastity. The examination of such arguments involved an examination of the factual claims, the adducing of fresh evidence, and the logical scrutiny of the structure of each argument. Things are very different here. The argument from tradition necessarily takes

[1] For more details of contemporary Catholic thinking about tradition, especially in its relation to Scripture, see, e.g., J. R. Geiselmann, 'Scripture, Tradition and the Church: An Ecumenical Problem", in *Christianity Divided*, Sheed and Ward Ltd., London (1961), p. 38–71.

for granted the framework of Catholic belief. It simply points to the agreement among theologians in the past that preventing the seed from being able to fertilize the woman is gravely sinful. The theologians themselves are not infallible, nor does the argument claim that they are; it is the constancy of their witness that matters, a witness to what has been taught and believed over the centuries by the pastors and members of Christ's Church. Would not a change now be a departure from their belief, a rejection of what was then preached as part of the faith? Can we hold both the invariability of the deposit of faith and the possibility of a change in the RP? Given the tradition of condemnation which exists, and (as we have seen) given the papal condemnations of it which explicitly deny that any alteration is possible, is there anything more to be said?

The stand taken in previous chapters against the various kinds of argument for the RP would not be impugned if I answered the question negatively and finished the book here and now. Tradition is a witness to what Christians have believed, but its force does not communicate validity to inconclusive arguments from reason used in its support. If we accept the RP as belonging to the deposit of faith, we shall certainly look at sexual intercourse differently, but the difference will not come from a reasoned reflection about sexuality. It will not be the result of observation and argument, though it may serve as a starting-point for new reflections. To accept the RP on the grounds of tradition is quite distinct from agreeing with the rational apologetic for it analysed in preceding chapters. But must we accept the RP in this way? Let us start by seeing what the tradition is.

2. *The tradition against contraception*

Since this book was finished, Professor Noonan's important history of Catholic attitudes to contraception has appeared, covering a much wider field than the incidental pieces of historical research in this chapter. I have decided to leave the text here untouched—for nothing, I was glad to see, needed withdrawing in the light of Noonan's discoveries—and to devote an appendix (Appendix C, pp. 235 ff. below) to a consideration of some themes in his book.

I shall begin, not with the comparatively recent papal pronouncements, but with the accumulated witness of the past. That there is such a witness is beyond any doubt. I am no expert in theological history, but I venture to offer what might be called a simple genealogical tree of the view that interference with the sexual act is wrong; the reader can then judge the matter for himself. We can take more recent moralists as read: those I mentioned in the first chapter (see p. 22) are agreed (for references, see Capello, §806) as is St Alphonsus Liguori. (6, §954.) Going back to Reginaldus, a seventeenth-century author quoted by Liguori, we find that any unnatural sin or spilling of seed is wrong. (*Praxis Fori Poenitentialis*. Lugduni (1620) and first published in 1615, liber 21, cap. 3, sect. 8; liber 31, cap. 43.) Reginaldus quotes Sanchez, whose *De Matrimonio* was first published in 1606, and the same prohibitions are found there. (lib. 9, disp. 20.) Both Reginaldus and Sanchez refer to Cajetan's famous commentary on the *Summa Theologiae* of Aquinas. This appeared about 1520, and in the remarks on 2/2.154.11 we read that any copulation or semination which of its nature cannot lead to procreation is unnatural, as the generative power and members are meant by nature to preserve the species. Nor is Cajetan's opinion any different from that in the text on which he is commenting; we have already mentioned the corresponding passage in Aquinas (see p. 7), which probably dates from 1271. Of St Thomas's predecessors, Alexander of Hales may be mentioned, as he is a source for the literary form of the *Summa*.[1] The same condemnation of both unnatural actions or incomplete acts like wasting the seed is found in his writings. (*Universae Theologiae Summa*, Venetiis (1676), pars 2, quaest. 143, membrum 9.) Both Alexander and Aquinas refer to the *Sentences* of Peter Lombard, an early medieval survey of theological questions whose rather meagre text served later writers (including Aquinas) as an occasion for more elaborate commentary. In the fourth book, Peter quotes with approval Augustine's condemnation of those "whose cruel lust or lustful cruelty leads them to take sterilizing poisons" and of intercourse "which has been turned into the unnatural use". (Distinction 31.) If it be thought that the *Sentences* are less explicit than theologians like

[1] For an account of the authorship and influence of works attributed to Alexander, see E. Gilson, *History of Christian Philosophy in the Middle Ages* (1955), 327–8.

Aquinas or Alexander, we can go back to the passages from Augustine which were quoted by Peter.[1] Intercourse for pleasure, Augustine writes, is "to be distinguished from intercourse in which the procreation of children is resisted by wicked desires or deeds.[2] Spouses who do this deserve that name no longer, they have lost the reality of marriage and are only using its honourable title to cover their shame." (*De Nuptiis et Concupiscentia*, 1, 15; 44/324.) He claims that their exposure of unwanted children betrays their secret vice, mentions their use of sterilizing poisons (which Peter Lombard repeats) and adds that they will procure abortions if their efforts to prevent conception prove unsuccessful. The second quotation from Augustine comes from *De Bono Conjugali*, cc. 10 and 11 (40/382): "Spouses turn away the mercy of God from themselves by turning the natural use of marriage into the unnatural. For this to be done in marriage has a special malice. Unnatural intercourse is abominable if performed with a harlot, and still worse if performed with one's wife." Again, in a passage quoted in our own time by Pius XI ("Marriage", *D* 3716) we read: "If a man has not the gift of continence, let him marry lawfully, lest he beget children shamefully or, still more shamefully, copulate without begetting. Though this is done even by those lawfully married: for it is unlawful and shameful to have intercourse even with one's own wife if the conception of children is avoided. Onan the Son of Judah did this and God slew him for it." (*De Conjugiis Adulterinis*, 2, 12; 40/479.)

The standard moralists today, Liguori, Reginaldus, Sanchez, Cajetan, Aquinas, Alexander of Hales, Peter Lombard, Augustine—the ancestry is long and the names could have been varied a score of times. Is it surprising that the very possibility of changing the RP is dismissed? Or that papal pronouncements speak with such confidence of the unchangeability of their condemnation? The question can be repeated: Is there anything left to be said? At all events, whatever is said cannot impugn the fact of this long-standing opposition to contraceptive practices. If—*per possibile vel per impossibile*—a change did take

[1] From now on, the sources of quotations from the Fathers will be followed by a pair of numbers like "44/324". These stand for volume and column in Migne's patrologies.

[2] ". . . voto sive opere malo resistitur."

place, there would be no denying that it was a change, no possibility of disproving a contrast between past and present. Is not this admission tantamount to a confession of defeat? Is it not inadmissible, given that such evidence exists, even to talk of change here?

3. Tradition and change

There would perhaps be precedents for doing so. The development of doctrine in the Church has on occasions proceeded abruptly, rather than by that gradual clarification and definition which usually mark it. For the moment I consider only one such example, the more liberal approach to Bible studies which is now becoming generally known in the Church. The opposition and disquiet it has caused show the novelty of what it suggests; the historicity and dogmatic force of texts seem compromised; administrative policies of the Church have been changed, and the force of past pronouncements conceded to be limited according to the time and place of their utterance. And we can go further. The witness of the past in the Church can be endlessly quoted against the new ideas: what we can think now of the Bible is not what the Fathers and medievals would have thought, nor what the vast majority of their successors would have thought either. What seemed securely bound up with the faith turns out to be detachable from it after all.

Yet a change like this is not held to compromise the preservation by the Church of the faith preached by the Apostles. We know now incomparably more of the past and of the disciplines needed to understand it than our forefathers did; we can accept that God spoke according to the condition of those who wrote the sacred books; we must, if we are to understand them aright, put ourselves into the position of writers whose circumstances and conceptual background were so different from ours. (cf. *D* 3830.) If our conclusions do not agree with those of the Fathers and the rest, we shall say that it is not on any unchangeable point that we differ, but on questions in which the deposit of faith is not compromised.

I have not talked about biblical criticism because I think that my remarks can be simply transferred to the condemnation of contraception. I am concerned only to point out how the acceptance of a change by theologians entails a change in their evaluation of past witness.[1] Weigel's statement about tradition and history (see p. 113) cuts both ways. If a Catholic theologian cannot approach the development of doctrine without presupposing the preservation of apostolic faith throughout the ages, it follows that his belief about this preservation will also affect his verdict on proved instances of doctrinal change. He might be said to have two schemes of inference at his disposal. The first is:

> The Church accepts no change which affects the deposit of faith.
> X is a change which affects the deposit of faith.
> So the Church cannot accept X,

and this is the point of what Weigel said. But there is another scheme of inference, just as valid, and with the same universal member:

> The Church accepts no change which affects the deposit of faith.
> The Church accepts X.
> So X is a change which does not affect the deposit of faith,

and this is the point of what is said about biblical criticism. It is important to understand that such an X may still be a great change. To admit that it is not in the deposit of faith is by no means the same as admitting that it is inconspicuous, or that it does not sharply contrast with what was once believed. Unfortunately, personal and diplomatic reasons can lead innovators to identify the two issues in the hope of making their suggestions more acceptable. Whatever advantage such policies bring can be no more than temporary—it would be better

[1] Without drawing too close an analogy, we might recall a passage by T. S. Eliot: "... the existing monuments form an ideal order among themselves, which is modified by the introduction of the new (the really new) work of art among them. The existing order is complete before the new work arrives; for order to persist after the supervention of novelty, the *whole* existing order must be, if ever so slightly, altered; and so the relations, proportions, values of each work of art toward the whole are readjusted; and this is conformity between the old and the new." ("Tradition and The Individual Talent", in *Selected Essays*, London (1958), p. 15.)

to admit the fact that a change of this kind has occurred. The changed approach to the Bible which has occurred in our own day has led to protests that it rejects Scripture as truth revealed by God. To offset these objections, biblical scholars insist that the human authors were often not concerned with historical truth in the way we are, that their attitude was different because their social and cultural surroundings were so different from our own. Those who can be persuaded to think this will not be shocked at abandoning belief in the historicity of some passages in the Bible, so I have every sympathy with the eagerness of orthodox but progressive writers to press the point. But I suggest that their quite understandable desire for respectability leads them to play down the very real novelty of what they are suggesting. What they ask us to believe is simply not what orthodox Christians used to believe. An excellent example has been suggested to me to show that it is not, and to show in consequence that a sharp change in belief about the status of biblical narrative is compatible with preservation of the essentials of faith.

One of the oldest elements in Christian iconography is the story of the "Three Children in the Fiery Furnace" and how God saved them from the King of Babylon's anger. (Dan. 3.) It is now held (or at all events, Catholics are free to hold) that the story is simply a pious fiction invented for the encouragement of the Jews during the persecution of Antiochus Epiphanes hundreds of years afterwards. Surely we cannot read the story now (apart from the all-important 18th verse) as earlier generations did? We talk here today of "literary forms" and of "the ancient orient". (cf. *D* 3830.) But the early Christians who painted the story so often in the Catacombs were not just interested in recreating a pious oriental legend; they really believed it all happened and were doubtlessly heartened during times of persecution by their belief. We do not believe it; is there any point in minimizing the difference? It may be objected that the story is a minor detail in the Bible, and no part of Christian belief. The objection misses the point—or rather, it begs the question by talking in terms that the traditional approach to the Bible would have rejected. Until our own day, orthodox Christians believed that biblical inspiration involved veracity in a way that we do not. Given that their faith included this, they could not draw distinctions in what their faith obliged them to accept as inspired. (See, for example, Leo XIII's *Providentissimus Deus, D* 3291.) "Minor details" do not come into it: "it nothing disgraceth the sacred historie that a smal matter being also true is recorded with the rest". (Note in the Douay Version, à propos of Tobias's dog wagging its tail.) I have taken the story of the Three Children as an instance where the modern talk of literary forms contrasts vividly with the older interpretation. Those who want other examples of the change might compare the outraged protests half a dozen years ago in the *Catholic Gazette* when a contributor questioned the historicity of the Flood narratives, with the tranquil reception in 1964 of remarks about the historicity of the Gospels.

But is there any parity between contraception and biblical criticism? I have not said that there is and my appeal to the latter does not of course, license us to think the same of the former. What we have gained is, I hope, a logical explicitation of how change can, if necessary, be accommodated to the Catholic belief that the deposit of faith is unalterable. To prove the existence of such necessity is quite another matter. In one sense, "proof" is out of the question, for the necessity does not arise until a change is accepted by the Church. The two schemes of inference on p. 119 are not alternatives offered to the individual Christian; rather, they express his acceptance of continuity and change in what the Church teaches him. It is only when the Church has accepted a change that he can (and must) say: "there has been a change; so what was believed cannot have been of essence of our faith". At the same time, the officia acceptance of any change is preceded by debate and argument—as indeed happened with biblical criticism. All that I can hope to do here is to make a contribution to the debate, and what I say cannot—logically cannot—be more than provisional. "Awaiting the judgement of the Church" is, as I have said, no ornamental flourish of piety here; it is an essential qualification to my thesis.

The change in what we think about the Bible did not appear spontaneously. Greater knowledge brought it about, a greater sense of history, and a greater understanding of human behaviour. The change is part of a development in what is known about the world and how the world is interpreted. Statements about the Bible now acceptable to Catholics were sometimes made in the first instance by men committed to the rejection of any divinely inspired work. The coincidence of view is no more than material, for the change in orthodox opinion does not nullify the respect and love for God's written word which earlier generations had, or condemn their use of it in argument. On the contrary, the new ideas can lead us closer to Scripture and give us a better grasp of its meaning. Our respect and love and employment of it will not be what those of earlier writers were; but we, like them, will accept it as God's word, even though our acceptance will not have the consequences for us that it had for them.

Let me now declare my intentions. I am going to suggest that it is not antecedently impossible for a change in the RP to become acceptable, because of the developments in knowledge and belief about marriage and the use of marriage which are characteristic of this period in the history of the Church. I offer no knock-down proof—as I have tried to show, knock-down proofs are necessarily excluded here. But if it appears that the Church's attitude to marriage and its use has changed and is changing, then at least the question can be put as to how far her views on contraception are part of her authentic patrimony of faith, and how far they are elements in an evaluation of marriage and of sexuality which has become obsolete. In other words, I submit that, faced with the proposition that the RP should be changed, we can ask which of the two schemes of inference is to be used. It would be grotesquely pretentious to attempt a complete survey of Christian attitudes to marriages over the ages. It would be easier, though unfair, to unearth eccentricities from the unread works of dead men, or from all that stock of folklore about what has been heard in sermons or taught in Catholic schools. I cannot aim at completeness, and I am not trying to be unfair. My intention is to say something about present opinions on marriage among Catholics, and of the tension in them between what is old and what is new (Section 4); to examine a few patristic opinions about sex (Section 5); to discuss what Aquinas has to say about it (Section 6); and to see how far his own arguments against frustrating the marriage act can be compared with the "appeal to nature" (Section 7). We shall then be able to examine the opinions of

Augustine (Section 8), to whom the rest of the tradition is so deeply indebted (Section 9). This survey of the general background of opinion against which the series of adverse judgements was given on contraception will enable some general conclusions to be drawn about the significance of the tradition (Section 10). What these conclusions are I will not say for the moment, as I am anxious for the information and criticism I offer in the following sections to be examined on their own merits, not just as part of a larger argument. Indeed, I think that they have an interest of their own which will not be affected by the reader's eventual verdict upon the conclusions I try to draw from them.

4. *Present tensions*

Nobody would deny that there has been in recent times a real development in the attitude shown to marriage in ecclesiastical writings, pronouncements and activities. Layfolk are being encouraged to see their status as something positive, as membership of God's people, not just as the mere absence of clerical privilege. In consequence, husbands and wives are being asked to treat their state of life as a vocation, as something more than just being neither virgins nor martyrs. The welcome given by Lestapis and many others to the safe period as a means of regulating conception is, as Lestapis himself admits, part of a whole approach to marriage in which the personal values of love between the spouses, in all the forms this can take, are accepted as having a place higher than that of accidental by-products to procreation. I may have disagreed with arguments used by Lestapis and other defenders of the RP: but I readily admit that they do acknowledge these values. I also admit—and insist—that in doing so they are saying something new, discovering riches in the theology of married life that were previously not explicated. One author frankly admits this. In commenting on the condemnation of the book on marriage *Sinn und Zweck der Ehe* by Herbert Doms, he says that by emphasizing the personal fulfilment marriage should bring to the spouses, the author has provided a complement to what is usually taught about the meaning and purpose of marriage. (*EOM* 223).[1] Lestapis makes a

[1] Doms was condemned for teaching that the "personal" ends of mar-

similar admission, though in excessively cautious phraseology.[1] Neither asks how far there is a conflict between present extollings of the married state and what used to be said about it. "Conflict" may seem too strong a word, but I can think of no other to describe the contrast between what is said about marriage in books like Marshall's and Suenens' with what is to be found in other works dealing with sexuality, works closely linked with the training of priests—upon whom, after all, the sacramental enforcing of the RP depends. I refer, of course, to manuals of moral theology. These are notoriously repetitive, and as such preserve in almost a fossilized form the attitudes and opinions of days gone by. So if it appears that there is a sharp contrast between what these contain and what is commonly said about marriage in more up-to-date works, we shall have to admit that a real step forward has been taken; and in doing so we shall have to evaluate what was previously taught.

Let us examine the phraseology in these textbooks used about sexual matters—it is sharply contrasted with what we have been accustomed to accept by more recent works. Here are a few examples. Capello, talking about love-play, says that the spouses may perform any incomplete *lustful* actions. (798.) These include oral-genital contacts, for these are still lawful, though *enormously obscene*. (807.) Génicot, for whom such actions are *most foul* and usually mortally sinful (546) (here he follows Liguori, 6, §935), speaks of the *lewd* actions permitted to the spouses, the *foul* words and looks, the touches upon the *decent*, *less decent* and *indecent* parts of the body. And Slater's readers are presented with a text from 1 Corinthians as a preface to a brief consideration of this *filthy* topic. (2, 218.) Of course, it all sounds less offensive in the academic obscurity of scholastic Latin—things often do. Given enough time spent in the study of, shall we say, Malprotesinervi's *De Usu et Abusu Matrimonii*, we shall find that *incompleta luxuria*, *enormiter*

---

riage were not subordinated to its generative purpose. Contrary to what is sometimes asserted, his book does not permit any interference with the sexual act; in this respect it shares in the RP.

[1] "It is in fact not impossible that, for reasons of a contingent character, certain more personal aspects of married life did not impinge to any great extent upon the awareness of a civilization that was less sensitive than our own to the subjective side of the question." (*L* 163.) *Chi va piano, va sano* . . .

obscœnus, *turpissimus*, *impudicus*, *turpis*, *inhonestus* and *foedus* impinge upon us only as technical terms. Nor are all moralists unaware of the impropriety of such expressions. An article by a Roman theologian shows a perceptive appreciation of the damage done by the practice.[1] But for every future priest who reads an article in a learned journal, twenty will read their textbooks. What conclusions will they draw? More important, what associations are being created for them by this misuse of language? Could not the authors of so many manuals have produced between them a vocabulary which did not equate the erotic with the sinful? It would be some consolation to know that the equation was only a matter of words, but unfortunately it seems to be more than verbal. To judge by these textbooks, love-making is carried on in what can only be described as an atmosphere of tolerated venial sin. Thus, while actions which assist generation are allowed and those which impede it are mortally sinful, actions which do neither (such as erotic conduct not aimed at copulation) are "at most venially sinful" (Génicot, 2, 548); for a married person to be aroused when alone at the sight of his or her own body, at the thought of past or future love-making, is "probably not gravely sinful" (Génicot, 2, 547); abandonment of what is regarded as the "natural posture" of man over woman is, even though no seed is lost, still "sinful unless there is a just cause". (Génicot, 2, 543.) These verdicts surely make as melancholy reading as the vocabulary. No-one blames moral theologians for tempering the wind to the shorn lamb, but venial sin, which appears so inextricably bound up with the use of marriage, is still an offence against God, not just a technical infringement of some trivial bye-law. The verdicts just given show little sign that married love is more than a tolerated foible that needs excusing not approbation, a way of displeasing God for which he will not hold us guilty of grievous sin.

Some moral theologians are, as I have said, aware of these defects. Attempts have been made to render the vocabulary less offensive, for which (as well as the article by Bertrams already mentioned) Lanza and Palazzini's *De Castitate et Luxuria* may be consulted. Their work (68) records a change which took place

[1] W. Bertrams, SJ, "De Efformando in Clericis Genuino Fundamento Caelibatus Suscipiendi" in *Periodica* (1958), pp. 3 f.

some years ago, when the bracketed words in the following sentence were omitted from a well-known manual: "Sexual pleasure was to attract man to something [filthy in itself and] burdensome in its consequences."[1] But it is just not possible to reconcile the picture of marriage presented by these textbooks with the prospects held out by the many sources that are trying to make husbands and wives aware of the dignity of their calling. It cannot be denied that a sharp change of attitude has taken place. The contrast between what we read in books like Marshall's or Suenens' and the curiosities from textbooks quoted in preceding paragraphs is not just a matter of vocabulary, as if words were purely adventitious labels to thought. Words are how we think: Marshall, Suenens, and their contemporaries have started to use different language because their opinions are different. And if we agree with these rather than with the older authors, we ought to admit that we have made a decision, have accepted a change in the evaluation of married life and of the use of marriage.

5. *Some patristic opinions*

The pejorative vocabulary and assertions about sex found in textbooks seem to perpetuate prejudices which are vaguely associated with the Fathers of the Church. We have a confused idea of sharp-tongued old men lashing the follies of the dying Roman Empire and exhorting men to leave all domestic ties and take to the desert—is there anything here more than a pictorial version of our own preconceptions? Did the Fathers really talk like this? The question has only to be put to be revealed as unanswerable. "Fathers of the Church" is an expression applicable to men who lived during a period of one thousand years, and who differed widely in temperament, ability and opinions: the fact that their writings can be found in uniformly bound patrologies should not trap us into rash generalities on so vast and unwieldy a subject. There were eccentrics among the Fathers as there are everywhere and it would be possible to find many oddities in what they wrote. Let us rather take some

[1] Noldin-Schmitt, §6 gives the amended text. For the author, incidentally, the "burdensome consequences" include children—a strange remark for one who defends the RP.

respectable examples, men whom we know to have taught that marriage is lawful, and to have rejected as blasphemous the view that sexuality is inherently corrupt. We can then see more clearly the consent of part of the tradition to which defenders of the RP appeal.

That matrimony as such is not sinful the Fathers are agreed, the odd eccentric apart, yet the concession turns out to mean disappointingly little, to judge by the pronouncements of some of the most venerated authorities among them. Not only is the use of marriage sinful during pregnancy (St Jerome, *Comm. in Eph. iii;* 26/657) or lactation (St Gregory in Bede's *Historia Ecclesiastica Gentis Anglorum*, 1.27; 95/64), but the very institution of marriage is due simply to the need for avoiding fornication. (St John Chrysostom, *Homily on I Cor.* 7.2; 51/210.) A greater evil is escaped by tolerating a lesser: it is bad to use marriage (for St Paul says it is good not to touch a woman), but worse to fornicate. (St Jerome, *Adv. Jovin.* 1.7; 23/229.) St John was not martyred, because he was unmarried, but St Peter, although he left his wife when he followed Christ, still wiped out the dirtiness of his marriage by shedding his blood. (1.26; 23/258.) For St Augustine—of whom we shall have more to say ni a later section—nothing casts down the manly spirit more than love making (*I Solil.*, 10; 32/878), though the shame attached to it is fallen man's penalty, not itself a sin (*De Nupt. et Conc.* I, 5 44/416), Augustine never, to my knowledge, claims that sexual activity is sinful as such. At the same time, he limits its sinlessness to when the action is performed for the procreation of children or to pay the marriage debt, not when it is done for mutual enjoyment (*De Bono Conj.* 6; 40/377). A papal endorsement to all this is given by St Gregory the Great in his letter to St Augustine of Canterbury from which the condemnation of intercourse during lactation has just been quoted. There is no fault in the pains of childbirth, he says, but there is in fleshy pleasure. After intercourse, a man may not enter a church without penance and washing, for till the fire of concupiscence has died down he is unworthy through the wickedness of his evil will. Marriage is not unlawful but its use is impossible without blameworthy desire.

I do not think that these examples are unfairly chosen, and indeed the hagiographer has put this outlook into popular and pictorial form, as anyone who has read Lives of the Saints (especially those of an older vintage) will acknowledge. Their seeming to take for granted that a call to God must be a call to sexual abstinence; their implied approval of sometimes repellent eccentricities to which this abstinence led; the married saints who either left their spouses, entered monasteries, or abstained from the use of marriage—the stories all point in the same direction. Excesses are of no great harm if they balance each other; the danger starts when all are on the one side. For instance, Roman Catholics often laugh at heretics who confuse the virginal conception of Christ with the sinless though not virginal conception of his mother. Yet the once popular *Visions of St Bridget*, a source of many pious legends and still mentioned in her mass, gets near to identifying the Immaculate Conception with a conception not due to sexual intercourse. It seems (bk. 1, ch. 9) that when Mary's parents, Joachim and Anne, were promised a child, they would rather have died than come together from fleshly love; and that their union was against their will, inspired only by their love of God. Somewhat inconsequentially, the legend also speaks of their grief at being childless—perhaps it was this inconsistency which led other hagiographers to say that Anne conceived after being kissed by Joachim. (See the *Acta Sanctorum* of the Bollandists (1729), 26 July, p. 237.)

The sexual pessimism of the Fathers is sometimes blamed on the decadence of the later Roman Empire. If this be so, then their reaction preserved—as reactions often do—the terms of the problem as stated by its adversaries. Eroticism without love, abjuration without discrimination—are not both extremes at one in regarding sexual feeling as an impersonal itch? For the one, amorous excitement is to be assuaged in any convenient way; for the other, incontinence is to be avoided through the outlet provided by marriage; for both, human sexuality appears as infra-personal and mechanical as the desire to urinate. Could an adequate theology of marriage be expected from either extreme? Jerome and Augustine were great men by any standards of achievement, but their historical setting and personal circumstances hardly allow us to give unqualified assent to their verdicts in this matter. Is not Jerome's harsh abuse of the married state, his pathological touchiness, all of a piece with the erotic hallucinations that tormented him in the desert (*Ep. xxii; 22/398*)? Augustine was a saint of commanding genius, perception and eloquence, the author of a great autobiography and the father of Western theology. To impugn his sensitivity in sexual matters may seem presumptuous, but I cannot help deploring the way in which his confessed erotic experiences have made an expert witness of him for later, celibate theologians. Does he show any perception more acute, any wider understanding of sexual matters, than Jerome, Chrysostom or Gregory the Great? As always, he will have more to say and it will be better put; but there seems little to show for the years before his conversion. He even has one passage more startlingly inadequate than anything the others wrote. For him it was not incongruous to illustrate the perfect control unfallen man had over his genital organs, by citing cases of people able to break wind at will or wiggle their ears. (*De Civitate Dei*, 14, 24; 41/432.) It would be harder to prove in fewer words a smaller understanding of what sex is about; and indeed, does the life of Augustine, for all its merits, entitle us to expect a theory less insufficient? Sexual experience for him took the form of fornication; the position was false from the start. *Ex falso sequitur quodlibet*—he could erect no scale of values without a starting-point, and what lesson was he to learn save repentance? But the greatness of his repentance does not entitle us to treat him as a mine of understanding. What do we find in the *Confessions*? He allows his affectionate and loyal mistress to be banished from him and from their child, in order to pave the way for his marriage, and promptly takes another woman till his child-bride is of age. (*Confessions*, 6, 15; 32/732.) "I was a slave of lust, not a lover of marriage", he adds, and we cannot help agreeing with him. That there might be a third way between debauchery and abstinence, a way laudable for its own sake and not tolerated as a poor second best, was something to which neither Jerome nor Augustine seems ever to have given a real assent.

The charge that the Fathers we have quoted said sex was sinful is, as it stands, too vague to be justified. But the cheerful denial commonly made to the charge is extremely misleading. True enough, the Fathers did attack heretics who taught that *marriage* was sinful; true also, they did not hold the act of marriage to be sinful *as such.* But they subordinated its use so severely to procreation that for fallen man to use his sexual faculties without sin turns out to be a difficult exercise in detachment rather than a gift of God used to love another of God's creatures to whom we have been united by him. If any reader thinks that my choice of texts from the Fathers has been tendentious, I offer a simple proof that their opinions have not been excessively misrepresented. Consult the massive seventeenth-century commentary of Cornelius à Lapide on the Bible, which is largely a compilation of patristic exegesis, and compare the treatment in it of two passages. The first is Numbers 31, where the Israelites massacre at God's command all adults and children of the Midianites, saving only the virgins for themselves. The commentary is less concerned with the slaughter (God is master of life and Midianite baby boys were saved from growing up to be sinners) than with the more curious question of how the virgins were to be picked out from the rest. (p. 900.) The second passage is the twelfth chapter of the Book of Judith and here no such easy dismissal is possible; after all, Judith is shown adorning herself to excite the passions of Holofernes prior to killing him. A half-hearted solution is suggested (if he had proposed marriage she would have accepted), but the conclusion firmly drawn is that woman's beauty is a snare and a delusion.[1] (p. 118.)

Faced with views like these, we find ourselves in very different company from that to which some modern works on marriage have accustomed us. If present-day Catholic thought gives more honourable a place to married sexuality than did the Fathers, are we entitled to doubt the value of appealing to them on questions about the purpose of marriage and its use? This is a point to which I shall return later in the chapter. For the moment let us examine the views on sex of one not associated with extremes of opinion—St Thomas Aquinas.

6. *Aquinas and sexuality*

What Aquinas has to say is usually worth reading whether we

[1] As a matter of interest, the *Dictionnaire de la Bible* of Vigouroux (1903) is just as worried about Judith and just as blasé about the Midianites.

agree with him or not, but we have a particular reason for examining his views on sexuality. With him is associated rational enquiry into theological and moral matters, and he is regarded in the Church as the patron of those who seek to use philosophical techniques at the service of theology. Even those of us who refuse him the oracular role he has been given by ecclesiastical authority must admit that the rational apologetic against contraception turns on the argument from nature. We saw in the first chapter (p. 6 f.) how Aquinas gives an account of the natural law against which this argument has to be understood. We also saw there that he condemns any exercise of the sexual function not ordered to the act of generation, for this is the purpose of the sexual organs. Have we not here the "appeal to nature" in a nutshell? But it was just this appeal to nature which was attacked in the third chapter: if what was said there was true, it is vitiated by an empiricist theory of meaning. Can the same objection be made against what Aquinas has to say about sex? Is he to be accounted a Locke or Hume *avant la lettre*? In this section I shall say something of the views that Aquinas holds about sexuality. To what extent he can be said to have used the argument from nature will be examined in the next section.

Appeal is often made to Aquinas in the face of pronouncements from the Fathers like those we have been examining. His philosophical equipment, more sophisticated than that of earlier writers, enables him to distinguish Christian faith from that defective anthropology which expresses the conflict between heavenly and earthly values in terms of soul and body. After the rhetorical exaggerations of some patristic writers, the views of Aquinas on sex seem to be distinguished by good sense and moderation. For him, man is created by God as an animal that thinks, and it does not make sense to treat any of man's functions, whether they are shared with other animals or belong to him alone, as wrong or shameful. (*ST* 1/2.98.2.) It is only when something fails to be what it is made to be that evil appears. (15 *DM* 1 ad 1.) Among the natural functions of man are nutrition and generation; the first ensures the continuing existence of the individual, the second provides for the perpetuation of the species. (*ST* 2/2.153.2.) It is impossible that sexual attraction should be sinful, for it is a universal inclination—impossible again, because the human species depends on it for its continuance. (*CG* 3.126.) Sex, like any other bodily activity, may raise our minds to God if performed properly, and for God's honour (*CG* 3.121; *4 Sent*. 26.1.4; S.49.4), and the pleasure which follows from it increases its moral worth. (cf. *ST* 1/2.24.3.) It is unreasonable to hold, with some authorities, that unfallen man would have multiplied asexually. He is an animal, and his physical make-up shows that he breeds by copulating. (*ST* 1.98.2.) Had man not fallen, all would have married, continence would not have been virtuous, there would still have been sexual reproduction, and the pleasure of it would have been greater than it now is because of the unfallen bodies' increased sensibility. (*ST* 1.98.2.) Nor was the fall of man brought about by sexual intercourse. (*ST* 1.98.2 ad 2.) Those who in our fallen state abstain from marriage for God's sake do not thereby assert that sexual activity is wrong: they sacrifice something which is good in order to leave themselves freer for the things of God, to the benefit of the rest of mankind. (*ST* 2/2.152.2 ad 1.)

Unfortunately, the views of Aquinas on sex are not quite so simply told. I do not question the genuineness of these texts, or assert that their contexts invalidate them. What I do submit is that he said other things about sex which give a different colour to the optimistic picture I have just drawn. It is a measure of the genius of Aquinas that his writings contain the seeds of later and better views of the married state, but an account of his own opinions cannot be so partial in its selection of passages. Yet if the quotations to be offered reveal defects in the opinions of Aquinas, I suggest that they will also eventually vindicate him from the charge of having taught the "argument from nature" in the sense in which it is used today by defenders of the RP. I shall start with an account of his views on the compensations of the married state and on sexuality before the Fall. Other opinions of his will be stated in the next section.

Aquinas thinks that the married state needs an excuse to justify it because of the intensity of the pleasure and absorbing nature of the passion attached to intercourse, and because family life brings with it such worries. (*ST* S.49.1.) From both these characteristics of marriage follows a certain disabling of the reason. The pleasure that accompanies the sexual act absorbs our attention to such an extent that we cannot exercise any intellectual activity during it (*ST* S.49.1, 2/2.153.2; *In Eth. Nic*, 7, lect. 11.) This absorption in itself is not sinful, or it would be wrong to fall asleep (*ST* 2/2.153.2 ad 2), but to choose a state of life of which an action bars us from the summit of virtue (*ST* 2/2.153.2) needs an excusing cause (*ST* S.49.1), as Scripture tells us. (*4 Sent*. 31. 2.2 ad 2; *ST* S.49.5 ad 2.)[1] The excuse or compensation lies in the good attributes or benefits of marriage (*bona matrimonii*). (*ST* S.49.2.) Looked at as a natural union, the use of marriage (like every other act) is made virtuous by the right intention of those who perform the action; so offspring (*proles*) is one benefit of marriage. Acts are virtuous also because the act is correctly applied to its object: so faithfulness (*fides*), by which a man has intercourse with his own wife and with no other, is another benefit. Looked at as a sacrament, marriage is not only good but holy, because it signifies by its indissolubility the union of Christ and the Church, and so being a sacrament (*sacramentum*) is the third benefit. These benefits make the married state good, but for the act of marriage to be good, one or both of the first two benefits must be actually intended by the spouses. In other words, the sexual act is good if performed by the spouses to pay the marriage debt (*fides*)—for instance, a wife accedes to her husband's request for intercourse; or if performed in order to beget children—(*proles*). (*ST* S.49.5.) No other motive by itself suffices to make the act of marriage good. If intercourse is prompted only by inclination then it is at least a venial sin. It cannot be saved from sinfulness by the benefit *sacramentum*, for this refers only to the *essence* of marriage—to the married state itself as indissoluble—not to the *use* of it. (*ST* S.49.5 ad 3.)[2] A wish to overcome temptations to unfaithfulness does not excuse intercourse from venial sin either—the means taken are unnecessary;[3] and if the motive is to preserve health, the method

[1] It does not, in fact. This is only the defective exegesis Augustine gave of 1 Cor. 7:6, to which I shall return later.

[2] The benefit *sacramentum* affects the goodness of the act of marriage only in the sense that the natural inclination to beget children must, for marital intercourse to be virtuous, be subordinated through an actual or habitual intention to the further purpose of raising up these children for God's service. (*ST* S. 49.5 ad 1.)

[3] *4 Sent* 31.2.2 ad 2, *ST* S.49.5 ad 2. Marietti's edition of the *Summa* has

adopted is equally inappropriate because not devised for this purpose; however, to consent to a partner who asks for intercourse from such insufficient motives is not itself sinful, as it can be counted as paying the marriage debt, which is *fides*, the second benefit of marriage. (*ST* S.49.5 ad 3, ad 4.) Nor is it sinful to admit the embraces of a partner who venially sins by seeking intercourse on a Holy Day—the consent, Aquinas assumes, will be unwilling and sorrowful. (*ST* S.64.7 ad 1.)

These texts darken the cheerful picture presented by the earlier statements Aquinas makes about sexuality and its place in man's life. Among these statements, it will be remembered, was the assertion that abstinence from sexual activity would not have been virtuous if man had not fallen. (*ST* 1.98.2.) Has the fall of man anything to do with what sex is now, in the opinion of Aquinas? To answer this, it will be necessary to collate the passages just quoted with what he says about sexuality *before* the fall of man, about sexuality as originally planned by God. Aquinas attributes what he calls the "filthiness of desire" now found in intercourse to our fallen state. (*ST* 1.98.2.) The sexual act makes us like beasts, for reason cannot govern the pleasure of intercourse and the heat of desire while it is taking place. (*ST* 1.98.2 ad 3.) In a state of unfallen nature, the pleasure would indeed have been greater absolutely speaking, owing to the superiority of our bodily parts. (*ST* 1.98.2.) But it would have been much less with respect to human reason, which would completely govern and control the pleasure, so that it would not be as fervent and superabundant as it is now. (*2 Sent*. 20.1.2 ad 2.) Reason would not then have been disturbed by sexual pleasure; as Augustine says, we should then have moved our genital parts as we chose, as calmly as we now move our hands or feet or other members of our body. (*ST* 1.98.2.) Aquinas here refers to the passage in *The City of God* from which the extraordinary analogies were quoted in the account of Augustine's opinions. (See p. 129.) In paradise, the context of it adds, semination would have been performed with no more disturbance to reason than when the hand of the sower scatters seed. (*De Civitate Dei*, 14, 24; 41/434.) Children would

---

the footnote: ". . . unnecessary because other means exist, more suitable and more in agreement with Christian moderation, such as prayer and fasting."

be procreated when and to the extent that was necessary, through genital organs moved by the will instead of by passion, which alone moves them now. The state of primal innocence entailed for Aquinas what he called a complete subjection of the lower powers to reason; there would be no need for continence as there would be no disordered desire to be shunned. (*ST* 1.98.2 ad 3.)

It is supremely important to disclose the ambiguity in the use of the word "reason" in these speculations. For Aquinas, the effect of the moral virtues is to make our appetites obey reason (*ST* 1/2.68.4), and the purpose of temperance is to remove us from inclinations which go against reason. (*ST* 2/2.141.2; and see above, p. 7.) In this sense, "reason" is nothing more than "that which is appropriate to man". He is a rational animal, so for him virtue consists in acting according to reason, according to his distinctively human good. (*ST* 2/2.141.1.) Take reason in this way, and the failure of fallen man's sexuality to measure up to the criterion of reasonableness is evident enough. Sexual desire can drive men to unfaithfulness, to treachery and meanness, to all manner of folly that their better judgement condemns and deplores. Even if effective resistance is made, the sting is still there: a husband resists a strong urge to commit adultery, but is still tormented by a desire whose blandishments he has conquered by the grace of God and at the behest of reason. Again, sexuality is supposed to be integrated into the whole practice of Christian marriage, yet here too the fallen state of our nature makes itself felt. Generosity in sexual matters, as in everything else, is a goal rather than a starting-point. Desire and instinct need to be disciplined, to be made really human, to be put at the service of two human beings who love each other.[1] If "reason" were used here only in this sense by Aquinas, experience would amply vindicate his assertions.

But he uses the word also in a second and narrower sense which cripples the force of much of what he says. "Reason" is also an activity of the mind which is interrupted by lovemaking; its greater power in unfallen man would keep the pleasure tightly in check, so that the genital parts could be aroused at will and as calmly as hands or feet are moved "Reason" here means much more than it did in the last paragraph. It is no

[1] The point has already been made in the preceding chapter (p. 105).

longer a synonym for "what is virtuous for human beings", it means rather a state of mind which is intellectual, calculating and cautious. Not, of course, that these are vicious attributes! There are many occasions in life where we have to be all these things—doing mental arithmetic, balancing accounts, dispensing medicines, building bridges. When our sums come out right, our books prove to be in order, our patients get better and our bridges stand up to traffic and tempest, then we have behaved *rationally*, not only in this narrower sense but in the wider sense of the word, because we have behaved as men should behave when they are doing these things. But men do other things as well; and "being rational" here will mean doing *them* as *they* ought to be done—which will not necessarily mean doing them intellectually, calculatingly and cautiously.[1]

It is precisely this confusion which makes the picture that Aquinas (following Augustine) offers of unfallen sexuality so distasteful. Controlling and using the genital parts as calmly as using one's hands and feet, combining intense pleasure with a rigid control by reason, reason which is able to persist throughout in intellectual activity—all this is not only so remote from human life as we know it as to make the speculation irrelevant to any understanding or evaluation of human sexuality, it is a degradation of what, even in our fallen state, sexuality ought to be. These hypotheses of Aquinas remind me uncomfortably of literary notorieties of the *ancien régime* like *Les Liaisons Dangereuses*. Obviously, it would be preposterous to institute a comparison in any *moral* sense; I wish it were as preposterous to speak of a resemblance in *psychology*, to see in that detached inquisitiveness and lack of passion in a Valmont a twisted reflection of the theories which have just been described. Of rationality in the calculating sense, there is enough and to spare in Laclos; of rationality in the sense of what is the *bonum hominis* there is not a trace. But is there so very much of it in what Augustine wrote and Aquinas adapted about the form sexuality took before man fell?

Sure enough, neither would presumably have claimed a direct

[1] If household articles are good when they do the job we buy them for, and good soap cleans our face, it does not follow that good shoe-polish will do the same. To commit this fallacy is, as Frege would say, to confuse values of a function with the function itself.

insight into how things would have worked out under that dispensation. Augustine explicitly says that our language cannot express the matter adequately. (*De Civ. Dei*, 12, 23; 41/430). Aquinas is less given to qualifications in his writing, but what he says about sexuality in paradise is part of a whole series of speculations about life there, and speculations which include the confident assertion that normal penetration and gestation would have been effected without damage to the hymen (*ST* 1.98.2 ad 4) are perhaps not meant to be more than conjecture. What is inescapable in the opinions, however we are supposed to take them, is a failure to understand that sexual love can be reasonable without being calculating. Reason, the distinctively human attribute, can and should have a place here just as it ought to have a place in every personal activity. Intercourse, far from making us like beasts, can be performed thoughtfully or carelessly, clumsily or tenderly, with affection for a loved partner or with impersonal curiosity towards a casual acquaintance. The excitement that goes with it cannot be discussed as if it were an unfortunate intrusion into an individual's private mental activity. The excitement is meant to turn the spouses towards each other, to help break down the barriers between them, to make them literally un-selfish. Not that the excitement and pleasure in themselves can do this: it would be folly to think that an adequate personal relationship can be founded just on shared sexual enjoyment, the marriage bond is far too complex for this. But is it not just as great folly to take the cool rationality of computation and speculation as the paradigm for what the sexual relation ought to be between husband and wife?[1]

With what we now know of the views of Aquinas on fallen and unfallen sexuality we can proceed to the next section and ask how far he was committed to the "appeal to nature". Answering this question will lead us to other opinions of his

[1] We may notice an illustration of this ambiguity of "reason" in a text of Aquinas. (*ST* 2/2.153.2 ad 2.) Answering the objection that intercourse is blameworthy because its pleasure interrupts reason, he starts by saying that the pleasure, even if very great, is not wrong if not unreasonable (*secundum quod convenit rationi rectae*). He goes on to say that a periodic quiescence of the intelligence (*rationis actus*) can reasonably occur (*secundum rationem fit*). He ends by saying that the rebellion of the sexual instincts against the dictates of reason (*imperio et moderationi rationis*) is due to original sin.

about sex, and to a better understanding of what distinguishes it from the views of those who defend the RP nowadays.

7. *Aquinas and the argument from nature*

I do not wish to take part here in the debate as to how far the philosophical views of Aquinas can be detached from the Cartesian form into which they have been systematized by neo-scholastics. It will be enough to see whether his opinions can be fairly said to include what is now meant by the "appeal to nature". My purpose in doing so is, of course, not purely historical. If the argument from nature (whatever we think of it) cannot be simply identified with what Aquinas taught (whatever we think of that), then we shall not be able, without qualification at least, to view this argument as embodying the speculations about marriage and sex of a leading witness to tradition. Its popularity today will be irrelevant to our estimate of what was taught by a theologian as important as St Thomas. On the other hand, if he turns out to have taught it, our rejection of it will have to be qualified by the admission that the use of such an argument by Aquinas gives an extrinsic, "traditional" suasion to what the appeal to nature ineffectively attempts to prove rationally. Whatever the answer is, it will be relevant to the ultimate purpose of these researches into the opinions of the Fathers and of Aquinas: what precisely is the content of the tradition about sexuality and marriage to which appeal is made?

Aquinas gets nearest to the argument from nature when he speaks about the purpose of human seed. While other secretions have no further object, seed is necessary for generation and must be used for it. To use seed in any other way is gravely sinful, because failure to follow the order of nature here is not a trifling matter, like walking on one's hands, but a blow at nature herself and an interference with the conservation of the human species. Indeed, as a sin, this abuse of seed (that is of potential human nature) stands second only to murder, which strikes at actually existent human nature. (*CG* 3.123.) At first sight there seems little to choose between this and the argument as used nowadays "from the very structure and purpose of intercourse". But a closer examination reveals an austere abstractness in what Aquinas says which is not found in the modern accounts. He does not talk in personal terms at all, not even to the extent of mentioning the act of intercourse itself; what he considers in this text is the seed and the seed alone; it has a purpose and we must respect that purpose. The treatment of sexual sins in the *Summa Theologiae* is just as abstract. "Human nature" becomes almost personified and is said to need sexual intercourse for its conservation, just as the conservation of the individual demands food.[1] The due employment of sexual activity is to be found in the fulfilment of this purpose, a purpose so important that misuse of sex is always sinful. (*ST* 2/2.153.2.)

To confirm the impersonal impression given by the method Aquinas uses to appraise sexuality, we may examine how he estimates the gravity of sexual sins. Any misuse of sex is against right reason, but acts like self-abuse, bestiality, sodomy, and failures to observe the due pattern of intercourse between man and woman, are acts which are said to be against nature as well. (*ST* 2/2.154.11.) Of all sins against chastity, these unnatural sins are the worst, for they corrupt the very principle from which all else follows. (*ST* 2/2.154.12.) It seems odd to have to say that self-abuse is worse than fornication or adultery, but odd only because we do not limit ourselves to the one criterion Aquinas takes into account. It is the generative use of the seed which is the norm of morality for Aquinas, and the extent to which the seed's use is corrupted measures for him the evil of what is done.

The estimate of Aquinas on this point is of a piece with other opinions of his about the use of marriage. We saw in the preceding section that *proles* and *fides* are justifying motives for having intercourse. (p. 133.) It must now be added that their status is not the same. *Fides* concerns the obligation each partner has to "pay the marriage-debt" to the other (*4 Sent*. 31.1.2; *ST* S.49.3 ad 3): it is not concerned with the grounds on which this debt is *demanded*. The intention of procreating children absolves the petitioner from venial sin. *Fides*, on the other hand, will excuse the partner who *pays* but not the partner who *asks*—unless we suppose that the petitioner seeks intercourse through *fides* in the sense of an abstract desire for his rights.[2] Both

[1] It is worth collating here what Schopenhauer has to say about species and the sexual instinct in *Die Welt als Wille und Vorstellung*, II, 44: "Metaphysik der Geschlechtsliebe".

[2] This suggestion is not as implausible as it seems. Aquinas says else-

spouses will be sinless in intercourse only when the petitioner demands it for the purpose of begetting children. An inevitable conclusion is that it is venially sinful to demand intercourse during pregnancy—one cannot intend to procreate a child when this is known to be impossible. I cannot find any explicit pronouncement of Aquinas on this point, but its morality may be estimated without difficulty from the principles already given: it is lawful to accede to the request, but (at least venially) sinful to make it.[1] What Aquinas says elsewhere might seem to allow a milder view. "If generation cannot follow *per accidens*, such as when the woman is sterile, then the action is not unnatural and not sinful." (*CG* 3.123.) But in this text Aquinas is talking of unnatural and so serious sins like sodomy and self-abuse; and his point is that what counts as natural is the conjunction itself, not the fact that the woman can or cannot have children. What he says in the *Summa Theologiae* about *fides* and *proles* takes all this for granted: it is concerned with the lawfulness of asking for intercourse inside marriage.

These views are understandable enough if the emitted seed is at the service of the conservation of human nature in the way Aquinas means this. Personal considerations like affection and love are then bound to be irrelevant, and indeed it may be wondered how far he thought of sexuality in such terms. He does speak of the shared activity (*communicatio operum*) between husband and wife, and holds it to be wholly directed to the upbringing of their children. (*4 Sent.* 31.1.2 ad 1.) Yet he does not suggest that a motive for having intercourse like the pre-

---

where that a husband may have an adulterous wife arrested and press for the death penalty, not from revenge, but from a dispassionate wish to see justice done. (*4 Sent.* 37.2.1.) It should be remembered that the demand for intercourse may be implicit. A wife known by her husband to want intercourse though too shy to ask for it may be said to be demanding the marriage-debt interpretatively. (*4 Sent.* 38.1.2 ad 4; *ST* S.53.1 ad 4.) If he accedes to her unspoken demand by requesting intercourse, he will not be sinning. She will, of course.

[1] He does record the opinion of Jerome that intercourse during pregnancy is sinful, and comments that Jerome did not think it to be mortally sinful, except perhaps when there is a reasonable fear of a miscarriage. (*4 Sent.* 31, Expos. Text.) It would, of course, be easy to cite medieval condemnations of such behaviour—a letter of St Peter Damiani, for instance. (*Ep.* 1.15; 44/432.)

servation of health is defective (see p. 134) because union should be inspired by affection rather than by self-interest. All that matters for him is that this is not what intercourse is *for*. Human nature, not human beings, is to be served by its exercise. In any case, Aquinas sets severe limits to the personal relationship which can exist between a man and a woman, thinking (like Augustine) that generation is the only matter in which a man is better helped by a woman than by another man. (*ST* 1.92.1.) A woman has by nature less use of reason than a man (*ST* 1.92.1 ad 2); she is, after all, a defective man, conceived because of weakness in the seed, or because a damp south wind was blowing at the time of conception (*ST* 1.92.1 ad 1.)

That Aquinas held such "abstractly generative" views on the sexual relationship may explain an odd silence of his on a topic readily canvassed by moralists in our own day—the lawfulness of *actus imperfecti*—erotic actions which do not lead either to intercourse or to a sexual climax. Theologians, as we have already pointed out, permit these if there is no immediate danger of either party's obtaining an orgasm outside the full sexual act. (See p. 12.) No consideration seems to be given by Aquinas anywhere in his works to the morality of such behaviour between husband and wife. He condemns them if they are done outside marriage, since the pleasure at which they aim is all one with the pleasure of sexual intercourse (*ST* 2/2.154.4), but as to their lawfulness when practised between husband and wife he says nothing. It is surely not surprising that he is silent on the point, for what place could such actions have within his view of sexual intercourse? They could obviously not be used for procreation, and hardly to pay the marriage debt, for this consists in intercourse itself. (*ST* S.41.4.) They would in fact be done to give pleasure, to express the love of the partners, and to make their relations more intimate. The first of these is not a sufficient excuse for allowing the perturbations of reason which goes with sexual activity (*4 Sent*. 31.1.2; *ST* S.49.5), and the others Aquinas does not even take into account—cannot, given what he says about the sexual union. It seems as if erotic contacts can be lawful only when part of a process culminating in full sexual union, for it is here alone that they do their job of helping to bring about that emission of seed required for the conserving of the human race. This assumes, of course, that the union is being carried out for the adequate motives of procreation or paying the debt.[1]

There is a consistency in what Aquinas says about sex which distinguishes it from the opinions and arguments of those who defend the RP today. We have seen at some length their recurrent and apparently insoluble difficulty. They propose a philosophy of sex which, so they claim, safeguards personal and human values, allows responsibility and self-control a place here as elsewhere in what men do, preserves the generative finality of sexual actions, and helps husbands and wives to live together as Christians should. But after all this, it turns out that the indispensable condition for any such activity to be lawful is that it should conform to a particular anatomical pattern in each and every instance; "use of marriage", "significance", "self-control", "responsibility", "generative finality" and the rest are all to be interpreted as functions of this pattern. Preserve the pattern, and there is in rhythm a way of separating the seminal emission from procreation which can be both lawful and efficient. Ignore the pattern, and no other considerations can repair the damage. We saw the various attempts made to resolve this discord. The most important of them was what we called the argument from nature. It was an appeal to the structure of the sexual act, and in it we detected a defective criterion of significance also found in the empiricists. In one sense, what Aquinas has to say is touched with the same fallacy—the complexity of the human sexual relationship is ruthlessly cut down by him to a statement about human seed. But—and the reservation is all-important—his defect is one of sensitivity and perception, not of philosophy or logic. For one reason or another, historical or personal, he shows no awareness of what married love means: and in this he is not alone among theologians. Yet he expounds his views, defective as they are, as logical consequences of his premise that human seed is for the conservation of the human race. For him, the starting-point is impersonal—perhaps transpersonal would be a better word. His *data* are Human Nature and Seed. I have graced the words with capitals because it is the exigencies of these two which

[1] I refer those who find my interpretation fanciful to the interesting article by J. Fuchs already mentioned (p. 21), where this and other difficulties are raised, and somewhat heroic efforts made to answer them.

determine the morality of how individual human beings behave. One might almost say that they are given antecedently to human individuals: the species is to be conserved and seed is there for that purpose. For the individual to waste it is an offence beyond any abuse of other parts of his body—the seed is not just for him, it is for the human race. Indeed, the individual seems almost a mere vehicle for something whose purpose outstrips his own duration and desires. This is unacceptable to us, and some of the consequences deduced from it seem to us wholly inappropriate: but the position itself is free from the empiricists' fallacy. There is no attempt at reducing significance to what can be seen or depicted at any one moment, no "peep-show" deduction of what sexuality is supposed to mean from the pattern of an individual act of intercourse. If anything, the position is idealistic in its giving pride of place to the species and its perpetuation in this way—hence my reference to Schopenhauer earlier in the section. Contrast this position of Aquinas with the argument from nature as expounded nowadays by those who defend the RP. They do not begin with the conservation of Human Nature by means of the unique secretion which is Seed, but with the copulatory actions of a human pair, and it is from the pattern of this union that they try to show its inalienable purpose to be generative. We have seen at considerable length that the pattern will yield what they want it to yield only when meaning and significance are treated in an impoverished manner. Aquinas can proceed without inconsistency from his presupposition, such as it is; our contemporaries have to introduce some dubious philosophy if they are to get where they want to be from where they have chosen to start. Whatever else Aquinas's conclusions are not, they are at least of a piece with his austere subordination of the individual to the task of transmitting seed and so perpetuating the species. Defenders of the RP (most of them at least) now have a fuller and higher idea of what part sex ought to play in marriage: but this estimate of theirs is yoked very uneasily to what they have chosen as the principal criterion of lawfulness. They have to keep appealing to personal considerations to give plausibility to their apologias, while restraining themselves from drawing the natural conclusions from these appeals. (See p. 69.) Aquinas is not obliged to perform such acts of intellectual legerdemain, for he has a view of what sexuality is for and he adheres to it.

This contrast between the delicate position of those who now appeal to nature in favour of the RP and the grim consistency of Aquinas is a revealing symptom of the difference between their views and his. It is one thing to treat the sexual relationship simply in terms of perpetuating the species, and quite another to see in it personal, emotional, and spiritual values which are not directly procreative. We have already seen how modern accounts of the RP admit these values but subordinate them to the "primary generative purpose". (See pp. 42–3 and 101–2.) The ambiguities detected there in the phrase can now be better understood. Whereas the RP now recognizes these "secondary ends" of marriage as legitimate reasons for its use, Aquinas holds that to seek intercourse for any reason other than procreation is at least venially sinful. The fact is acknowledged by some defenders of the RP, but its consequences do not seem to have been deduced as they should. The function of procreation in marriage cannot be the same in two theories, one of which makes it the only legitimate reason for seeking intercourse, while the other allows inclination and love to be motives as well. To think that questions about purpose and significance must admit of mosaic-like answers in which one element may be removed without affecting the rest, is all of a piece with the empiricist fallacy analysed in the third chapter. We cannot assume *a priori* that it is possible to abandon the strictly procreative norm Aquinas laid down as the reason for seeking intercourse, while leaving untouched what he says about the purpose of sexual activities. Notice, I do not say that we *cannot* do this, only that its possibility needs proving. And the phrase so often found in defences of the RP ("essential subordination of secondary to primary ends") is certainly not such a proof, it is only an assertion.

If the views of Aquinas were something peculiar to his own system or cast of thought, then our judgement of the tradition against contraception would not be seriously affected—we should have proved only that the "appeal to nature" cannot be laid at his door. But there is nothing out of the ordinary in his views. They are shared to a greater or lesser extent by all the authors quoted earlier as witnessing the tradition against contraception. In the next two sections I shall try to prove this, first of Augustine, then of the rest. I hope that the examination of their views will throw light, not only on the tradition against contraception, but upon the RP as taught in our own day.

8. *Augustine and the use of marriage*

Three works of Augustine were the most ancient of the sources I quoted when offering a list of authorities opposed to contraception (see pp. 116 f.). His opinions were appealed to by the succeeding writers and can be discerned in the views they offer about sex and its place in marriage. As for Augustine's own views on the subject, there can be no mistaking them. Any use of sex not motivated by the object of procreation is sinful—and it is only the state of marriage which saves it from being mortally sinful. "Other things are to be tolerated in marriage, lest heinous crimes like fornication or adultery follow. To avoid this evil, even marital embraces done, not for procreation but for the service of overpowering desire, are not commanded, but conceded with pardon. These are the embraces of which the spouses are not to deprive each other lest Satan tempt them for their incontinence . . . 'I say this according to pardon, not by command'. [1 Cor. 7, 6.] Where pardon is to be given, the existence of a fault cannot be denied." He goes on to say that sexual pleasure is pardoned because of marriage: we have a new reason for praising marriage—it secures pardon for matters intrinsic to it. (*De Nuptiis et Concupiscentia*, 1, 14; 14/423.) Only when the procreation of children is intended is there no fault, for sexual intercourse is here being used for its purpose. (*De Bono Conjugali*, 9; 40/381.) If desire prompts it, then pardon is needed, and a venial fault is committed. (10; 40/381.)[1] Here, as so often, Augustine emphasizes that it is not

[1] It can be noticed here that Augustine relies on a Latin translation of the Epistle to the Corinthians which translates Paul's κατὰ συγγνώμην as *secundum veniam*, where *secundum permissionem* or *secundum permissum* would have avoided the impression that the Apostle was forgiving or pardoning those who used marriage because of desire. What in fact Paul means is simply, "I permit, I do not command." The Vulgate renders it as *secundum indulgentiam*, which does little to mend matters, and Augustine's exegesis echoes down the centuries. An instance of it in Aquinas is to be found at *4 Sent*. 31.2.2 ad 2. (See p. 133.)

marriage that needs pardon, nor the use of it for procreation; only the use which is prompted by desire.

The recital of this series of opinions held by Augustine throws light on the remarks we saw made about sexuality by other Fathers of the Church in the fifth section of this chapter (p. 127). Their reservations about motives for intercourse, their depreciation of sexual pleasure, their speculations about intercourse in the unfallen state—all these are not simply accidental quirks and verbal infelicities in men who, after all, shared the views held nowadays by Christians about sex. Nor are they just symptoms of celibate prejudice against married life. Talk of prejudices or quirks or verbal infelicities is not in order here, and does little credit to the intellectual integrity of men like Jerome, Gregory and Augustine: the talk should be rather of principles and theories. Augustine and the other Fathers quoted spoke as they did simply because they did not evaluate the use of marriage as we do. If we do not feel at ease with what they taught, our uneasiness will not be exorcized by any explanation couched in terms of "emphasis" or "exaggeration". We shall have to face up to differing from them in questions of nature—and purpose.

The key to these opinions of Augustine lies in what he says about unfallen sexuality, for here he is concerned with sex as God meant it to be, with sex purged of the rebellious concupiscence that characterizes it in our fallen state. We have already seen how Augustine thought the sexual organs would then be used (p. 129); let us now ask why and when they would be used. The answer occurs at the beginning of the same chapter in the *City of God*: "Man would sow offspring with his genital parts and woman receive them into hers when and to the extent that this was necessary. Their parts would be moved by reason, not desire." (*De Civitate Dei*, 14, 24; 41/432.) Sexual behaviour then, in the ideal state, was dictated simply by the wish to procreate; this motive will still make it sinless; but it may also be motivated by desire, which is sinful. (See the quotations on p. 127.) Our instinctive disagreement with such a statement may lead us to overlook the most extraordinary thing of all in what Augustine says. His choice of motives seems to be either procreation (when both partners are sinless) or because we are asked (when at most one will be sinning) or desire (when both may be sinning). There is not a word said about love or affection as motives for intercourse; the spouses are supposed either to want to procreate, or to appease desire. We ought to be amazed, not at the evaluation of desire by Augustine, but by the poverty of the choice in motives that he offers. And yet, if we reflect for a moment, he is quite consistent with his principles. God made man and wished him to multiply; to the procreative act he attached pleasure; man was to perform the act as the need for procreation demanded, and in doing so was to enjoy the pleasure. Man fell, and his reason no longer securely controlled the bodily parts concerned with begetting; so marriage serves to prevent rebellious desire from leading to great crimes like fornication. Given that Augustine believes all this—and thinks that this is all there is to believe—he is not likely to think that intercourse can serve to deepen the love and intimacy between the spouses. The very opposite is true. If sexual pleasure is now only a spiritually disturbing phenomenon incidental to the generative act, then it is bound to be just as impervious to integration into the shared personal life of the spouses as, say, the pleasure incidental to scratching one's back. It is something infra-rational, an irreducible surd in married life due to our fallen state. That pleasure now inspires a man to demand intercourse is a testimony to this fallen state, not a fact about human beings which has to be incorporated into a just view of what marriage and sexuality ought to be. It is our proneness to sexual sin that we confess when we seek the remedy of marital intercourse, and the impetuous demands of sexual desire are channelled by the institution of marriage, so that what would be mortally sinful seeking of pleasure becomes a venial fault. But it is still a fault; to use marriage as God wants it to be used, virtuously and without sin, we must not seek intercourse except in the cause of procreation, though we may lawfully accede to the demands of our partner, even when these are venially sinful in him.

We must not fall into the trap of identifying the distinction made by Augustine between seeking intercourse for procreation and seeking it for pleasure, with the distinction proposed by defenders of the RP nowadays between the primary and secondary objects of intercourse. To begin with, the RP now has a much richer stock of purposes for marriage and its uses. I must repeat here my admission that Lestapis, like many others, is genuinely concerned to show how the sexual relationship in marriage can be put at the service of the human and supernatural relationship which joins husband and wife.[1] What the modern writers say cannot be reduced to the stark choice of procreation—paying-the-debt—pleasure. Their writings show a conceptual structure of the theology of marriage which is finer drawn, so that by its side the Augustinian theory seems not so much over-rigid as clumsy and imperceptive: one is reminded of a comparison between a crude sketch and an accurate piece of draughtsmanship. If I may draw an analogy with philosophy, the use by Augustine of "desire" as a reason for having intercourse is reminiscent, in its covering of varied cases with one blanket-like term, of the attempts of philosophers to persuade us that "all we ever see are sense-data", "all we ever know is the present" and so on. But there is a greater difference still to be considered. For the RP, these secondary effects of marriage can now be lawful reasons for its use, provided that the primary effect is not obstructed. In other words, these secondary effects have their own part to play in the married life of Christians, they can in their own way bring husbands and wives nearer to each other and nearer to God. This idea is not in the least Augustinian: for Augustine, pardon and excuse were needed for those who wished to use marriage for purposes other than procreation. Using it to avoid fornication, or for the sake of sexual pleasure, were faults. (I point out here that the Augustinian condemnation of intercourse for the sake of pleasure cannot be equated with the condemnation of seeking one's own gratification in the sexual act and nothing else, so ignoring the personal affection which should inspire it. To say that intercourse should not be dictated by the quest for pleasure is in this sense very true—but talk like this is quite beyond the scope of what Augustine says. As far as I know, he—like so many other theologians—never raises the question of sexual selfishness at all.) For him, intercourse performed for these non-procreative

[1] As a sign of how the wind is blowing nowadays, we can compare extracts from the index to two editions of Denzinger's *Enchiridion*. The edition of 1942 states "the purpose of matrimony is the corporeal increase of the Church". The edition of 1963, on the other hand, begins its account of the purpose of marriage with "the reason and primary cause of marriage is the mutual interior *growing together* of the spouses".

purposes was not a serious fault, but it could not be integrated into the Christian's life, except in the sense that his married state saved him from sinning mortally thereby. Such intercourse could not bring him closer to God; it would at most, by the sacrament of matrimony, be stopped from depriving him of his grace. It was procreation alone that made the demand for intercourse virtuous, and there alone could the use of marriage draw men to God. The distinction drawn now in the RP between the primary and secondary purposes of marriage is wholly alien to Augustine's thought, for which "virtuous or venial" would be a more relevant distinction.

The RP must allow all these motives to be lawful, while still making one of them a necessary condition of the acceptableness of the others. More sophisticated expositions of the distinction will assert that the subordination is transcendental, or absolute, or something of the sort. (*EOM* 205.) I have already discussed the ambiguities in the RP's assertion that procreation is the primary purpose of marriage. (See pp. 42–44.) We saw that it called for the natural pattern of intercourse to be preserved—a request which turned out to be a demand for a particular kind of anatomical conjunction as the standard of lawfulness. In this way the defenders of the RP hope to be able to accommodate those who in fact seek intercourse for non-procreative purposes, by allowing them a method of ensuring that their desires do not lead to conception. But for Augustine, there can be no virtuous sundering of intercourse from procreation—procreation is what intercourse is for. The pardon given by God to those who have other motives for using it does not make what they do pleasing to him; if it did, why would he be pardoning them? Intercourse is robbed of its point and place in God's design if its procreative effect is obstructed. When the inferior motives inspire a man to seek intercourse, he sins by so seeking something whose original significance is purely procreative. For him to obstruct this purpose would be to abandon the only thing that gives intercourse goodness.

Now this is not what the RP says, even though both defenders of the RP and Augustine would condemn contraceptive procedures. The RP holds that non-procreative motives for demanding intercourse are virtuous, but that the act of sexual union is of its nature designed for procreation. This means, so the argument goes, that its physiological structure must be respected, whatever our motives may be and whenever we may decide to have intercourse. Augustine, on the other hand, holds that non-procreative motives are not virtuous but venially sinful, that intercourse is designed simply for procreation, so that to obstruct this purpose is to depart from the design of God. The RP is ready to allow intercourse to be confined to times when the chances of procreation are held to be virtually non-existent. We obviously cannot ask Augustine for his opinion on the safe period, but what he says about sexuality surely makes the question unnecessary.[1] A couple who deliberately confine their sexual relations to those occasions when procreation is least likely can obviously not be coming together in order to procreate. They are motivated by a desire for pleasure or by a wish to avoid fornication, and so are sinning venially. But we can go further. Are not such a couple not only sinning venially, but deliberately frustrating the purpose of sexual union? Have they not lost what Augustine calls "the reality of marriage"? (See p. 117.) For Augustine, the purpose of marriage is simply generation, and he seems to think that even a desire for no procreation is wrong ("*voto* malo sive opere malo resistitur"—see the same quotation from Augustine). But procreation is exactly what the couple are trying to avoid. They are not like husbands and wives who have intercourse during pregnancy or when the woman is past childbearing, for these only *know* that conception will not follow. The couple who use rhythm *set out to prevent conception*, set out to obstruct the achievement of what intercourse is meant to achieve. "They behave in such a way as to impede the offspring which marriage demands". (*De Nuptiis et Concupiscentia*, 1, 14; 44/423.) Consequently, their action falls under Augustine's condemnation in *De Conjugiis Adulterinis* already quoted (p. 117), that intercourse with one's wife is shameful "when the conception of offspring is avoided".[2] It is no use here saying that they are still respecting

[1] We can ask Augustine such a question, after all! Noonan has discovered a text in which the practice is mentioned—and, of course, condemned. (See Appendix C to Chapter 7, p. 337 below.)

[2] It is worth noticing that the English version of "Marriage" published by the Catholic Truth Society mistranslates this passage from Augustine (quoted correctly by Pius XI), rendering "ubi prolis conceptio devitatur" as "where the conception of the offspring is *prevented*". (Italics mine.)

the natural pattern of sexual conjunction—this is a concept alien to Augustine's thought in the matter. He *does* indeed talk about unnatural actions, but all he means here is sodomitic intercourse. There is no question of his reading off some indelible purpose from a particular kind of biological pattern. He condemns "the unnatural use of women" and his condemnation of it is deliberately put into the phraseology of the Epistle to the Romans. (See *De Bono Conjugali*, 2; 40/382, on p. 117.) To see how unreal it is to impose on Augustine the philosophical abstraction of later writers, notice how his statement that "sodomitic intercourse cuts spouses off from God's mercy" appears coupled with a statement that failure to abstain at times of prayer does so as well. The wastage of seed by withdrawal is not called unnatural by Augustine. It is wicked simply because it is against procreation, which is the purpose of marriage: hence it is condemned by God. (See quotation from *De Conjugiis Adulterinis* just mentioned.)

Augustine's position has a simplicity and consistency which are lacking in apologias for the RP nowadays. We saw that the preservation of the biological structure of the sexual act appeared many times in earlier chapters as the hidden mainspring in statements about marriage made by those who, while anxious to present a positive view of the married state, still hold the RP. Their insistence on this preservation of structure is no mere scruple or fancy; it is the one link between what they teach themselves and the very different doctrines taught by others whom they regard with veneration. Augustine and the Fathers subordinated marital relations to procreation in a way that apologists nowadays do not, so the apologists transfer the subordination from the purpose and practice of intercourse to the particular biological pattern taken by intercourse, and as long as the pattern is not tampered with, hold that the generative subordination is not infringed. The Fathers would have been just as opposed to such tampering, but their opposition would be due to an idea they had about the purpose of marriage. Their successors today have dropped the idea but still forbid the tampering. They give intercourse a different place and finality in the Christian's life, but they still prohibit any interference with its biological structure. An opinion of the Fathers, in other respects rejected, is enshrined in this prohibition; to adapt a phrase of Berkeley's[1] what is this sacrosanctity of the biological pattern in intercourse but the ghost of a departed finality?

9. *The followers of Augustine*

The title of this section does not commit me to the claim that all later theologians who wrote against contraception were "Augustinians" in any technical sense of the word. What I do think and hope to show is that, despite modifying and elaborating what Augustine wrote about the use of marriage, they remained faithful to the principles he took for granted about it. Having seen what Augustine taught, we can now appreciate how deeply Aquinas was affected by him.[2] Now let us see how the rest of the witnesses quoted against contraception accept the Augustinian restrictions on the morality of marital intercourse.

Peter Lombard cites with approval passages from Augustine similar to those already mentioned. He also quotes a passage from Augustine's commentary on Psalm 147: "Whoever does not demand the marriage debt, but pays it to his wife out of pity for her carnal weakness; or who through his own weakness has married, lamenting rather his need of a wife than rejoicing in having secured one, may safely look forward to the last day." (*Enarr. in Ps cxlvii;* 37/1917.) For Alexander of Hales, the wish to avoid fornication may be added to *proles* and *fides* as a legitimate motive for intercourse, though sexual relations prompted by desire are still venial sins. (*Summa* 2.147.1.) The pleasure sought must be "under God", or the sin is not merely venial: it is mortally sinful to satisfy one's desires with one's wife by "harlot-like caresses" (3.35.8), or if the passion is great and impetuous enough. (2.143.3.) In his allowing the avoidance of fornication to be a good motive, and in his clear statement that seeking pleasure (under God) is no more than a venial fault in many cases, Alexander shows himself more liberal than Aquinas,

[1] *The Analyst*, §35.

[2] A full account of the views of Augustine and Aquinas would among other things bring out the important clarification Aquinas brought to the doctrine of original sin, whose transmission Augustine binds uncomfortably close to sexual desire. To have given an exposition of this part of Augustine's teaching would have provided me with relevant material, but it would also have led too far afield.

whose opinions on these points have already been mentioned. (See p. 133.) But Aquinas was not a rigorist by the standards of his age; we get an indication of severer views in this passage of his contemporary St Bonaventure: "In the opinion of some authorities, if a man copulates with his wife with the principal intention of having that wretched pleasure which is said to be in intercourse, he sins mortally. It would be as if someone preached simply from vainglory. If he copulates with some other principal intention, but is gratified *en passant* with the sexual pleasure, they say he sins venially. For the marriage act to be sinless, the pleasure must not gratify but rather offend the reason." (*4 Sent*. 31.2.3.) Bonaventure thinks the opinion probable but too severe. His own view seems to differ only in that he makes erotic activity between husband and wife to be venially and not mortally sinful.[1] Cajetan (*In* 2/2, 153.2) roundly rejects the opinion Bonaventure thinks probable ("whoever behaves like this is either frigid or a fool") and says that pleasure may lawfully be taken in intercourse "which is otherwise properly motivated, such as for offspring etc." I cannot give a closer account of Cajetan's opinion (he never commented on the supplement to the *Summa*), but his phraseology assumes that the proper motive lies elsewhere than in pleasure. Sanchez—and Reginaldus only repeats his opinions—allows *proles* and *fides* to be legitimate reasons for having intercourse. He takes a middle way between Alexander and Aquinas when he says that the wish to avoid fornication is a legitimate motive *if no other means are adequate*—otherwise, to have intercourse for this reason is venially sinful. And he says the same about the preservation of health as a motive. He also makes a significant concession. For him it is not necessary for those who have intercourse to have an actual intention of procreating or paying the debt. In order that their action be virtuous, a habitual intention is enough, since what they are doing is of its nature destined to generate. Sanchez does not elaborate this point and its exact sense remains obscure, for he admits with the rest that to have intercourse for the sake of pleasure is sinful. (9.9, 9.10: and see

[1] For an account of some of these rigorists see "Duae opiniones heterodoxae circa honestatem usus matrimonii vigentes initio saeculi XIV" by A. Mruk in *Periodica* (1963), pp. 19–35. Aquinas mentions such a theory at this point in his commentary on the Sentences, and dissents from it.

Reginaldus 31,44.) Liguori makes the seeking of intercourse for pleasure a venial sin (6.§912) and says the same of health, if this be the only motive (6.§927) but the avoidance of incontinence he allows to be a sinless motive (6.§927).

In all these authors there is just the same defective catalogue of reasons for intercourse as there was in Augustine. Some of them show a more liberal attitude to the motives of avoiding fornication or preserving health, one makes a distinction between actual and habitual intentions but does not develop it; none gets beyond the methodology of Augustine. None talks as if intercourse might have something to do with love and affection, none offers a view of marriage which measures up to what we are nowadays exhorted to think about it. Even Aquinas remains inside these Augustinian postulates—postulates which indeed constitute the "defect in sensitivity and perception" which we detected in what he writes. (See above, p. 142.) What Aquinas does contribute is a more elaborate philosophical framework for Augustine's thought. We have already seen how it takes a quasi-idealistic form, an exaltation of the species and of its preservation by the transmission of seed at the expense of the individual. The concept of "nature" can now be extended from the non-philosophical sense given it by Augustine to any sexual actions which do not provide this seminal transmission. As I have already criticized Aquinas's theory, and tried to show that its defective notion of what marriage is for cannot be identified with the "appeal to nature", I refer the reader to those passages. (pp. 138 ff.)

These defects in sensitivity and perception can be illustrated if we return for a moment to a topic already considered. Earlier in this chapter I mentioned the verdict of a recent author on abandoning what he considered to be the natural posture in intercourse. (p. 125.) It is worth tracing this opinion to earlier sources. For Alexander of Hales, (*ST* 2.15.3), *coitus a tergo* is "against the rational mode of natural copulation", even though the seed is not frustrated of its destination. To have intercourse in this way is a very grave sin; if there is real need to do so (for example, advanced pregnancy in the woman) the sin is only venial. Alexander's condemnation is shared by Reginaldus, but with a less severe verdict—it is not a mortal sin but only "a very grave venial sin" and confessors, he says, should dissuade penitents from such brute-like behaviour (*brutalitas*). (Lib. 21, cap. 3, sect. 8.) Sanchez allows this or any other change of posture only when done for a good reason, not when done for pleasure (Lib. 9, disp. 16), and Liguori follows him, with the modification that lapses here are venial, not mortal. (6. §917.)[1] But the degree of severity in the authors is less significant than the detached and impersonal approach they all share in evaluating this question. That such matters fall within the competence of academic theologians; that the concept of nature goes down into such particulars; that emotion and inclination in the spouses need not be so much as mentioned; that intercourse can admit of no variety and no personal initiative—these are the common and unquestioned presuppositions of them all. And it is precisely such insensitivity I had in mind when speaking earlier of the views of Aquinas. There is no logical defect in what he says about the purpose of sex, no falling into the ambiguities of the "appeal to nature". It is his understanding of married love itself that betrays him, not fraudulent reasoning about the biological pattern of individual acts of sexual union.[2]

Aquinas and the rest share with Augustine a view of inter-

[1] The opinion of Aquinas in the *Summa* cannot be stated with certainty. Writing in *ST* 2/2.154.11 of unnatural sexual actions, he describes them as those "against the use of sex proper to the human species", and distinguishes four classes: masturbation, bestiality, sodomy, and "failure to observe the natural mode of intercourse". This in turn is subdivided into use of the wrong organ (*instrumentum non debitum*) and "other monstrous or bestial ways of having intercourse". It would be natural to conclude that the former of these referred to *coitus per anum* and the latter to such actions as *coitus a tergo*: for in phrases reminiscent of Alexander's, Aquinas in speaking of a defect in the *mode* of intercourse, a defect which lies in its not being the use *proper to the human species*. Against this it can be urged that the third objection in this article assumes (nor does its answer deny) that generation cannot follow from unnatural actions. On the other hand, Aquinas admits a double use of "unnatural" in 15 *DM*, 1 ad 7; in one sense, an action is unnatural if against generation, and this applies to all animals. In another sense, what is unnatural for man is what is against his specific nature; and in this sense fornication is against nature. Perhaps this ambiguity is present in the text of the *Summa*, where the next article distinguishes "failure with respect to the organ" from the lesser offence of "other things to do with the mode of intercourse". (2/2.154.12 ad 4.) Certainly he condemned such actions in *4 Sent*. 31 Expos. Text.

[2] I have not written this paragraph to defend "marriage manuals", which have received such hard words from some defenders of the RP (would not the analogy often traced by the latter between eating and sexuality oblige them to condemn cookery-books as well?). Some of the manuals certainly share the fallacy of the appeal to nature—they presume

course which subordinates its virtuous practice to generation. The contrast I pointed out between Augustine's opinion and the opinions held now by many who defend the RP could just as well have been pointed out between what these other writers taught and what is taught nowadays. In other words, the authors from Augustine down to Reginaldus selected as witnesses against contraception also made statements about married life which simply do not square with what is now taught by reputable theologians. Their statements are not the fruit of chance prejudice: they make excellent sense if taken in the context of their presuppositions about the purpose of marriage and the nature of the sexual relationship. For us who do not share these presuppositions, the opinions retailed in the foregoing sections seem inhuman and irrelevant, seem to identify the service of God with a mistrust of one of his gifts. How far, we cannot help asking, is the witness quoted from these authors against contraception bound up with their defective attitude towards sexuality as a whole? Can it be detached from historical and now obsolete circumstances, and accepted as the unfailing tradition of the Church? Or must it be subjected to a revising process, just as so much else that the authors said has been subjected? These are questions I shall try to answer in the next (and final) section of this chapter.

10. The tradition revalued

Although I have distinguished opinions about marriage held by older writers from those accepted today, it would be quite unjustified to infer that we do not share a very substantial part

---

that the significance and purpose of sexuality is statable in terms of what I have called "corporeal geography". Yet many people who marry are sexually ignorant. Doubtless, they should consult a doctor, but in fact many will not; could not reading at least help? It seems hardly fair to dismiss the literature as "pornographic or semi-pornographic" (Keenan and Ryan, 197)—their humourless solemnity would be worthier of attack. The vehement statement of Pius XII about books which openly discussed "secrets of conjugal intimacy before which even classical paganism seemed to stop short with respect" (allocution to a pilgrimage of "Pères de famille", September 1951, 733) can hardly be quoted in argument here, for it must have been motivated by very unusual publications indeed—classical paganism leaves remarkably little unsaid.

of what was taught by those whose doctrines we find in some measure to be defective. Whatever reservations we make about the teaching of earlier authorities, we have too much in common with them ever to regard what they say as wholly alien to us, and concentration upon disputed matters should not make us lose sight of those truths of creation and salvation that are our heritage as well as theirs. Even the points of dissent disclose shared convictions. We may object to the way in which they describe sexuality in fallen man—we cannot object to their insistence on the fall of man, and on the difference it has made to the way he must treat God's gifts. When Aquinas describes our fallen sexuality in ways which leave us unsatisfied, we must remember that he also places the vocation of continence for Christ's sake as an essentially post-lapsarian virtue. There would have been no such vocation if man had not fallen; but now that he has, the Christian life cannot escape the note of struggle and restriction: we are not dispassionate holders of the mean, we are an army on the march. We cannot promise ourselves that we shall always take kindly to the precepts inculcated in the Scriptures concerning the use of sex: and whatever our state of life may be, we shall not live worthily in it without the grace of God. If sex is God's gift it must be used on his terms. And neither sex nor any other created thing can stand as a substitute for his love.

When all this has been said, we can still acknowledge that the disagreement exists; but the disagreement does not of itself determine what our own position should be. The older subordinating of intercourse to procreation we do not accept, and regard it as unworthy of the ideals now held up to husbands and wives. But the rejection of so extreme a position does not specify what is to be substituted for it. B and C may be both incompatible with A without either of them following from the negation of A. So here, we may proceed from the denial of the earlier views to this assertion: "Intercourse is not only for procreation, it has many uses and may be used for these at our choice." Or we may substitute: "Intercourse is primarily for procreation, and cannot be used virtuously unless we fulfil that duty as we ought." And a third choice is: "Intercourse is primarily for procreation and cannot be used virtuously unless we preserve the physiological pattern of union uninterrupted."

The first of these propositions is outside our consideration; it presumes an independence of man in his behaviour that Christians cannot accept. It is hardly necessary by now to say that the second opinion represents the burden of much that I have said, while the third is the RP. The second has the advantage over the third in that it simply widens the Augustinian account of what intercourse is for, and then, without further adjustment, is open to the personal and vocational considerations which distinguish the theology of marriage today from what it was in the past. The third has the disadvantage of having to combine these same personal and vocational considerations with a purely biological criterion: but it has the advantage, the all-important advantage, of traditional and papal support.

I have been suggesting in the preceding sections that the patristic subordination of intercourse to generation cannot be abandoned without calling into question the unlawfulness of obstructing the generative effect of that action by contraceptive means. I pointed to the pronouncements of Augustine about sexual desire, to the austere abstractions of Aquinas, to the united front presented by these and the rest against the moral worth of intercourse for enjoyment, and to their universal silence about the place of love and affection in married sexuality. I submitted that they all subordinated intercourse to procreation in a manner not taught today in defences of the RP. I submitted that to abandon this generative subordination isolates the present absolute ban on interference with the generative pattern of intercourse from the foundations it originally possessed. I submitted that the concept of "nature" so readily appealed to is not to be found in Augustine, and that in Aquinas it has a significance quite distinct from that now given it. But for all my submissions, there are Roman pronouncements enough and to spare which tell to the contrary. Pius XI in his encyclical on marriage spoke of the inter-personal relations of "a common growth in the interior life, and unflagging zeal to better each other", and went as far as to call them "in a real sense the primary purpose of marriage, as long as marriage is considered in the wider sense of a life-long companionship and society, not in the stricter sense as instituted for the begetting and rearing of children." (*D* 3707.)[1] The Pope explicitly denied

[1] This passage in the encyclical so embarrassed some commentators

that spouses are in any way forbidden to seek the secondary ends of intercourse (which he lists as "mutual help, the cherishing of mutual love, and the quieting of desire"), but he lays down as a necessary condition "that they preserve the intrinsic nature of the act, and in consequence the due ordering of it to its purpose". (*D* 3718.) As I have already quoted utterances of Pius XII to the same effect, I refer the reader to them (p. 42), as I do to another passage from Pius XI's encyclical previously cited (p. 42). The matter could be summed up in a passage from Pius XII's allocution to the midwives:

> If the exclusive aim of nature, or at least its primary aim, had been the mutual giving and possessing of husband and wife in joy and delight; if nature had arranged that act only to make their personal experience happy in the highest possible degree, and not as an incentive in the service of life, then the Creator would have made use of another plan in the formation and constitution of the natural act. Instead, the act is completely subordinate and ordered to the great and unique law, "*generatio et educatio prolis*" (the generating and educating of children), that is, to the fulfilment of the primary end of marriage as the origin and source of life. ("Midwives", 62.)

To these can be added several pronouncements of Roman Congregations in the last century. (*D* 2715 etc.)

If I may digress for the moment, I find it puzzling that no earlier condemnations of "onanism" are to be found. We have seen how moral theologians denounced the practice, yet the earliest reference to it in Denzinger's *Enchiridion* dates only from 1822. Nor can there have been many others to hand. Thus the Holy Office asserted in 1851 (*D* 2792) that onanism was against the natural law, but cited no precedent for its decision except "an implicit condemnation by Innocent the Eleventh" (*D* 2149) which in fact refers to solitary sin. The reply of the Sacred Penitentiary to the Bishop of Le Mans in 1842 (*D* 2758) was prompted by an enquiry that deserves attention—the

---

that a falsified translation was circulated in England, and a well-known account of the encyclical glossed over the discrepancy. (See the article by D. Cloud in *CR* [June 1962], p. 358.)

bishop's question is not printed in Denzinger, but can be found in Marietti's edition of the *Summa Theologiae* where it is given in a footnote to 2/2.154.11. Apparently he reported to Rome the complaints of his flock that the prohibition of contraception was something new—our fathers were no chaster than us, the plea ran, but their families were no larger. They cannot be persuaded, says the bishop, that contraception (as distinct from adultery and abortion) is wrong. Nor can they be convinced that they must either observe continence in marriage or run the risk of begetting numberless offspring. What was the situation in that diocese? Could it be that confessors had just started to condemn "protectives" as distinct from *coitus interruptus*? Or had vaccination begun to lower the infant morality rate? Or were the laity simply chancing their arm with the bishop? At all events the Roman reply was quite uncompromising as to the illicitness of contraception, though ambiguous about the obligation of disturbing the good faith of penitents. Whether earlier statements exist, and if not why not, might be an interesting study for historians of theology. Perhaps the simplest explanation is that the constant teaching of theologians made Roman condemnations unnecessary; on the other hand, contraceptives were being used already by the end of the seventeenth century, and it is strange that nothing is said of them for so long. The catechism of the Council of Trent (*De Matrimonii Sacramento*, 8, 15) denounces those who use drugs in order to impede conception or procure abortion and the latter is identified with murder.[1] What remains for us to see is how the force of these official pronouncements is to be estimated.

There are two ways in which this series of authoritative statements could prove the RP to be involved in the tradition of the Church. One or more of them could be in themselves infallible decrees; and if so, they would by themselves be sufficient proof. On the other hand, if none of them is an infallible decree in

[1] "Quare fit, ut illorum sit scelus gravissimum, qui matrimonio juncti, medicamentis vel conceptum impediunt vel partum abigunt: haec enim homicidarum impia conspiratio existimanda est."

I owe this reference to the Catechism of the Council of Trent to Dwyer (p. 5), who also mentions a condemnation of anticonceptional practices in a Catholic prayer book used in England in 1786. (It may be pointed out that the Catechism of the Council of Trent does not share the status of conciliar decrees.)

itself, they can all still lend their support—decisive support perhaps—to the long succession of denunciations already quoted. That is to say, they would, taken together, represent a constancy in the day-to-day teaching of the Church which would admit of no rescinding. Which course is to be taken here? The obvious candidate for an infallible pronouncement is Pius XI's encyclical on marriage, for the tone of the language used seems to commit the Pope to a full exercise of his magisterial power:

> The Catholic Church, to whom God himself gave the task of teaching and defending moral honesty and virtue, placed as she is amid this decay of morality, preserves the chastity of the nuptial bond from this foul corruption, by raising aloud her voice through our mouth as a sign of her divine mission and proclaiming yet again: any use of marriage at all in which the act is deprived by human effort of its natural procreative force, offends the law of God and of nature, and those who so behave are guilty of grave sin. [*D* 3717.]

If the document (or the relevant portion of it) is infallible, then the debate is at an end. But exactly how this is to be shown is not easy to say. Let us remember first of all that the authoritative language and magisterial diction of papal encyclicals do not furnish of themselves, if I may use the expression, infallible inferences to infallibility. As Pius XII said in *Humani Generis*, encyclicals, although not exercises of the supreme magisterial office of the Pope, demand reverential submission, so that "if Popes expressly pronounce in encyclical letters on matters previously debated, it is obvious to all that the question—according to the mind and intention of those Popes—can no longer be regarded as open to free discussion among theologians." (*D* 3885.) Clearly a document which demands such reverential submission will naturally adopt a commanding mode of expression, whether or not it enjoys the plenitude of divine guidance. Pius XII's innumerable addresses are couched in such language, but no-one suggests they are in themselves infallible; their value and strength lie in the expression they give to what is then being believed and taught in the Church. If limitations in papal (or Roman) documents come to be admitted, their literary form does not, in the long run, hinder their reappraisal.

One thinks of utterances so disparate and yet all so forcibly expressed as Boniface VIII on Church and State (*D* 870 ff.), Leo XII on the reading of scripture, Pius IX's *Syllabus* (*D* 2901 ff.), and Pius XI on socialism. (*D* 3742 ff.)[1]

In the case we are considering, appeal is naturally made to the passages in Pius XI's encyclical. Its force and the reverence which it demands from Catholics are repeatedly and rightly stressed. But I have yet to find a work which explicitly claims that it is an infallible pronouncement. And, after all, let us put the question the other way round: Would there be so much debate and argument if the decree were infallible? Would not the mere citation of the document put an end, not of course to the practice of contraception, but to debates and arguments over the RP? Yet even in a discussion of the subject which recently appeared in a Catholic periodical, the defender of the RP would say no more than "although it may be held that they [i.e., Pius XI and Pius XII] were not speaking *ex cathedra*, I should be extremely surprised if their verdicts were ever reversed about contraception."[2] In this situation, we must insist that there is a general point of logic to be made: given what Roman Catholics believe about infallibility, there can be no degrees in it. *Humani Generis* has condemned the idea of dividing papal pronouncements into those we must obey (because they are infallible) and the rest (to which we need not submit). But to say that non-infallible statements must be obeyed is not to say that they are infallible. Obedience, silence, belief, inward and outward submission—all these may be demanded by and given to papal declarations, whether infallible or not. They are no more equivalent to the truth guaranteed by infallibility than our certitude, persuasion, assuredness and peace of mind when we assert the statement A are equivalent to A's being the case. To think that they are blurs the frontiers of logic and psychology in a way which has already been rejected at some length. It is logically possible, though not usual, to have to correct that of which we were completely certain; it is logically impossible to have to correct what is true.

[1] Leo XII's pronouncement is to be found at 1607 in older editions of Denzinger's *Enchiridion*. The latest edition omits it, without comment.

[2] The Rev. A. McCormack answering M. de la Bedoyère in *Search* (November 1963). I shall refer to this debate in the next chapter.

This is not due to some special firmness in human knowledge—it is just a matter of what we mean by "true". Thus, from another passage in *Humani Generis* (*D* 3897) we might conclude that Catholics may not defend publicly or privately, or even favour inwardly, the theory of polygenism. We cannot conclude from it that polygenism is false unless we first show that the passage in *Humani Generis* is infallible.

Yet even if the pronouncements in *Casti Connubii* are not infallible, they still sum up and combine with all the other authoritative statements and theological opinions to form a weighty testimony against any change. This I readily concede—which is why I admitted at the very beginning of this chapter that the appeal to tradition is the strongest argument of all. Let me admit more than this. There can be no question of matching the weight of tradition with contrary testimony, as if diligent search might reveal a series of authors who taught the opposite. All that can be done—all I have tried to do—is to question how far the *de facto* existence of this tradition entails a *de jure* and so unchangeable attitude. I have suggested that it might not, on the grounds that the tradition is *not simply about contraception but about the whole purpose and morality of the use of marriage.* The abandonment of the tradition with respect to these other topics makes appeal to it with respect to contraception no longer decisive evidence, but a partial selection of testimony which itself needs justifying. In earlier chapters I raised objections to rational arguments for the RP which appealed to human and divine values, to chastity, to the natural structure of intercourse, and to distinctions between different types of sterility. If what I have written is well founded, then the presence of such gaps and faults in the apologetic defences of the RP nowadays may be turned against the traditional appeal as well. I am, of course, not suggesting that a doctrine cannot be part of the faith if bad arguments are used in its favour—much of Christian belief would be invalidated by such a criterion. Rather, the defects and poverty of the defence point to a radical equivocation in what is being defended. Equivocations have already been detected in the rational arguments, as the earlier chapters have tried to show at some length; and the present chapter has traced equivocations in the appeal to tradition. Both sets of ambiguities are relevant to an appraisal of the argument for the RP which bases itself on traditional belief. If the defences of the RP were purely extrinsic to the position itself, strains and equivocations in them would be of no great moment; the use of sex would be accepted as divinely revealed, and the arguments themselves would be treated as quite distinct pieces of apologetic. But the RP is never—even in Roman documents—simply imposed on the grounds that it is revealed. The arguments, rational or traditional, form part of its presentation. Consequently, equivocations in them point to weaknesses and strains in the position itself. What the strain is we know well enough—it is a tension between old and new opinions on marriage, which the defective use of "nature" is a vain attempt to resolve. Even pronouncements of the Holy See cannot wholly escape such strains, for the simple reason that they defend a position which is not that of the authorities to whom they look back.

When wholly virtuous intercourse was simply for procreation, there was no such tension—hence my refusal to attribute to Aquinas the fallacies of the "argument from nature". Difficulties begin when the conclusions of the older theory have to be grafted on to a theory that would not in the normal course of argument lead to them. When Augustine says that intercourse with one's own wife is wrong when conception is avoided, he is talking in terms of beliefs not shared by Pius XI, who quotes him. ("Marriage", *D* 3716; see above, p. 117.) When Pius XI talks of "depriving the generative action of its natural procreative force" (*D* 3717, see p. 161), his later concessions about the legitimacy of intercourse for other reasons and his rather vague approval of the safe period (*D* 3718) give what he says a restricted sense alien to what Augustine believed; and when he says that depriving the marriage act of its natural generative force is wicked because the act is "of its nature intended to produce offspring" (*D* 3716), the use of "nature" in the reason he offers is, I have tried to show, not only different from Augustine's, but philosophically ambiguous. The same ambiguities can be detected even more clearly in pronouncements of Pius XII already quoted. (See pp. 101–159.) A verbal coincidence with earlier writers in phrases like "completely subordinate and ordered to the great and unique law *generatio et educatio prolis*" conceals a profound difference in the place given to sexual relations in marriage. Expressions like this would make excellent sense in Augustine; others like "incentive in the service of life" or "neither ought they to subject themselves unrestrainably to their sensual appetite" are quite acceptable even to those who reject the RP: it is the attempt to reconcile the two extremes by a physiological criterion that makes the interpretation of them so strained. The Pope cannot be repeating the doctrine of Augustine and limiting intercourse to the occasions when procreation is desired, for he allows in the same address the periods of natural sterility to be used for due reason ("Midwives", 36; see above, p. 60): Augustinian language has to be taken in a non-Augustinian sense. In the same address he condemns those who "extol the sexual relationship independently of the purpose of offspring" and "who for the moral obligation to master our passions would substitute freedom to make use of the whims and inclinations of nature blindly and without restraint". ("Midwives", 61.) Excellently said—but one can applaud this condemnation without agreeing with the RP! In consequence, the allocution has to identify disagreement with the RP with just this hedonistic philosophy of sexuality that divorces it from procreation and, ultimately, from restraint and rationality altogether. Such a philosophy of sex may be widespread, but disagreement with the RP does not entail it. It is a measure of the ambiguity and strain in the RP itself that the argument just quoted has to assert that this entailment exists, so identifying the adversary's view with self-indulgence, while at the same time leaving the door open for anti-conceptional procedures that can give the sexual relationship just the same independence of procreative consequences. Yet this ambiguity is built into the RP as it stands today.[1]

Having said all this, let me add a disclaimer. I do not consider myself to have offered a clinching proof that the traditional teaching on contraception can be abandoned. Not only am I doubtful as to how far rational argument can ever provide clinching proofs in theology; the position I have adopted precludes my making any such claim for what I have written. Arguments may suggest the possibility of change, but the Church alone can prove its possibility by actually making it. The second scheme of inference I gave on p. 119 can be used

[1] I have already mentioned a related confusion in the same discourse between self-control and the use of rhythm (see p. 101).

only in terms of this teaching, not as a licence for believing what one pleases. What I do think I have done is to put up a case that deserves answering; I think I have shown that the appeal to tradition is not quite as open-and-shut a business as it seems at first sight. And to have done this much is something. If the conclusion be authoritatively drawn that the tradition stands firm and can be disengaged from these relics of the past, I naturally accept it and have nothing more to say—except that my argument may have disclosed both the necessity for such disengagement and the fact that not all sources have so far succeeded in bringing it about.

But might not another conclusion be drawn? Might we not see in these ambiguities and equivocations, in this tension between old and new, a sign that the RP was still open to development, a development that would preserve what was essential while leaving behind these encumbrances of the past? Does the suggestion seem wholly unacceptable, and the Church too deeply committed for it even to be considered? Then think for a moment of another point of doctrine. Citations from Augustine's work *De Nuptiis et Concupiscentia* have often been given here, as author after author has repeated its teaching. (See, for example, p. 117.) Should we now wish to repeat the teaching Augustine gave in the first chapter of it, where he asserts that any apparently virtuous pagan marriage is and must be secretly vicious? (1, 3; 44/415.) Presumably not—but many older authorities would. We subscribe to the formula *extra Ecclesiam nulla salus* as they would: but we do not interpret it as they did. Changes over the last hundred years (see *D* 2865–6, 3821, 3886 ff.) have so accustomed us to the newer meaning given the phrase, that we find it hard to believe that men like Francis Xavier and Vincent de Paul accepted it in the most uncompromising form. When we look back on past beliefs in this matter we do not reject them outright. On the contary, we see in them a praiseworthy determination to hold certain doctrines fast—the gratuity and mysteriousness of saving grace, the insufficiency of nature, the central place of Christ and the Church, the perils of indifference. We must hold fast to these doctrines as well, and we differ from our predecessors only in that we have come to see more clearly how they can be reconciled with other beliefs about salvation. Even the defects of the past are significant. The long time the change was in coming, its slow and tentative nature, the contrived and imperfect solutions proposed (see, for example, Aquinas, *De Veritate* 14.11 ad 1)—all these witness to the tensions and dilemmas which faced theologians anxious for both orthodoxy and for the eternal salvation of separated brethren, as they threaded their way through a maze of opposed errors. No wonder that instinct ran ahead of argument.[1] But if there has been such progress in this doctrine, against so forceful a weight of tradition, may there not be a change in the RP? We do not accept what Augustine said about pagan marriages, though we do accept the distinction between nature and grace; we do not accept what he said about the value of married sexuality, though we do accept the fall and its consequences; must it be out of the question for us one day to cease to accept what he said about interference with the seed, while accepting that the use of marriage must not be divorced from procreation and must be subject to the Christian practice of temperance? Of course, the air has cleared now about the salvation of infidels and we can see the way through; which is exactly what it is hard to do in the matter of interference with the seed. The peculiar force of the argument from tradition is that it can ultimately be by-passed only by an authoritatively admitted change in belief. *Solvitur ambulando* is here the only refutation which can count in the last analysis, and an individual's argument can do no more than throw out the idea that walking might be possible.

I have mentioned Bible studies and salvation outside the Church as examples of accepted changes. There is yet another example which might be taken and which I now offer to the consideration of others. Unfortunately, I know too little about the history of controversies over the lawfulness of usury to be able to cite this change with any elaboration as a possible analogy to changes in the RP.[2] Let me make four suggestions which I think are significant. (1) Medieval theologians condemn

[1] Thus, a life of Pius X tells of the scandal he gave his secretary by saying the *De Profundis* on passing a Jewish cemetery. To the objection of his secretary, the saint had no better—or worse—answer to give than (I quote from memory) "You have your theology, and it is good; but God has his own theology too."

[2] The article "Usure" in the *Dictionnaire de théologie catholique* gives a wide selection of source material.

usury on the grounds, not of Bible texts, but of a rational argument about the nature of money. (e.g., *ST* 2/2.78.1.) (2) Its condemnation was vehement and repeated, and official prohibitions appealed to the tradition of Church teaching against it. (*D* 1355, 1442, 2140, 2546.) (3) Pronouncements against it petered out into advice to confessors not to disturb the conscience of penitents (*D* 2743 etc.)[1] (4) Explanations now given of the development in doctrine state that changes in the external situation allowed a new understanding of the nature of money. (See, e.g., Davis, 2, 375.) The first two points seem to give a fair parallel to our case—Why not the last two as well, in course of time? *Videant periti et judicent*!

Yet another analogy might be drawn, which would illustrate a point peculiar to our subject matter and perhaps throw light on the present state of the question. The elevation of marriage to a sacrament by Christ gives the Church power over the marriages of the baptized. (Code of Canon Law, 1016.) There have been interventions in matrimonial law in the history of the Church for which no adequate precedent can be given—they were themselves their own justification, they were not deducible from previous practice, but rather illuminated and extended belief about the nature of marriage and the powers of the Church over it. I refer, of course, to three seventeenth-century constitutions about the marriages of infidels which substantially extended the "Pauline Privilege".[2]

Church practice has since then further developed these to the stage when only a consummated sacramental marriage is held to be indissoluble. If the power of the Church is so great concerning the substance of marriage, is it wholly unreasonable to suggest that a similar power might be enjoyed by her with respect to the use of marriage? Clearly, the suggestion is unacceptable if we look on contraception as "prohibited by the natural law". But if my attacks on the radical ambiguities of the phrase are well founded, why should an intervention of the Church here be out of the question? The growth of under-

[1] For a liberal selection of texts on the whole question, see Marietti's edition of the *Summa Theologiae*, at 2/2.78.1.

[2] That is, the constitutions of Paul III, Pius V, and Gregory XIII respectively. These can all be found in the appendices to the Code of Canon Law. For shorter extracts, see *D* 1497, 1983, 1988.

standing among Christians about marriage and sexuality would leave its mark on the practice of the Church; her decision would be one which did not simply repeat past decrees, but developed the law of marriage by being added to it, much as a crucial decision in the courts affects the sense of the law. (See above, p. 14.) Obviously it would be foolish to dogmatize about such speculations, and I attach no great importance to this analogy. I mention it simply because it might be of some use in expounding the distinction between loyal obedience to what the Church's law is, and belief that this law cannot be changed. And—perhaps a point more pastorally useful—it would prevent the disastrous consequence of passing from a questioning of the RP to a rejection of Church discipline altogether.

A very natural objection against the practical importance of any of these proposals of mine is furnished by the length of time required for change in the Church. After the centuries that went by before the present views on the salvation of those outside the Church were reached, or before the persistent condemnations of usury lapsed into oblivion, is it not presumptuous to expect the status of the RP to change within the foreseeable future? Once more, answers here can be little more than conjecture. All I can suggest is that the rate of change in the Church—its second differential as it were—is itself increasing. The position of non-Catholic Christians, liturgy, the place of bishops, the place of the Bible—so much is happening and has been happening that we are in danger of forgetting how much and how quickly. Consider, for instance, the extremely guarded commendation of the safe period by Pius XII in his address to the midwives, its mass of qualifications and hypotheses, and the warnings against hedonism which accompanied it, and compare all this with something written recently by J. Fuchs, a lecturer at the Gregorian University, Rome:

> If the Priest or Confessor is asked about the Safe Period, he will explain its lawfulness; he will do the same even if not asked, to those married or about to enter marriage who will probably have difficulties. He will even urge the use of the method where there would otherwise be danger of sin, or would be if pregnancies kept following each other. Quite a few truly Catholic husbands and wives who have been well

instructed build up their families in a Christian and rational way by following the method proposed.[1]

Or compare what is said and done nowadays about those outside the Church, not just with what was said and done one hundred years ago, but what was written in Pius XII's encyclical *Mystici Corporis*. (e.g., *D* 3821.) Not that we reject what the Pope wrote: but the Church has progressed, and at an ever-increasing rate.[2] What makes the changes easy to overlook is not only the pace at which they occur but the desire of any organization to present a united front with the past, even at the cost of "benign interpretations" of it. The effect is to disguise the extent of change by forms of words which preserve the appearance of identity with older and now abandoned views. Capello for instance, wishing to defend the lawfulness of pleasure as a motive for intercourse, is faced with the condemnation by the Blessed Innocent XI (1676–89) of the opinion that intercourse so performed is free from venial blame (*D* 2109)[3]—a condemnation which of course simply re-echoes earlier teaching. Here as elsewhere, the pronouncement is accepted but its force is interpreted away. For Capello, this venial sin is committed only when the couple make a positive exclusion of all motives except pleasure. (800.) Reasonably enough, he thinks such sins would be difficult to commit. But did Innocent XI wish to condemn anything so recondite? Such methods of interpretation are neither unusual nor uncandid. The *stilus curiae* demanded, e.g., that the famous letter to Cardinal Suhard on biblical criticism should describe some earlier pronouncements of the Biblical Commission as "in no way opposed to a further and really scientific examination in the light of what has been learnt over the last forty years". (*D* 3862.) Do not let us mistake these diplomacies of officialdom for statements of historical fact.[4]

[1] I translate part of an extract from an article by Fuchs printed in A. McCormack "Family Planning, A Pastoral Problem", *CR* (March 1964).

[2] For this point see Appendix to chap. 7, pp. 207 f.

[3] Note that the Sanchez to whom the condemned opinion is ascribed in Denzinger is not the Sanchez whose opinions we have quoted.

[4] "This wasn't hypocrisy. It was the kind of formal language that Crawford had been brought up in. It was not very different from the formal language of officials. It meant something like the opposite of what it said. It meant that such thoughts were in everyone's mind: and that for reasons

To have questioned the force of a tradition is one thing; to suggest what changes in it might be made and how they might come about is quite another. In this chapter I have been concerned with what might be called the theory of change—what is tradition, what theology does about changes in belief, what sort of tradition is opposed to contraception, what other traditional beliefs in Catholicism furnish an analogy with its prohibition. There still remains what we can call the practice of change—how the RP stands at present, how the teaching Church speaks of it, what suggestions have been made for modifying it, and in what direction the RP is likely to develop. These topics will be considered in the next chapter. It will be possible then, in the final chapter, to lay down some principles and methods for future discussion of this topic.

---

of prudence, face-saving and perhaps a sort of corporate kindness, the thoughts had to be pushed away." C. P. Snow, *The Affair* (1960), 358.

7

Methodological

1. The limits of any solution

When Kant had finished his examination of human reason, he gave some practical conclusions about its use in what he called the "Doctrine of Method". Among these was the *discipline* of pure reason, in which checks and barriers were laid down against the tendency of reason to go beyond its province; and also its *canon*, in which its valid and proper use was inculcated. I have ventured to adapt Kant's title for this final chapter. In it I want to state briefly some conclusions about the nature and limits of profitable argument about the RP. And the first point to be made concerns what we are entitled to hope from such argument.

A common presupposition of many early works in favour of anti-conceptional practices was that the invention of an efficient and acceptable contraceptive would be a panacea for matrimonial problems. If we are not so naïve nowadays, we may still need to remind ourselves after seven chapters spent arguing about the RP, that there is more than the control of conception to sexual happiness, more than sexual happiness to marriage, more than marriage to life, and more than life to being a Christian. Given the imperfect and complicated character of human beings, we have no right to assume that easy solutions are likely in a matter so delicate as the use of marriage. Indeed, the repeated appeals in these pages for a view of sex that takes into account the whole marital condition of husband and wife are themselves a warning that the relationship between them cannot be solved on an infra-personal level, as if a suitable anti-conceptional method would of itself achieve something which calls for love and understanding from both husband and wife, in all aspects of their life together.

Arguments about controlling conception can continue until both sides unwittingly adopt a quasi-Freudian position in which sex becomes the one key to human behaviour. This is, I think, due to something more than the myopia which concentration on a single topic so often generates—the RP itself is partly responsible. The primary norm it has taken for licit sexual activity between husband and wife prescinds of its very nature from their status as human persons. In other matters of their life together, they consider their human situation as a whole, and appeal to norms which take into account who and what they are. Their sexual activity, on the other hand, has to be governed in the first place by questions that properly belong, not to a distinctively human behaviour, but to physiology. That the husband and wife manage to adapt themselves to this physiological standard does not alter its status. However well they manage to use the fertility-cycle, the norm for their coming together remains something which needs accepting and integrating into their whole marital condition, like traffic noises in the street or the barrenness of an apple-tree in their garden. It is not itself something by which that condition is enriched, like children, friendship, or responsibility. If they cannot adapt themselves to the cycle, then their sexual activity, by the very element of chance and unreliability it brings into their married life, resists all the more any incorporation into the human and rational pattern they try, under God, to impose on that life. It will offer them chances for self-abnegation and heroism; it will not of itself serve to build up a complete human and loving relation between them. In either case, sex has to be discussed as something standing apart from the rest of the activities which go to make up their shared life together. If the use of marriage has, unlike so much else in their lives, to be governed by so extrinsic and biological a norm, we must not be surprised if sexuality assumes a prominence in debates over their married life that does not belong to it.[1]

[1] A correspondent in *Search* for January 1964 makes this pertinent comment: "What does Fr McCormack mean when he says the use of the Safe Period should be considered as an attitude to life? This seems to me to assume a constant preoccupation with sexual intercourse, instead of allowing sexual desire to surprise husband and wife suddenly and unexpectedly into a rapture of love, as I believe God intended. The deliberate and constant use of the Safe Period may be possible to some, advantageous to many, but how unlovely! Is it really the only solution the Church has to offer?"

2. *Verdicts on the past*

The best reason for thinking that the use of marriage has to be governed by so biological and extrinsic a norm is that tradition says it must. By admitting this, and by devoting a chapter to the examination of tradition, I tried to remove the crux of the debate about the RP from philosophy to theology. Its resolution was now to rest, not on appeals to reason and common sense, but on appeals to God's revelation as shown in the witness of the faith over the years. But the admission does not mean that I must play Dr Pangloss to Church history. To say that a doctrine is in the strong sense part of tradition certainly commits one to believing it, but it does not commit one to admiring all the forms which the doctrine has taken, still less all the motives of those who have defended it. To admit that an appeal to tradition about the use of marriage is in order here does not excuse us from making as coolly rational a scrutiny as we can of what has actually been taught. If we end by accepting the appeal and believing the RP, we shall (if we wish) still be able to concede that the true metal of faith has had to be purged of dross and impurity. On the other hand, if we do not accept the appeal, our rejection of the RP will be bound up with our verdict on the forms it has taken and on the presuppositions with which it has been bound up. In either case the tradition itself needs examination. The importance attached to what the tradition supports must not become an excuse for ignoring less desirable elements in the tradition itself.

My own remarks in a preceding chapter about the tradition against contraception lead naturally enough to all this. I make the point again because those who defend the RP may find themselves ending up by defending other things as well, things of which their own reason and conscience would not, outside the heat of polemic, have them approve. For instance, we read much at the moment of the need for rational control of conception, for instruction to be given to Catholics as to how they can regard their married lives as a vocation, and express their love in their marriage while controlling its procreative consequences. We can be glad that all this is being said; but what used to be said? Were not the Catholics of a generation ago just as much in need of this advice? Has the need for it just arisen? Life moves quickly enough nowadays, and change succeeds change with sufficient rapidity, for an illusion to be generated that a sudden upsurge of population after the war was providentially met by the Church with a modification of her teaching about the values of married life and with a more favourable outlook on the safe period. This may be comforting self-deception, but it passes over too many awkward facts. What advice was offered the Catholics of a century ago? True enough, the infant mortality rate was then higher, but was there not just as much need for family limitation, to respect the health of the mother, the often small accommodation available, the scanty wages of the father? We cannot applaud today's attempts at a new theology of marriage without sitting in judgement on what that theology was yesterday. When Father McCormack says (*Search*, November 1963) that complete continence is, outside exceptional cases, "not worthy of serious consideration", he is presuming the existence of what he thinks is a licit and effective way of regulating conception, of separating intercourse from its generative effect. He goes on to say that it is only since 1960 that the real "breakthrough" has been made in predicting the cycle. Bliss is it in our day to be alive—but what of the days that are past? What are we to think about the situation imposed on the faithful who lacked our knowledge? If we regard the safe period as a poor second-best, things would not be so awkward—we should applaud past behaviour, and greet the new technique with coolness and caution.[1] But it is not possible to welcome the safe period as an integral part of the philosophy of Christian marriage without wondering at the odd situation by which generations of Catholics had to use sex on such widely different terms, with no third choice between unregulated procreation and absolute continence. A writer like Suenens (p. 70) points out the mistake of young married couples who think that continence means they have to live "as brother and sister", and says they should be told that there is another way which is easier. He says that living as "brother and sister" is "more than some couples with good intentions are capable of", and that this

[1] Kelly (see above, p. 91) would not be perturbed. He quotes with approval (p. 53) an author who compares the position of a husband and wife who say they will have no more than six children with that of an ordinand who says he will become a priest on condition he never has to say Mass or preach.

solution is "not the normal or usual one". But to talk like this is to pass an implicit verdict on what used to be said, upon the tradition which imposed the burdens it did, burdens of which the same author says "We have no right to rest content with placing upon men an obligation in God's name without at the same time telling them how to meet the obligation and without encouraging them at every step along the way." (p. 52.)

"Earlier ages had no choice", it may be answered: "No licit method of controlling conception other than complete abstinence was then known." An honest avowal like this demands respect, but we must be quite clear as to what it commits us to admitting. To say that no generation previous to our own has been able to reconcile as we can the three elements of family limitation, obedience to God's law, and the use of marriage, is to make a very bold claim indeed, for the change it says has come about radically effects the practical consequences of the obligation to preserve chastity in marriage. To make this alleviation depend upon a fortunate invention of our time comes very near to a position I have already mentioned (p. 192), which would base the licitness of alterations in moral principles on the novelty of what is being considered. In other words, to claim so unique a position for our own time gets very close to saying that the attitude in the Church to the use of marriage is unchanged, but that—*o fortunatos nimium*!—Catholics of our generation have, thanks to science, a way round the law. I do not accuse defenders of the RP of holding so crude an opinion; but I do suggest that they have not considered enough how the admission of the safe period has affected, not just the married lives of Catholics, but the Catholic teaching on marriage itself. They have not, I submit, sufficiently explicitated the verdicts on the past which their admission of the safe period implicitly involves. As I have already tried to show (pp. 149 ff.), the non-procreative use of intercourse afforded by the safe period is not compatible with the views held by many of the authorities on whom the tradition against contraception depends. To admit the safe period entails a rethinking of that tradition. In other words, to say that up to now no method other than complete continence existed for controlling conception is misleading. It suggests that moralists sought anxiously but in vain for some such process, much as Pius XII expressed the hope that it would be possible to make the calculation of the infertile period still more accurate and reliable. ("Family Campaign", 15.) How could they have done anything of the sort, when they subordinated the use of marriage to procreation as rigorously as they did? Was it not this attitude of theirs, rather than the defects of knowledge, which was the reason why no alternative to complete continence was suggested? If so, is it not time that the appearance of the safe period should be considered, not just as a providential means of circumventing a traditional prohibition, but as an occasion for examining the traditional prohibition itself? In other words, the rethinking of the theology of married life which is now going on must not proceed as if the RP had been determined prematurely but irreversibly in earlier and defective ages, so that revision could affect only incidentals. Doctrines cannot become *de fide* through absentmindedness or lack of perception. The Church is not like a builder who regretfully decides that, although some concrete has set too quickly, subsequent building operations cannot extend to removing it. If the view of the use of marriage has changed, there is a *prima facie* case for reviewing the tradition as a whole. Talk of the changelessness of tradition does not in itself exclude this, as I have tried to show by my "schemes of inference". (p. 119.)

I suspect that defenders of the RP are not altogether easy about the matter themselves, for how else can one explain their neglect of the argument from tradition? After all, they are addressing their remarks to Roman Catholics, to an audience which acknowledges the legitimacy of such an argument. For all the philosophical tone of apologetic for the RP, no-one suggests that this apologetic is going to change the practice of the world at large; it is in fact strictly for home consumption. Why, then, is this apologetic not based squarely on the indisputably long tradition of opposition to interference with the procreative act? Might it not be that the apologists realize what diverse and dubious elements the tradition contains? And that they shun the aid it could give them—*non tali auxilio, nec defensoribus istis*? The argument from nature, for all its sophistry, has at least the merit of seeming to place the morality of contraception outside Church tradition altogether. In consequence, an apologetic based upon this argument can ignore past theological opinions, or allow them only a material coincidence with conclusions reached by reason alone. It would be more honest, if less comforting, to face the legacy of tradition—more profitable as well, for the scrutiny might show how far the appeal to nature is only a rationalization of prejudice. My suspicions are confirmed by the attitude displayed by defenders of the RP to what its consequences used to be in the days before family planning became respectable for Catholics. An article by the Rev. A. McCormack already quoted (*CR* (March 1964)) shows a sympathetic understanding towards the problems faced today by Catholic husbands and wives in this matter. I wish he had shown the same degree of sympathy for the problems of the past, for here a tone of uncertainty appears in the article. Thus, while admitting the drawbacks of some large families, he writes, "Times have changed since a Catholic couple was prepared to raise ten or fifteen children in a tenement, a flat or house meant for four or five. A modern young couple are not to be blamed if they feel unequal or unwilling to face this task, or to feel that in such circumstances they could not really bring up their children well." "Times have changed", "not to be blamed", "unequal" or "unwilling"—these are oddly ambiguous phrases. Does Father McCormack want us to believe that the older order was good in itself or bad in itself? To be wistfully remembered, or looked back on in anger? Does he want us to regard the situation of the Catholic couple nowadays as something to be tolerated, or as something to be praised? I do not want to carp at his article, which contains some welcome and still all too rare sympathy. But I cannot help noticing in it a certain disparity between what is said of the large "traditional" Catholic family, and what is said of the smaller Catholic family. He reminds us that large families are not to be "blamed" and that having a large family "is extremely praiseworthy and the couple can well rely with confidence on providence for special graces in their difficulties and special blessings on their home". He emphasizes that parents of large families must never be made to feel rejected, "as if they were unwise or feckless". All that he will say of those who choose to have small families is that "they should not be looked down on, regarded as second-class citizens of the Kingdom of God, or be thought of as lacking trust in His providence". All this not only identifies a personal preference for the larger family with the law of God; it is hardly consistent with what the author writes elsewhere in the article. He admits that past treatment of penitents was often harsh and cold, lacking in sympathy and understanding; that they were greeted with rebuke, and given confused and unreal answers far removed from the realities of everyday married life. He cannot have it both ways. It was this confessional and pastoral practice of priests that produced the traditionally large Catholic family of which he writes so eloquently. It is all very well for him to blame the confessors of the past; *he* now has what he regards as a safe and licit method of separating procreation from sexual intercourse. *They* had not—what were they to do? Is there not a basic confusion here between two quite distinct things: what the Catholic approach to matrimonial problems of this sort should be; and the actual existence of a method by which sexuality may be exercised and conception simultaneously controlled?

Is not the change of policy mentioned by Father McCormack something more than the simple enactment of a positive law, like changes in the eucharistic fast? But if it is more, it surely must oblige us to pass judgement on what used to be taught and said? After all, there has been no abrupt break in human life and needs to necessitate so profound a change. Nor is it any piece of distant history which is in question, where logical difficulties about moral verdicts on the remote past could be raised. The day-to-day teaching of the Church is involved, a teaching on which rests just that appeal to tradition which is the strongest argument for the RP. And note, an adverse verdict on this tradition would in no way reflect upon the heroic virtue that was formerly displayed; it would question only the preaching and teaching that made such virtue necessary. Father McCormack—and so many others—speaks of these virtues shown in the old days among the Catholics of our own country. I wonder what other motives affected the pastoral denunciations of birth control and—more importantly—commendation of large families, apart from the desire of preserving what was believed to be the faith? The usual accusation made against the Roman Church in this matter, that its teaching on contraception comes from celibate prejudice against sex, seems quite inadequate: there were surely other forces at work. Did not holding out to husbands and wives the ideal of large families (with all that this entailed for people who were not rich to begin with) amount to committing them to a life in which all their physical and mental energies would be devoted to family matters? A life in which there would be little chance of those energies being used in wider contexts? Is it unfair to say that for the clergy in England, the paradigm Catholic family has traditionally been large, docile, and working-class? And that the matrimonial ideals inculcated in pulpit and confessional have not only been modelled on the social *mores* and habits of the working class, but have militated both against the intellectual and social betterment of the faithful and against their having spare time and initiative for public affairs? These are not just rhetorical questions—I should like to know the answers to them, because the tradition supporting the RP has social and political presuppositions that have not been examined as they should. As things are, one can only hazard guesses that do not seem wholly implausible.

If the traditional witness to the RP is entangled with prejudices and presuppositions that are no longer in fashion, its defenders will need some technique of decanting the pure doctrine they wish to preserve from the dregs they are anxious to discard. It is worth noting that the word "Jansenism" has proved very useful for those who want the RP of today set apart from less acceptable elements in its heritage. Any aspect of past teaching which now offends can be comfortably attributed to the Jansenists, leaving the true doctrine uncompromised. But an examination of alleged instances of such Jansenism will show that rhetorical need rather than historical investigation has dictated their choice. Lestapis, for instance, asserts that, had it not been for "the Jansenist crisis", the optimism of St Francis de Sales regarding the values of married life would have affected Catholic teaching more than it did. (*L*, 163, footnote 4.) I share Lestapis' admiration for the saint. Unfortunately, the part of his teaching on marriage which has stuck in my mind is his story from Pliny about the elephant's habit of copulating only when offspring is needed, and of washing his body after doing so—for Francis, this is a pattern to be held up for admiration to husbands and wives (*Intr. à la Vie Dévote*, 3.39.) One hardly knows what to smile at more, the theology or the zoology, but how much optimism about the values of married life does the story convey? It is just as unhistorical to connect Jansenism with restrictions on sexuality taught by many of the older authors, restrictions that go back to days long before Jansenism was ever thought of. The prohibition of intercourse during pregnancy we have already encountered, and understood it as a natural consequence of a restricted view of married life. If the Jansenists taught this, they said nothing new. And if they did say it, they were not alone in doing so. Liguori himself taught that only the danger of incontinence excuses intercourse during pregnancy from venial fault (6, §924)—he means, presumably, that intercourse at such a time can be tolerated only as an antidote to adultery or self-abuse. Was Liguori a Jansenist? Or, to take an example from a Roman document, Pius X's decree on Frequent Communion described the "plague" and "poison" of Jansenism as leading to the exclusions from the Holy Table of whole classes of Christians, like merchants and married people. (*D* 3376.) But the Blessed Innocent XI set merchants and married people aside from the rest as classes whose access to the altar should be subject to the decision of their confessors "who search the secrets of their hearts" and who should warn husbands and wives to abstain more than ever from intercourse before receiving communion. (*D* 2090–2.) Was the Blessed Innocent a Jansenist?

He was not. Neither was Liguori, for whom Communion the morning after intercourse performed for the sake of pleasure was usually a venial sin. (6, §273.) Neither was De Smedt, who as late as 1920 wrote that for intercourse to be morally perfect, the couple must explicitly intend to procreate children. (*De Sponsalibus et Matrimonio*, Bruges 1920, §279.) These, like so many others, simply did not think as the Church now encourages us to think, and "Jansenism" is an expression which, if used in a sufficiently nebulous way, can temper the force of what was once said and now needs unsaying. The technique is reminiscent of Capello's *interpretatio benigna* of what Innocent XI said about sexual pleasure (p. 170); the force of the past utterance is removed while the form of the past utterance is preserved. I hold no brief for Jansenism, and I suppose I ought to welcome so handy an overworking of the word as a device for quietly disposing of what is obsolete. But a warning already given needs repeating—we must face the past if we are to estimate the force of tradition. Otherwise, the harmless fiction of pronouncing awkward elements in it to be Jansenistic can become an excuse for not submitting the whole tradition and legacy of the past to rigorous scrutiny. Caution may use forms of words to lend grace to withdrawals. Something more than caution is needed if the nature and consequences of the withdrawal are to be understood.

3. *The displaying of moral criteria*

Defenders of the RP have been known to accuse its opponents of appealing to over-population in remote lands as an excuse for self-indulgence in their own. The accusation, if addressed as it is to inhabitants of a grossly overcrowded country like England, is ill-conceived: but it usefully displays a fact about ethical arguments in general. No satisfactory solution of moral problems will be obtained by *ex tempore* dispensations and exceptions. Christians ought to accept this without difficulty, as an examination of religious morality has shown (pp. 36–7), but the principle should commend itself to all who want to argue seriously about how we must live. There is a universality involved in the passing of moral judgements which is not compatible with treating each situation as some brand-new subject for discussion, without reference to past decisions. How far this view of morality and of moral argument has been questioned by some recent theories (see above, pp. 49, 71) does not concern us here: what I have to say, like my criticisms of the RP, is addressed to those who accept that morality must be something more than a series of verdicts without precedents.

Proposals whose acceptance involves a change in moral judgements cannot, then, be judged simply by appeals to isolated cases of tragedy or inconvenience caused by the present system of moral judgements. They demand an investigation into the grounds on which these present principles are based, the truths and beliefs they suppose, and their compatibility with other principles. I hope that the examination of arguments used to support the RP has done something towards this, but I think that at all events it will have performed one important service. It will have displayed the "moral centre of gravity" of the RP, displayed it as lying in the status accorded to the physiological structure of intercourse. If nothing else is proved by all that I have written, this displaying of moral criteria would be a worthwhile result. Debate over moral beliefs cannot even begin until both sides are quite clear as to what these beliefs are. I have said that an appeal to tragic results of present moral principles is not of itself a sufficient warrant for their abandonment. On the other hand, the frequency or inevitability of tragic results may justify second thoughts about principles, on the grounds that they can have such consequences. And if the frequency seems almost built into the principles themselves, then, if no overriding consideration like divine commands is involved, the principles not only can but ought to be rescrutinized. "Hard cases make bad law" is true; but more precisely, it has two senses, both of which may be true. Not only does appeal to exceptions destroy the rule; the rule itself may need revising if its consequences prove to be disastrous.

The philosopher Ramsey once said that many of our arguments are of the following pattern: A: "I went to Grantchester this afternoon." B: "No, I didn't." (*The Foundations of Mathematics*, p. 289.) Discussion of the RP has been bedevilled by *ignorationes elenchi* to an extent unusual even in theological or philosophical debate. Lack of food in Calcutta is not solved by the use of the safe period in Nantes, and over-fertility in Hong-Kong is irrelevant to matrimonial problems in Liverpool. What advice we give in Liverpool and Calcutta will depend on what our verdict is on the RP: the verdict itself cannot be based just on what is going on in those two cities, any more than it can be based on some promised invention for growing wheat in the Sahara, colonizing the North Pole, regulating the female cycle with mathematical precision, or constructing artificial satellites in which the surplus population of the earth can be housed.[1] Our verdict on the RP will have to be reached in terms of what men and women are, in terms of what sexuality ought to mean in marriage. It must be based upon something more than spontaneous compassion for those in difficulty, even though that compassion may have urged us in the first place to review our ideas about the control of conception. Evidence of hardship is still evidence, but it is not a judicial directive to the jury for a verdict. It needs weighing with the rest of what we know, it must play its part in helping us to decide the one issue really at stake —what power *homo sapiens* is to have over his generative faculties.

[1] The last, according to Rock (p. 19), is a suggestion of Mr Colin Clark.

But if moral principles cannot be impugned simply by appeals to hard cases, they cannot be defended either by appeals to what has only emotional relevance to them. I have already conceded that the impersonal and biological norm imposed by the RP is not good material for persuasive apologetic, and that the temptation to adorn it with more human and personal considerations must be very great. (pp. 69 f.) But the adornment is still only adornment; sophistry in fact, if more is claimed for it. Those who defend the RP, and those who attack it, must be quite clear that they are not, in the last analysis, arguing about the spiritual nature of man, or the proclamation of chastity, or the protection of family life. They may well agree on all these without agreeing on the RP. The real point of issue lies in the physiological criterion, and nowhere else. For the defenders, of course, this criterion is readily invoked as a kind of safety-net beneath other precarious arguments. The French theologian Père Tesson provides us with a good example of this technique:

> In man, [the supremacy of spirit] is achieved only by submitting himself to the plan itself which is written in his nature and expresses his likeness to God. Thus his body becomes an instrument of the soul, a value which lifts it above the level of a mere animal body. (Quoted by Cavanagh, p. 322.)

Even if we pass the highly dubious philosophy embedded in this, what more is Tesson saying than that we must preserve the corporeal geography of husband and wife in intercourse? His use of spiritualistic terminology is a piece of rhetoric designed to reinforce the association of the RP with the service of God. But if we question the position itself, we thereby question its claim to be a service to God, and the use of spiritualistic terminology now begs the question. As I have already pointed out (pp. 26–7), it is idle to talk of man's special relationship with God as a proof of the RP without first proving that this special relationship affects him in the relevant way. Tesson can do no more than reinforce emotional and religious associations; but, reinforce associations as we please, we do not turn them into rational arguments. Defenders of the RP who lard their proofs with appeals to the spirit are just as guilty—and just as excusable—as opponents of the position who lard theirs with denunciations of celibate fanaticism. Each is substituting a partial glimpse for an all-round view of the facts. Each forsakes the arduous task of reasoned debate for the easier (and perhaps more successful) occupation of playing on prejudice and habit.

This is only another reason for my plea that the RP should be thoroughly re-examined, not just improved by patching over the debris of the past. The first step to this re-examination is, as I have said, to state quite clearly what criteria are essential to the RP, and what are merely ornamental. If we display moral criteria as we should, present apologetic for the RP seems trapped between the alternatives of defending a narrow view of sexuality by bad philosophy or making it palatable with irrelevancies. Is there no other form the defence might take? Are my objections to the RP such that the position is, under any hypothesis, indefensible? The questions deserve an answer, which I shall try to give in this next section.

4. *A possible apologia for the* RP

The rational arguments for the RP which I have examined attempted to pass from facts about human sexuality to human obligations in the use of it, or from the need to preserve certain values to the necessity of accepting the RP in order to do so. For those who propose these pieces of reasoning, the appeal to tradition only confirmed their conclusions, only showed that divine revelation taught what was already rationally inferred about human procreation from its divinely ordained structure. I have given at some length my objections to the rational arguments and my reservations about the appeal to tradition. After all that I have written, I can hardly now put forward a probative apologetic for the RP. Let me rather suggest to its defenders a way of presenting their thesis as an awkward but inescapable fact about the human condition as it now is, a way which does not impose a proof but rather invites resignation—in short, an apologetic that really does apologize. I have put what follows into inverted commas; *timeant Danaos*.

"The sexual instinct in human beings takes many forms and can be stimulated in many ways. Its use for procreative purposes is important, but cannot itself be elevated into the only worthy use. Differences of culture, upbringing and physical make-up will give it different patterns; what seems repulsive to some will delight others. But sex is a powerful instinct, and the fallen state of man means that its control will entail effort and abstinence. At the same time its procreative, social, and emotional consequences demand that this effort be made. God has spoken to us by Scripture and Tradition as to how he wants this instinct to find expression. An instinct so polymorphous could well have been governed by other norms, but we must follow the pattern imposed on our sexuality by him to whom we owe the gift of our life. Faith in God tells us that obedience to his laws gives to him honour and to ourselves the only happiness that counts in the last analysis; it also tells us that he denies no-one the help needed to obey these laws of his. We cannot expect to find the obedience easy; we cannot even expect that obedience will assure us a balanced and fully human use of our faculties. We have a fallen nature, and the healing grace of God leaves much in us awry—much that may have to be sacrificed if we are to be his friends. He has promised victory to those who trust in him. He has not promised that the victors will emerge from the struggle unscathed. He has called us, we believe, to be something more than human—can we be surprised at tensions between our Christian vocation and many inclinations of ours, legitimate in themselves?

"The wound of original sin touches even that witness of his Church which enshrines his revelation. The prejudice against sex in Christian tradition is only the dark side of what is good in that tradition—its preaching of the need to forsake all things if God's service demands, of the struggle needed to serve him, and its praise of continence accepted for the Kingdom of Heaven's sake. Christians are imperfect like all other human beings—like other human beings their virtues and vices come in groups and not singly, so their good qualities are likely to bring less desirable characteristics in their train. Legitimate stress upon one important truth may all too often lead to the neglect of another: neither truth is invalidated by this overemphasis, nor is the tradition itself rendered of no effect. The witness of tradition, like the witness of God's written word, has the unambiguous clarity of any effective command. The 'mechanically verifiable' norm laid down for marital intercourse cuts short all debate and prevents any abuse dictated by human weakness and selfishness.

The norm is imperfect in the sense that it is not tailor-made to individuals, but is a plain command whose very impersonality leaves no room for doubt as to whether it is being obeyed or not. Nor can the use of the infertile period affect the substance of what God has commanded. The whole point of divine laws is that they must be respected *as they stand*; it is not for us to take on the burden of amending them, or to suppose that they have become ineffective because we have learnt how to separate intercourse from procreation. If such a way exists, we can take it as long as we do not infringe the existing commands of God. Our use of the safe period will have to respect the needs of procreation, because this is an important consequence of intercourse, but the method itself is not 'cheating' or 'underhand'. Words like this are out of place, they presume that there is a primary purpose for intercourse and that we are avoiding it. No claim is made in this apologia about primary purposes; what matters is the specific commands God has given about sex. They and nothing else are restrictions on our liberty. The imperfection of our bodies—itself a result of original sin—means that rhythm can be used by some and not by others; that some will have to abstain for lengthy periods and some very little. But a law cannot be clear and straightforward without creating such inequalities, and a law for the imperfect needs to be so unequivocal that they cannot distort it for their own ends. 'What sex is for' is a consideration not immediately relevant to Christian morality, for it does not take into account the fact that such morality is essentially a makeshift. We are not just rational animals who must respect the innate finality of things. We were made in God's image, lost his grace through sin, and have been summoned from our fallen state to be his children. There is no 'book of instructions' to be followed as a sure guide to self-fulfilment; books of instructions presume that the mechanism is in order, is as it was designed to be, and this is just what human beings are not. A question like 'What is sex for?' can have two senses. It may be concerned with purpose, as shown by a general survey of human needs, emotions and habits; or it may be concerned with purpose in the sense of how we must use sex. The question in its second sense can be asked only within the boundaries laid down by God's commands. Given what these commands are and what men are, we have no right to expect that the answer to the question in this sense will coincide with the answer to it posed in the first sense. Rationality can go only part of the way: it must start from what God has said and submit itself to that."

I do not claim that an apologetic like this would convince those who were not already receptive to the Church's teaching. But it has the merit of saying something about the present state of man and about the nature of divine commands which is, I would suggest, unquestionably relevant to the point at issue. True enough, it offers only cold comfort to believers—but then what else can be offered, even by those who propound apologetics based on nature, chastity and the rest? More important, this apologetic of mine respects the integrity of human reason. We have to do enough violence to our inclinations if we are to accept the RP without having to do violence to our critical faculties as well. Bad arguments for what is true are not strengthened by the truth of their conclusions. Certainly, the badness does not compromise the truth of the conclusions in themselves, but it may well do so in the eyes of those who are already disposed to reject these conclusions. We do our faith no honour by supposing it to need such untrustworthy crutches. Aquinas made the point once for all about another question, and his words deserve quotation: "We can believe the proposition, we cannot prove it or know it to be true. The point is worth bearing in mind, to prevent inconclusive proofs being used in attempts to demonstrate what is a matter of faith. Proofs like that succeed only in providing amusement for unbelievers, who conclude that our belief in articles of faith must rest on such grounds." (*ST* 1.46.2.) But the apologia has, I think, a further interest. In its insistence that we accept the facts of sexuality and the tradition about it as they are, and do not take to ourselves the task of changing them, it approaches an objection that has been made to my general thesis by more than one critic. A consideration of this objection will lead naturally enough to what concluding remarks I have to make.

5. *The need for discussion*

It has been put to me that the organic nature of man sets a limit to the modifications to which he can submit his bodily functions.

Man is not a pure spirit using a body as a morally neutral instrument, his form of existence is that of a rational animal, and this has its own exigencies. How far, it may be asked, can the manifestations of sexual love between husband and wife exercise a dominion over the bodily forms of their human spirit? Are these methods of treating biological organs which are not in accordance with the human, no matter what humane motives are entertained? Does not the way I have argued drive a wedge between personal values and the type of existence which the persons themselves possess? These questions might be put in a terminology used in several passages of the book—what degree of inviolability does the human sexual function enjoy? We have seen that much argument in favour of the RP rests on a postulate that no obstruction or disturbance of the pattern of union can be allowed. If this postulate is questioned, is not man given a dominion over his sexual faculties that would permit, say, homosexual actions in virtue of personal needs and values that would morally justify something supposedly in itself indifferent?

I have already considered the principles raised by these objections: perhaps a statement of my views here will clarify them. I begin by recalling that my critique of the RP was not written by one who was ethically uncommitted. Distinctions between religious and non-religious morality have been explicitly drawn, and the peculiar characteristics and exigencies of Christian teaching on sexual behaviour have not been noted at some length. (pp. 34–40.) More than once I have stated my assumption that Christians who speculate about the use of marriage must take monogamous heterosexual union as the starting-point imposed by their religion. (e.g. p. 39.) My reasons for doing this were not just that I was arguing as one Roman Catholic with others, though this postulate was also explicitly made (pp. 4–5): the very nature of arguments about sexual morality was involved.

Ethical assertions and the arguments to which they can lead seem to take justice as their paradigm, and are most persuasive as they approach that paradigm. Ill treatment of the innocent, theft, or lying, are obviously wrong because they are seen to infringe rights, to go against what people are entitled to expect. The same paradigmatic position of justice can be detected in those appeals to the common good, to the basic necessities for human society, to social harmfulness, and so on, which are made in moral disputes. Each party is taken to pay at least lip-service to a tag like "give each his due", or the dispute is felt to be hopeless, or nothing more than an exercise in philosophical dexterity. Now, to repeat what has been said elsewhere, not all assertions about sexual behaviour get close to the paradigm. The condemnation of adultery, which does approach it, cannot be equiparated with the condemnation of actions like stealing or breaking contracts. (See p. 38.)

I make these points again here because I want to repeat that arguments according to what I have called "the justice paradigm" are not able, as I see it, to provide an adequate apologetic for the absolute and (if I may recall the phrase) "perspicuously concrete" commands about sexual behaviour that are imposed by Christianity. Such arguments may suggest or persuade, they may offer answers to objections raised against Christian teaching: I do not think they can do more.

That is why I am doubtful as to how far the limits of man's power over his bodily functions can be decided, I do not say outside a religious code of law, that is too positivistic and formal a description, but outside a tradition in which an experience of and insight into what man is, can be interpreted under grace so as to issue in decisions about the extent of his powers. I have spent a chapter and an appendix pointing out what I think are deficiencies in the Christian tradition about sex: but I have admitted there, and repeat the admission here, that changes in the tradition need to come as developments of it, not rejections. (p. 167.) If, as I have suggested, the tradition can so develop as to allow the prevention of intercourse from leading to insemination, the tradition itself still remains, and the guidance it gives is still necessary—all the more necessary, in fact, if the once simply reproductive evaluation of sex is deepened, and gives a place to personal and emotional values it did not formerly give. The change, if it does come, will illustrate (just as the changes which have already come have illustrated) the growth of tradition, not its annulment.

But having said all this, I should like to turn aside from the question of tradition for a moment and repeat both my original denial that permitting contraception entails the permission of homosexual practices, and my surprise that anyone should assert such entailment. (See p. 66.) Let us forget for a moment the Christian prohibition of such actions; let us for the sake of argument prescind altogether from their moral status. Surely what matters for the non-entailment with which I am concerned is that contraception and homosexuality are so *different*—one is between a man and a woman, and one between people of the same sex. The two actions seem to me incommensurable, for I can see no common standard in the fact that both can lead to non-generative semination. Obviously, if someone condemns any such semination he will condemn both activities, but equally obviously, it does not follow that if he allows one type of action which involves it he must *thereby* allow the other. He would have to do this only if there were no relevant differences between the two. For me, the two resemble each other *only* in their non-generativeness; and if (rightly or wrongly) I have abandoned non-generativeness as a deciding factor, I can hardly be blamed for refusing to set any store by this resemblance between the two acts.

The objection could be and has been put in a stronger form than this suggested analogy with homosexuality: I should like now to state and discuss this stronger form. In earlier chapters the RP has been characterized as an insistence on preserving the physiological structure of the sexual act, and the adequacy of this criterion has been attacked at some length. But if the physiological norm is abandoned, what grounds are left for not thereby permitting deviations like oral or anal coitus that Christian tradition forbids? The difficulty I feel in answering this question is part of the general difficulty that, I have suggested, is attached to debates about sexual morality. The revulsion which such practices can inspire is not of itself sufficient to condemn them. The danger of basing verdicts about sexual behaviour on aesthetic grounds has already been noted (p. 199), and for that reason the apologia of the preceding section included a reminder that what revolts some may not revolt others. (p. 264.) Besides, the "incomplete" use of at least some such acts is not now prohibited by moral theologians as it once was (p. 124), so the condemnation cannot be directed against the contacts as such. Are they, then, condemned for the non-generative semination they involve? This will certainly have contributed to their condemnations, but I cannot think that it was the sole and precise reason for it. To show why I cannot admit this, let me consider for a moment the attack on contraception which lays most stress on the anti-procreative volition it demands in the partners—the theory of Dr Grisez which has already been examined. (pp. 224–234.)

Suppose it were argued that Grisez's defence of the RP allowed such deviant actions. After all, it might be said, the will of the couple becomes relevantly opposed to the procreative good when "intercourse is carried to the point when procreation might follow unless [they] act to prevent it." (Grisez, p. 90.) However, the couple who practise the deviant contacts are not just embarking on an action which might lead to procreation if they did not stop it doing so by interposing a barrier: their action is different in kind from the start, not an interruption of possible fertilization. What they do is obviously non-generative, but the very difference in what they are doing from what the contraceptive couple are doing means that their volition is not opposed to procreation in the direct way that the volition of the other couple is. Whatever we thought of this reasoning (and whatever Grisez might think of it), it would surely not commit us to accepting the deviations. We should still have the right to object on the grounds that the departure from the normal pattern was too great, that the deviant couple were, to use the words of the original objection, treating biological organs in a way not in accordance with the human.

We have refused to locate the condemnation of these actions solely in their non-generativeness. But is not the refusal based upon an appeal to just that physiological norm which has already been criticized as inadequate? And does not the appeal oblige us in consequence to reinstate the RP? The questions cannot be answered, I think, outside the context of the tradition I recalled at the beginning of this section. The point at issue is, to repeat a phrase used earlier, "what control man is to have over his generative functions" (p. 261), and I concede that exclusion of the deviant acts from the zone of control does involve a physiological criterion. Involves, I say, for I cannot see that the criterion can be purely physiological—if it were, all "imperfect" contacts of these species would be forbidden, which is not the case. (See parallel reasoning in *ST* 2/2, 1544 about the prohibition of imperfect sexual acts by those for whom intercourse itself is forbidden.) But does not any involvement of physiology in the exclusion demand that we no longer reject the physiological criterion in the RP? A further recalling of the scope of this book will show, I think, that this is not the case.

Preceding chapters have tried to locate the precise force of the RP as taught nowadays, and to display the historical development of its verdicts. If the contentions there are correct, the focus of the prohibition is not on the vocational obligations of marriage, nor on fecundity, nor on self-indulgence, but on preventing the seminal emission from reaching its destination; while the history behind the RP shows that a rigid subordination of sexuality to procreation has recently been tempered by the admission of other values. My arguments have pointed out that the admission of these values, and the changes in practice which have come with them, leave the prohibition of putting barriers in the seed's path an impersonal factor divorced from the purely generative context that originally gave it meaning. In consequence, I have been led to question the unchangeability of a tradition that has already changed so much: but I have also been at pains to point out that an individual's speculations are not of themselves sufficient to declare that the tradition has been modified in this respect. (p. 165.) In other words, I have been arguing inside the tradition in favour of a modification of it here. Since I was arguing inside the tradition for its development, and not outside it in favour of its abandonment, my starting-point was the normal copulatory and inseminatory act between husband and wife, and my speculations were confined to questioning the immunity of this act from the interposition of devices in the path of the seed. My starting-point, in other words, took physiology for granted, and the action I considered was already physiologically defined. I suggested that the interposition of devices might be licit: such interpositions obstruct—frustrate, put it as you please—the ordinary marital act. But the obstruction and frustration are concerned with this ordinary act, they are not on a par with the performance of another kind of physiological conjunction altogether. The contraceptive and the deviant act will have non-generativeness in common; they will also have in common the physiological fact that the emitted seed does not reach its destination; but I fail to see how two actions so diverse can be said to be necessarily connected morally simply because of these two common elements. I have (once more, rightly or wrongly) already declined to accept non-generativeness as a sufficient criterion; and the physiological element of obstructed semination occurs in two contexts of which one departs altogether from the fundamental pattern preserved by the other.

Of course, I have not *proved* the consistency of my position. All I have done is suggested that it does make sense to impugn the inviolability of copulation from interference with the seed's transference, without thereby having to license sexual conjunctions of a physically different pattern: and the basis for my suggestion is precisely this physical difference between the two types of action. Naturally, the suggestion can be rejected. Those who do reject it will be able to reinforce their acceptance of the RP by saying that its abandonment over contraception gives no reasonable grounds for not allowing further departures. (They will be able to use the phrases about "mechanically verifiable limits" that occur in the apologia of the preceding section.)

But I do not think that either side can offer a clinching proof for the position adopted in a matter of this kind. Neither party to the dispute can resolve such questions outside the tradition which, while criticizing, I have endeavoured to keep as the wider context of what I had to say. If the debate is over what dominion man has over his generative functions, a decision cannot be reached apart from tradition as to this dominion's extent. I think that my critique of the RP has cogency, and that the distinction I have drawn between contraceptive and deviant coitus is valid: but it would be going against an integral part of my thesis to assert either the cogency or the validity without qualification.

It is this characteristic of the debate that confirms what has been said in an earlier chapter about church tradition; and the explicitation of this point will be a suitable conclusion of the whole book. I have tried to suggest (pp. 246–8) that tradition, while involving the grace of God, also involves the presence of that grace among men. It is something more than an isolated repository of information which can be consulted at intervals by those privileged to do so. Membership of the Church calls for obedience to the witness made by the Church to the gospel, but the witness is complex in its manifestations. It includes not only extraordinary acts of teaching like councils or definitions, but the day-to-day proclamation of the gospel by bishops, and the researches and debates by which the faith of Christians seeks understanding. To admit this complexity is not to confer a charisma of infallibility on these day-to-day proclamations and debates, but it does entail an acknowledgement that, if discussion and investigation are suppressed, the Church is the poorer.

The greater understanding of marital values which distinguishes theology today did not appear spontaneously: reasoned debate was a necessary condition of it. Nor is the presence of this greater understanding simply a piece of good fortune for our age. It also represents an obligation on members of the Church to integrate this understanding with what was traditionally taught, and to scrutinize the traditional teaching in the light of what is now better understood. I have already acknowledged the difficulties which can be caused by open discussion (p. 246), and have suggested that worse consequences follow from the lack of it (p. 248)—there is no need to repeat the points here. But if my contention is true that the RP is a mixture of discordant attitudes widely different in origin, and that it is defended by a heterogeneous apologetic whose elements are widely different in value, then surely the acknowledgement of the need for sincere and informed discussion of the subject between those who share the same faith is not only desirable but urgently necessary.

But discussion, however sincere and informed, will not of itself solve the problem, for more is involved than what sincerity or information can determine unaided. A change in perception and evaluation in the Church is not reducible to the particular interventions and suggestions that have brought it about. Such changes have already taken place in the Catholic attitude to marriage, and the "negative capability" of the Church to disregard the obsolete (see pp. 170–1) makes it necessary to remind ourselves of their extent. In the present state of uncertainty, dogmatism and prophecy are equally inapposite, but there is a general fact about theological development mentioned earlier that can bear repetition as a conclusion. In Chapter 6 I took biblical criticism as an example of a development in the faith that was compatible with sharp contrast between old and new. What needs remembering is that the development was not brought about by a disinterested theological analysis of the conceptof inspiration. Once the development has been acknowledged, analysis by theologians can accommodate it to the inherited tradition—indeed, it would be more accurate to say that such analysis is part of the process of acknowledgement. But the origins of the development lie elsewhere. The first to broach the critical ideas we now take for granted also proposed theories that were bound up with presuppositions and beliefs then as now incompatible with the faith; but the pointed and rebarbative dissidence of their suggestions led towards future change as dutiful repetition of the commonplace could never have done. When the change came, it did not involve an undiscriminating acceptance of everything bound up with those suggestions, but it did involve a rethinking of church tradition in the light of them. I have suggested that there is a valid analogy between developments in biblical studies and the debate on moral issues to which this book has been devoted. If this is so, to identify a questioning of the RP with a total abandonment of the traditional teaching on marriage is just as unreasonable as identifying a Catholic scholar's verdict today on Genesis with what Voltaire had to say about the book in his *La Bible enfin expliquée*. But would the Catholic think now as he does if Voltaire had not written as he did? Theology is like an oyster: it secretes its pearls only in response to irritants.

I have put up a case against the RP which I think deserves an answer—I claim no more for it than that. As I went to Plato for my motto, let me end with a sobering epigram from Aquinas:

> His presuming to argue about matters of pure faith which exceed the scope of philosophy is a sign of over-confidence. . . . He might by the same token extend the debate to the Trinity, the Incarnation, and similar topics, where he could only be purblind in his pronouncements. [*De Unitate Intellectus*, 5.]

Although I have no ambition to debate about the Trinity, the Incarnation, and similar topics, I may still have been purblind in my pronouncements. Perhaps someone will tell me where.

Index of sources and references

Index of sources and references

N.B.—This index is divided into three main sections: (1) biblical, patristic, and theological sources; (2) official church authorities; and (3) other authorities and sources consulted, periodicals, and references. The first two of these sections concern primary sources, and full details are given of authors, works, work references, and (where appropriate) secondary-source references. The third section, however, concerns principally commentators and non-official sources, and so—for the sake of brevity and the reader's convenience—details of works are here omitted, and only authors' and periodicals' names given.

The index should be used in conjunction with the list of abbreviations on p. (x) above, and with the bibliographical Appendix to Chapter 1 on pp. 19–24 above, where important supplementary information is provided.

1. *Biblical, patristic, and theological sources*

A. Bible

B. Church fathers

C. Classic writers on moral theology

2. *Official church authorities*

Note: Throughout this section double references to Denzinger's *Enchiridion Symbolorum* are given. The first reference in each case is, as in the text, to editions by Schönmetzer (editions 32 and following). The second reference, in square brackets, has been added for the convenience of readers using earlier editions, in which a different numbering system was employed.

A. Conciliar decrees and catechisms

B. Papal encyclicals, decrees, and addresses

C. Curial decrees, replies, and letters